# Praise for *The Behavioral Code*

"The law is an embarrassment for its failure to account for the facts about how or whether its rules actually work. This brilliant and foundational text, beautifully written and compelling, will launch a long-needed movement. . . . The current system is deeply unjust; this book points a clear way to making it much more just."

—LAWRENCE LESSIG, Roy L. Furman Professor of
Law and Leadership, Harvard Law School

"In an engaging, scientifically grounded fashion, van Rooij and Fine expertly link the findings of behavioral science with evidence of how people respond to laws, regulations, and legal sanctions. An excellent and urgent reminder of how behavioral science is essential to our understanding of law."

—ROBERT B. CIALDINI, author of *Influence* and *Pre-Suasion*

"If you've ever dreamed of a legal system that's informed by behavioral science, this book could very well move us one step closer to making your dream a reality."

—ADAM GRANT, author of *Think Again* and
host of the TED podcast *WorkLife*

"Accessible, timely, and compelling, *The Behavioral Code* explores the vast literature concerning punishment and provides a blueprint for reforming the criminal justice system—one where we can better understand just how effective our laws may or may not be."

—ERWIN CHEMERINSKY, dean, UC Berkeley School of
Law, and author of *The Case Against the Supreme Court*

"Sometimes we follow the law, and sometimes we don't—but why do we pick and choose which rules are worth following? Van Rooij and Fine tackle this complex question by using our contemporary understanding of behavioral ethics to predict human responses to laws. Through fresh and fascinating analysis, *The Behavioral Code* has the potential to lead policymakers to make wiser decisions to pass laws that make the most sense given how humans actually behave."

—MAX H. BAZERMAN, author of *Better, Not Perfect* and *Blind Spots*

"Laws come in so many flavors: universal versus parochial ones; those obeyed versus those blithely ignored or heroically resisted; bureaucratic nonsense versus laws that save lives or proclaim sacred values. *The Behavioral Code* explores the factors that shape when people do or don't obey laws, with writing that is clear, science-based, and even-handed. A fascinating book with crucial implications—from the successes and dysfunctions of entire societies to our own everyday behavior."

—ROBERT M. SAPOLSKY, author of *Behave: The Biology of Humans at Our Best and Worst*

"With research informed but enlivened by real-world accounts, this work unlocks the secrets to using the law to advance the commonweal. . . . This is a book to be studied carefully and then shared with others as a 'must-read'—but do so with the proviso that the volume be returned so as to occupy a prominent and permanent place in your library."

—FRANCIS T. CULLEN, Distinguished Research Professor Emeritus, University of Cincinnati, and past president, American Society of Criminology

"Irrespective of whether the issue is wearing a face mask, complying with a police request, or accepting the results of an election, the ability to motivate people to follow rules is central to the viability of our own, or any other, society. But why do people follow or break rules? Anyone interested in knowing will benefit from reading *The Behavioral Code*. An engagingly written, timely, and compelling read."

—TOM TYLER, Macklin Fleming Professor of Law and professor of psychology, Yale University

"This book draws on a broad swathe of behavioral research and is essential reading for anyone who assumes either that rules are necessarily the best way to alter behavior or that compliance follows automatically."

—MALCOLM K. SPARROW, professor, Harvard Kennedy School

"*The Behavioral Code* is a fantastically engaging look at how legal codes—from how we drive to how we serve food to how we reduce harm—guide every aspect of our lives. Van Rooij and Fine draw on fascinating examples of laws that worked (and ones that failed) to teach us new ways to impact behavior. Anyone who cares about making our society a safer place should read this book."

—ELIZABETH F. LOFTUS, former president,
Association for Psychological Science

"This superb book is the best comprehensive treatment of the new field of law and behavior. Groundbreaking and highly accessible, this book will set the agenda for law reform for the next decade."

—DAVID LEVI-FAUR, professor, Hebrew University of
Jerusalem, and founding editor of *Regulation and Governance*

"*The Behavioral Code* is readily accessible to both scholars and the general public and will change the way you think. This is interdisciplinary integration at its very best."

—SALLY S. SIMPSON, past president,
American Society of Criminology

"Most books about the American criminal justice system show how deeply unjust and biased it is. *The Behavioral Code* reveals a startling truth: it actually fails to fight crime. Offering a witty and accessible tour de force of the science of crime, this must-read book shows us how to reduce our reliance on brutal punishment and build a more humane and effective justice system that can actually protect us."

—L. SONG RICHARDSON, president, Colorado College

"Van Rooij and Fine's engaging book offers a blueprint of how we can begin designing laws to create the outcomes we want as a society. A compelling call to action that should be read by all policymakers and regulators."

—EUGENE SOLTES, professor, Harvard Business School, and author
of *Why They Do It: Inside the Mind of the White-Collar Criminal*

"Anyone interested in understanding how to use law and regulation more effectively to solve social and economic problems will benefit from van Rooij and Fine's engaging masterpiece."

—CARY COGLIANESE, director of the Penn Program
on Regulation, University of Pennsylvania

"*The Behavioral Code* is a marvelous book full of striking stories and insightful science that help us see the law through a different lens—what difference it makes in everyday life, and how it can and must do better."

—CHRISTINE PARKER, professor, Melbourne Law School

"The faith of modern societies in the ability of laws to shape behavior by words alone remains astonishingly strong, as our pandemic experience now attests. *The Behavioral Code* brilliantly decodes a century's worth of human science to show both how terrifyingly misguided that faith is and what we actually know about how to change behavior."

—JONATHAN SIMON, Lance Robbins Professor of Criminal Justice Law, UC Berkeley, School of Law

"Using engaging stories, insightful resources, and practical guidance, this book picks up where the law leaves off for all those who are interested in understanding noncompliant and criminal behaviors."

—HUI CHEN, former Compliance Counsel Expert, US Department of Justice

"By summarizing hundreds of studies, weaving in catchy examples, and delivering an insightful and informative guide on the effect of law on behavior, *The Behavioral Code* is an incredible feat that challenges what we think we know about the law."

—YUVAL FELDMAN, author of *The Law of Good People*

"Van Rooij and Fine provide a master class on the intersection between social science and the law, and their insights will reshape how we think of the law."

—DAVID DEMATTEO, former president, American Psychology-Law Society

"*The Behavioral Code* convincingly concludes that building more prisons does not work; what does is reducing poverty and building motivation for, and pathways to, compliance within fair legal institutions."

—JOHN BRAITHWAITE, emeritus professor, Australian National University

# The
# Behavioral
# Code

## THE HIDDEN WAYS
## THE LAW MAKES US BETTER
## . . . OR WORSE

## BENJAMIN VAN ROOIJ
## *and* ADAM FINE

Beacon Press
Boston

BEACON PRESS
Boston, Massachusetts
www.beacon.org

Beacon Press books
are published under the auspices of
the Unitarian Universalist Association of Congregations.

24 23 22 21    8 7 6 5 4 3 2 1

This book is printed on acid-free paper that meets the uncoated paper
ANSI/NISO specifications for permanence as revised in 1992.

Text design and composition by Kim Arney

*Library of Congress Cataloging-in-Publication Data*
Names: Rooij, Benjamin van, author. | Fine, Adam, author.
Title: The behavioral code : the hidden ways the law makes us better . . .
    or worse / Benjamin van Rooij and Adam Fine.
Description: Boston : Beacon Press, 2021. | Includes bibliographical
    references and index.
Identifiers: LCCN 2021017587 (print) | LCCN 2021017588 (ebook) |
    ISBN 9780807049082 (hardcover) | ISBN 9780807049099 (ebook)
Subjects: LCSH: Disorderly conduct. | Transgression (Ethics) | Law—
    Social aspects.
Classification: LCC HV6486 .R66 2021 (print) | LCC HV6486 (ebook) |
    DDC 364.1—dc23
LC record available at https://lccn.loc.gov/2021017587
LC ebook record available at https://lccn.loc.gov/2021017588

*To Janine, Max, and Mare*

———————

*To Reaghan and my girls*

# Contents

# CHAPTER 1

# A Tale of Two Codes

Imagine that you could take a pill, a red pill, a little like the one Morpheus offered Neo in *The Matrix*. The pill promises to show you the world as it really is.

Before today, every morning, you would turn off your alarm, get dressed, make your coffee, and get in your car to drive to work. But this morning, just before you leave your house, you take the red pill. You drink some water to wash it down. At first, nothing changes, but just as you're backing your car out of your driveway in the beautiful California sunshine, suddenly fine-print snippets of text begin appearing as though they are attached to everything you see. Underneath the speed limit sign across the street, you see text that reads "A person shall not drive a vehicle upon a highway with a speed limit established pursuant to Section 22349 or 22356 at a speed greater than that speed limit."

The text continues, "No person may drive a vehicle upon a highway at a speed greater than 65 miles per hour." You rub your eyes and then focus on it again: "No person shall drive a vehicle upon a highway at a speed greater than is reasonable or prudent having due regard for weather, visibility, the traffic on, and the surface and width of, the highway, and in no event at a speed which endangers the safety of persons or property."

You note that each of these texts has small lettering at the end, indicating its source: the California Vehicle Code.

As the pill's effects begin to intensify, you start to notice that the little texts are popping up everywhere. Rules, rules, and more rules, wherever you look. These little scrolling snippets of text are all over your car. There are rules that explain that you must have a driver's license to operate a car, rules about the usage of handheld devices, and rules about driving under the influence. You already knew the gist of these rules, but the amount of detail you now see all around you is staggering.

You find texts about things that you sort of knew you should not do but were never really sure were illegal. One text explains that you are not allowed to throw out your window "any bottle, can, garbage, glass, nail, offal, paper, wire, any substance likely to injure or damage traffic using the highway, or any noisome, nauseous, or offensive matter of any kind." So, would throwing an apple core out of your window into the bushes break the law? You guess it depends whether people see that as "offensive matter of any kind" or if it constitutes "offal," whatever that is. ("Offal" are entrails, decomposing animal flesh, or just waste in general.)

The inside of the car is too overwhelming, so you pull over, get out, and lean against the hood. But a flurry of texts is cluttered around your headlights. You read a few. Some just state the obvious: "A motor vehicle, other than a motorcycle, shall be equipped with at least two headlamps, with at least one on each side of the front of the vehicle." That makes sense. But others provide details you never heard of: "The headlamps and every light source in any headlamp unit shall be located at a height of not more than 54 inches nor less than 22 inches." Another explains that "any motor vehicle may be equipped with not to exceed two auxiliary driving lamps mounted on the front at a height of not less than 16 inches nor more than 42 inches." It continues to explain that "driving lamps are lamps designed for supplementing the upper beam from headlamps and may not be lighted with the lower beam." Does that mean you can't use your driving lamps and headlamps at the same time? What's the difference again?

None of these rules were on your driver's license test. But now that the law has revealed itself, you realize that there are an enormous number of very specific legal rules. Who knew there were such detailed rules about car lights? These are only a fraction of the texts such a magic red pill would reveal. The California Vehicle Code alone has over one thousand pages filled with dense rules on virtually every aspect of operating and driving motor vehicles.[1] And these are only the applicable state rules about driving. They do not include the state and federal laws and regulations that guide the manufacturing and selling of cars. A magic pill would show a staggering number of legal rules in relation to car production tort liability, vehicle emissions, automobile safety standards, occupational health and safety standards for vehicle factory workers, and competition rules, let alone the thousands and thousands of pages of the US tax code as they apply to the production and sale of cars.

The red pill would reveal that laws and legal rules are omnipresent. Wherever you looked, you would see stacks and stacks of legal rules.

We live in a world of code—legal code—that guides every aspect of our lives. This code is everywhere. It's there when we are at work, when we watch television, when we grow food, when we serve food, when we play sports, and when we build homes. It's there when we date and fall in love, when we go online, and even when we sleep.

Legal code is as old as humanity. We clearly see it in our ancient religious texts such as those in the Bible and the Quran. Originally everyone knew the code. They were the rules of the community, the Code of Hammurabi, the rules escribed in the Zhou dynasty's bronze cauldrons, and the Ten Commandments. They were the customs of the group or the laws of the city. But as legal systems and societies grew larger and more complex, legal code itself grew and grew. And each time there was a new risk or a new problem, people called for new rules, and more laws and more regulations were adopted.

In our everyday lives, we only see snippets of the code. After each new mass shooting, we learn about different gun laws on assault weapons, bump stocks, and background checks. After Bernie Madoff's massive Ponzi scheme, we learned about fraud rules and securities regulation. After Purdue and Johnson & Johnson settled historic lawsuits in the wake of the opioid crisis in the United States, we learned about tort law and product liability.

But in all of this, the average person gets only tiny elements of the full legal code that surrounds us. Its size and complexity has made it impossible to grasp its entirety. Not even trained lawyers can see the full code as it truly exists. Lawyers themselves have to do hours of legal research and delve into databases of legal rules and case law. Even then, the picture is fuzzy at best. Because the legal system has become so vast and complex, we are unable to see the intricate web of rules that to some degree shapes every aspect of our lives.

It may seem nonsensical to have such a massive system of legal rules that guides our everyday existence. But most rules have a reason for existing: they are intended to keep us safe from harm.

Consider how the US used laws, rules, and regulations to respond to some of its biggest challenges in the twentieth century. In the 1960s and 1970s, two-thirds of American lakes, rivers, and coasts were so polluted that they had become unsafe for fishing and swimming. As a result, Congress adopted the Clean Water Act in 1972. This new law sought to fundamentally curb water pollution and make the waterways safe for both fishing and recreation. Or head back to the 1930s. In the wake of the Great Depression, Congress enacted the Glass-Steagall Act to separate high-risk investment banking from ordinary commercial banking activities. It created the Federal Deposit Insurance Corporation, which protected people by insuring bank deposits, to help maintain the overall stability of the nation's banking system.

Whenever our society faces a harm or risk, we continue to develop rules that we adopt into the legal code. Not everyone always agrees on what the damages and risks are, what causes them, or what the best legislative response might be. But when there is sufficient consensus and political support, we end up with new legal rules to address the risks our societies, markets, and environments face.

Certainly, laws are necessary. Without effective legal rules, our property wouldn't be protected from theft. Our small businesses would be swallowed whole by large monopolies and unfair lending practices. Our environment would be even more degraded and the climate even warmer. Much of our food would be unsafe to eat. Our public schools would close since the government would no longer be able to collect taxes. Our bosses could harass us as much as they wanted.

Legal code is what makes contemporary society possible. Yet, in their everyday lives, people seldom think about how the legal code actually works. Once we see the legal code as it exists, we see a massive system of rules designed to keep us safe. Surely, not all legal rules serve these purposes, and there are clear historical examples, from Nazi Germany to the crack-cocaine sentencing disparities in the US, where legal rules served injustice and caused more harm. And of course for the law to work well, the law itself must be just. But when the legal code does intend to make our lives better, it only works if people comply with these rules, if the code actually changes behavior.


Interstate 405 in Los Angeles and Orange County has a speed limit of sixty-five miles per hour. When massive traffic jams aren't plaguing the region, virtually everyone drives at least seventy miles per hour. California drivers know the rules. There are signs on every road that remind them what the limits are. They may know the fines and penalties for speeding and even that they can lose their license if they get caught too many times. Yet most drivers on I-405 speed every time they get the chance.

There are countless examples of legal code failing to change behavior. During Prohibition in the 1920s, US leaders introduced laws and even amended the Constitution to eradicate alcohol consumption. Yet it completely failed to change American drinking habits.[2] The law is remembered for creating black markets and breeding organized crime. It did not just fail: it actually created more crime.

History has repeated itself with the War on Drugs. US legislators have introduced ever-more-stringent laws banning the use, production, and sale of recreational drugs (with the exception of recent changes in rules on marijuana). And since 1971, law enforcement has been fighting battle after battle in the War on Drugs.[3] But American drug abuse is as rampant as ever. While laws ban heroin and harshly punish drug offenders, the opioid epidemic rages on, killing more Americans each year than died in combat during the entire Vietnam War.[4]

Law also has had trouble changing corporate conduct. Almost every week, the media expose yet another major corporation's egregious violation of the law. Recall the revelations of how Facebook tried to silence and attack its critics, the emissions scandals at Volkswagen, or the massive fraud at Wells Fargo. Consider that Bank of America has received over $56 billion in fines across twenty-nine cases, yet despite punishment after punishment, it has continued to break the law.[5] Due to violations of occupational safety laws, over a hundred Americans die at work every week.[6] In fact, a greater number of Americans die at work each year than were killed in Iraq from 2003 to 2010.[7]

Everyday news is replete with other examples of how legal code fails to keep us safe. Laws prohibit police from shooting unarmed civilians, yet viral videos continue to emerge monthly of them doing just this. Laws ban performance-enhancing substances in sports, yet Olympians continue to test dirty for doping—even the ones wearing "I Don't Do Doping" sweatshirts. Laws forbid sexual assault and harassment, yet from Hollywood to Congress, from churches to even our courts, sexual predators are uncovered almost daily.

Our legal code clearly does not always work. At worst, it fails to change harmful behavior and does not provide us the protections that we were promised. When that happens, all we have is a massive system of written rules that does little to keep our lives, societies, markets, and environments safe. So, the key question, the one that this book is dedicated to answering, is this: why does law fail to improve human conduct?

Standing in front of a class of law students, we place a little book version of the US Constitution on the podium. We ask them to tell us what it is.

Several students say, "It's the Constitution."

"No," we say. "Look more carefully."

"Our basic rights," tries another one. No, look again.

"It's the law," another says.

No, not exactly. "What do you really see? What, precisely, is it?"

"A set of fundamental legal rules." "Our core social fabric."

No. Anyone else? On and on it goes, until finally one student gives the answer we are looking for.

"It is a stack of paper."

Exactly: words printed on paper. In the end, that is what the legal code is, or at least what it always was until we developed digital legal databases and it became words represented by zeros and ones. And once we see what the legal code really is, its failures to change behavior do not seem so surprising. Simply by writing a text, legislators somehow hope to change real everyday behavior. But how can text, whether printed or digital, affect our behavior? How can law in the books become law in action? This is no easy feat.

To understand how this set of paper rules shapes behavior, we must change the perspective. Rather than take a magic pill and see the rules, we must come to see the way people respond to such rules. This lets us see a very different code, a code of behavioral mechanisms: *the behavioral code.*

Consider seatbelts. Whenever you get into your car, you buckle up. You are not really aware of it. It's not really a conscious decision. Nor do you ever really think about the specific law that requires you to use it. This was not always the case. For decades, the vast majority of drivers and automobile passengers did not use their seatbelts.

By 1968, US law required all vehicles to have seatbelts.[8] Yet well into the 1980s, only one in ten Americans actually used them.[9] Law changed this. In 1984, New York became the first state to require drivers to use seatbelts. Soon all states—except the "Live Free or Die" state of New Hampshire—followed suit, and seatbelt usage across the country shot up from 10 percent to 50 percent—a 400 percent increase.[10] Simply introducing the law mandating seatbelt usage hugely impacted people's driving safety habits.

But half of Americans still weren't buckling up. In response, states began organizing enforcement campaigns with catchy slogans like "Click It or Ticket." Seatbelt slackers were warned that they could face fines if they failed to comply with the new laws. Fines were low, mostly well below a hundred dollars, especially compared with speeding tickets, which were typically much more expensive. Concurrently, authorities broadcast public service announcements showing unbuckled, lifelike crash-test dummies to warn about the potential gruesome effects of not wearing seatbelts. And car manufacturers installed those seatbelt warning alarms, reminding (or really just irritating) us into buckling up.[11] With all of these combined, today about 90 percent of American drivers and car passengers wear a seatbelt.[12] And most strap in automatically.

Now let us try to discern what behavioral mechanisms were at play here. The first two are easy to miss. The simple fact that a new legal rule was adopted changed behavior tremendously. From a behavioral perspective, this means two things. First, people learned what the new rules were and what behavior they required. All too often this is not the case. Much of the legal code remains unknown and therefore largely ineffective. Second, simply by changing the rule, people started to change their behavior. They did so even though there was no clear enforcement effort yet, and thus they responded to the mere fact that it was the law. Therefore, a sense of duty toward the law and the legitimacy of the legal system played a major role here.

Several other behavioral mechanisms also kicked in. By instituting a fine, the law made people fear the repercussions of not buckling up. But what is interesting here is that the fines were quite low, much lower than for speeding, where fines do not seem to work. Somehow these low fines triggered the desired behavioral responses.

Next came persuasion through public messaging campaigns that convinced people that buckling up was in their own interest. Such campaigns sought to move seatbelt decisions from an extrinsic motivation ("I don't want to get punished") to an intrinsic motivation ("it's in my own self-interest, so I don't get hurt").

Then came the warning beeps. These annoying beeps created a practical obstacle for those who were still not buckling up. This added a behavioral layer on top of the duty, fear of punishment, and intrinsic motivation. If all of those failed, one would be beeped into submission. In effect, these warning beeps made it very hard, or at least very annoying, to drive without using a seatbelt.

As more and more people began buckling up, using a seatbelt became more normal than not using one. The behavior became sustained socially as people started to take cues from others. Finally buckling up became habitual and automatic. The behavior became so deeply internalized that it was no longer a decision. We barely notice that we are automatically obeying the law.

There it is: one example of a successful marriage between the legal and the behavioral code.

In this and other cases, we may see some of the interventions, such as punishment and public messaging campaigns, but other ways that legal code shapes behavior remain obscure. We do not see people's sense of duty or how they view the legitimacy of the legal system. We have trouble understanding what people's motivations are and how they might respond to public messaging campaigns. We don't always know how people perceive punishment and how fear of punishment shapes their conduct. We rarely think about how much people take cues from others or how practical obstacles might influence misconduct, let alone how forms of automation take over even when we think we are making conscious, rational decisions.

To improve our laws and make them more effective, we need to understand the behavioral code. Here social science is key. Decades of research have unearthed the behavioral mechanisms that shape human responses to legal rules. Science has made the invisible behavioral code visible. It has shown how our laws can shape people's motivations and adapt their situations to improve compliance and prevent harm. Over the last four decades, scientific insights have revolutionized our understanding of how humans act and why they misbehave. But the science has yet to be adopted in our laws. Locked behind the paywalls of academic journals and obscured by scholarly jargon, many of these insights have remained as hidden as the behavioral code itself.

Bad behavior undermines our societies, our safety, our markets, our ecology, and our way of life. We have erected a complex legal code to address different forms of damaging behavior, and clearly the legal code is intended to shape behavior. Lawyers play a crucial role in all of this. As legislators, lawyers draft the language in our codified laws and choose what gets passed. As prosecutors and regulators, they make key decisions about if and how the law is enforced. Lawyers are hired to draw up contracts and design organizational rules, inserting the legal code into business transactions. Lawyers act as judges and apply the law to disputes, and in doing so interpret and shape the future meaning of the law. And as law professors and legal experts, they shape public debate about what the law is and what it should be.

As such, we leave the design and crucial decision-making within our legal system to lawyers, yet they have hardly any knowledge of the social science underlying human behavior. Law school curricula have almost entirely ignored the behavioral revolution that has rocked fields like economics and ethics.[13] Because lawyers who design and operate our legal code rarely receive any mandatory training in social and behavioral sciences, they are forced to rely on their own intuitions about human misbehavior, many of which have been proven false by empirical studies. We have left the most important coding of human conduct, the legal code, in the hands of behavioral novices.

But it's not just the lawmakers' fault. Our laws tend to originate in a political process that is shaped by public opinion. But few of us understand the behavioral code, let alone the social science that has mapped it. Instead we rely on our gut responses when we hear of a brutal murder, when we hear of a multinational corporation bribing national governments, when we hear of yet another shocking #MeToo case, or when we see that car zooming by dangerously above the speed limit. And these visceral, instinctive responses ultimately shape public opinion and law-making. If we truly care about making law more effective, we must learn to understand the behavioral code. We must delve into the social science that shows us what has remained hidden. Only by understanding human behavior will the law truly fulfill its function and keep us safe.

# CHAPTER 2

# The Punishment Delusion

S hermie and Shelby have been driving their family crazy.[1] Every day, the five-year-old boy and his four-year-old sister run around the house screaming. They climb on everything, from doors to kitchen counters to trees in their backyard. In the car, they are out of control, shouting and kicking each other and getting out of their seat belts. Little Shelby is overly dramatic, crying and wailing at the top of her lungs whenever she does not get what she wants. Shermie is aggressive, pushing and shoving anyone who gets in his way. He is particularly violent with his little sister; he hits and kicks her constantly and sometimes even chokes her.

Finally it gets to the point where their parents can't take it anymore, so they send a video of their kids to a TV show called *Supernanny.* They plead for help from Supernanny herself, Jo Frost, a British celebrity parenting guru. As Supernanny, Jo visits the family's house and, in the children's absence, watches videos of Shermie and Shelby terrorizing their parents. She wonders out loud, "What is going on here?"

After a period of observation, Supernanny confronts Mom and Dad about their inability to respond properly to their kids' misbehavior: "The lack of respect towards the pair of you is never followed through with discipline. . . . Your children don't know what discipline is. Is it the bedroom, a spanking, or is it one, two, three, four? Or what is it? I don't know, 'cause I never saw any. How can you expect your children to meet your expectations when you set no boundaries?"

Supernanny begins teaching Mom and Dad how to use discipline effectively. Her recipe, which is virtually the same in every episode, is simple: the family needs to set clear rules and there must be consequences when the rules are broken. The rules themselves are quite simple, consisting of a clear daily schedule with allotted times when the kids can watch TV and play video games. She asks the parents to place "no go zone" signs throughout the house to indicate where Shermie and Shelby are not allowed to go or climb.

Supernanny also teaches the parents how to punish their kids when they do, inevitably, break the rules. They are instructed to designate an area of the house for timeouts, which she calls the "naughty corner." The parents are to place their kids in this corner for the same number of minutes as they are aged, so five minutes for Shermie and four for Shelby. And, perhaps most importantly, the parents have to explain to Shermie and Shelby *why* they are placed there—both before and after their timeout.

Shermie and Shelby's mom, Joelle, is not convinced that this will work. She worries especially about Shermie, as she explains that he is "very strong-willed." Just as Joelle expresses her concerns, Shermie runs off and hides under the table, screaming. Shermie refuses to come out. Joelle gets an immediate chance to try out the new technique. She drags her son to the naughty corner and, as instructed, explains, "Shermie, I am putting you in the naughty corner because you did not listen. You will stay here for five minutes."

Did it work? Nope. Joelle was right about her little boy. Within a minute, Shermie runs off again, and his mom chases him through the house and into the garden. Joelle is desperate. "Now I don't know what to do. Now I am going to be chasing him through the neighborhood." Seconds later, Shermie climbs up a tree outside the reach of his mother and Supernanny.

Finally, by warning Shermie that he will lose his video-game time, his mom is able to get him back into the house and into the naughty corner. Shermie is left crying in the corner as his mother sets the timer for five minutes. And, lo and behold, little Shermie stays put in the naughty corner for the whole five minutes. When the five minutes are up, Joelle explains to Shermie why she had put him there: "Mommy put you in the naughty corner because you were not behaving nicely. Now I would like to get an apology, and I will let you up." In tears, little Shermie sobs, "Sorry."

The naughty corner works miracles. Rage-driven toddlers and aggressive kindergarteners quickly learn to follow family rules. It might not work the first time, but parents themselves learn that consistent and well-explained punishment eventually changes their kids' behavior. On TV it looks so easy—just set the rule, and when violations occur, explain the rule and punish both quickly and consistently.

The naughty corner is naturally appealing. There is nothing strange about using discipline to correct bad behavior. From our earliest years, our parents and teachers punish us when we misbehave. Just like Supernanny, many of us think that punishment can change behavior and keep us from breaking rules. In fact, if you look, you will find that the naughty corner is all around us, in our families, schools, and workplaces. It is also deeply ingrained in our legal system and political and public calls for how the law should respond to bad behavior. From everyday child misbehavior to serious crimes in the community, using punishment to correct misbehavior feels natural, even intuitive. And thus many of us have what we call a *punitive intuition*.

"Enough is enough," US senator Elizabeth Warren wrote on her Facebook page in February 2016.[2] Prosecutors had reached yet another settlement with yet another big Wall Street bank (this time Morgan Stanley) for criminal misconduct. As she explained, "These guys broke the law, and they did for the oldest reason in the books: to make more money." In her eyes, the settlement wasn't enough. "The company will pay a fine, and tonight every executive who plotted, planned and scammed can go home to his family, spend his fat bonus and smile all the way—no arrest, no prosecution, no jail time." In an earlier op-ed in the *New York Times* she had argued, "Justice cannot mean a prison sentence for a teenager who steals a car, but nothing more than a sideways glance at a C.E.O. who quietly engineers the theft of billions of dollars."[3] The op-ed referred to her own review of twenty cases of corporations caught breaking the law. In only one of those twenty cases was an executive sentenced to jail. The case concerned a corporate executive, responsible for a mine accident that killed twenty-nine people, who was sentenced to a mere three months in jail.[4]

A few months after her Facebook post and *New York Times* op-ed, Senator Warren wrote an open letter to the Department of Justice criticizing it for not prosecuting nine individuals who were implicated in serious violations of federal securities and other laws in relation to the 2008 financial crisis. In the letter she noted, "Not one of the nine has gone to prison or been convicted of a criminal offense. Not a single one has even been indicted or brought to trial." She explained, "Key companies and individuals that were responsible for the financial crisis and were the cause of substantial hardship for millions of Americans faced no criminal charges. This failure is outrageous."[5]

Warren's calls for tougher punishment came when official prosecution policies had been changing. By late 2015, the Obama administration's Department of Justice (DOJ) had already committed to major changes in how it would address corporate crime. Under its corporate crime policy, which Deputy Attorney General Sally Q. Yates introduced in a memo on September 9, 2015, the DOJ would begin prioritizing the prosecution of individual executives. As the memo explained, "One of the most effective ways to combat corporate misconduct is by seeking accountability from the individuals who perpetrated the wrongdoing. Such accountability is important for several reasons: it deters future illegal activity, it incentivizes changes in corporate behavior, it ensures that the proper parties are held responsible for their actions, and it promotes the public's confidence in our justice system."[6] Not even two months later, the DOJ already had its first guilty verdict against two bank executives for twenty-eight counts of fraud and conspiracy.[7]

The calls for punishing executives more strongly and the overall shift in DOJ policy were clearly premised on the idea that punishment will change behavior. When punishment is meted out, corporate behavior is supposed to become more compliant, which should prevent the next financial crisis or major environmental disaster. The logic is clear. If there is damaging and law-violating misbehavior, we can change it by instituting stronger punishments.

Conservatives certainly have the punitive intuition. In 1973, President Nixon remarked, "When we fail to make the criminal pay for his crime, we encourage him to think that crime will pay."[8] President Reagan routinely echoed Nixon: "For too many years, the scales of criminal justice were tilted toward protecting rights of criminals. Too many sentences today are inadequate and the time served too short."[9] President George H. W. Bush in 1989 said, "We won't have safe neighborhoods unless we're tough on drug criminals—much tougher than we are now."[10]

Democrats also developed their own tough-on-street-crime rhetoric. President Bill Clinton signed the 1994 Violent Crime Control and Law Enforcement Act, authored by Democratic senator Joe Biden. At over 356 pages, it was the largest crime bill in the history of the US. As Clinton explained when he announced the bill, "It will put police on the street and criminals in jail. It expands the federal death penalty to let criminals know that if they are guilty, they will be punished. It lets law-abiding citizens know that we are working to give them the safety they deserve."[11]

Politicians love punishment. Maybe they disagree on who deserves to be punished, but punishment itself is their favorite response for bad behavior. Politicians often claim that they have to support stronger punishment because the public demands it. Twenty years after Clinton's crime bill was signed into law, NPR's Carrie Johnson quoted Vera Institute of Justice president Nicholas Turner's explanation of the tough-on-crime policies and the nation's punitive instincts: "Criminal justice policy was very much driven by public sentiment and a political instinct to appeal to the more negative punitive elements of public sentiment rather than to be driven by the facts." Johnson added, "That public sentiment called for filling up the nation's prisons, a key part of the 1994 crime bill."[12]

Public sentiment is said to have driven politics. We, the public, were so afraid of crime that politicians began cracking down harder on crime to assuage our fears. Yet the above analysis omits the fact that the relation between public sentiment and politicians' actions is not a one-way street. It does not acknowledge how decades of political speeches on crime preceding the bill likely increased the public's fears and fed our punitive intuition. Presidential national addresses over the decades told us to be afraid of crime and that stronger, tougher punishment was the only way to keep us safe. The truth is that politicians both respond to and stimulate the public's punitive intuition.

This is not just an American phenomenon. Consider how politicians such as President Rodrigo Duterte in the Philippines and President Jair Bolsonaro in Brazil have been able to get popular support by promising to reduce crime through brutally tough punishment. Even a liberal democracy like the Netherlands puts faith in punishment to reduce unwanted behavior. In just three weeks in the fall of 2019, Dutch minister of justice Ferdinand Grapperhaus introduced two bills to enhance sentences for public misconduct. The first bill sought to increase sentences for driving under the influence from three months to one year. And the second sought to mandate imprisonment for people found guilty of assaulting ambulance, fire, or police personnel.[13] Equally liberal Denmark also has had a populist politics turn toward stronger punishment. It instituted a new law in 2018 doubling the punishment for crimes committed by people from twenty-five residential areas where residents are heavily low-income and Muslim. The law calls the designated areas "ghettos."[14]

Senator Warren is right that it is unfair that corporate executives receive far more lenient punishments than people who commit minor street or drug offenses, if they even get punished at all. But wouldn't it be much better if these corporate executives never broke the law in the first place? Isn't the core function of law to prevent harm? For law to truly keep us safe, we must look at punishment in a different way. Rather than just assess whether punishment is fair or justified, we must ask whether and how punishment shapes behavior and reduces crime.

## FEARING PUNISHMENT

Cesare Beccaria had been afraid that the world was not ready for his ideas. He feared that his short treatise on criminal justice reform would make him a pariah and subject to governmental reprisal. So he chose to publish his work *On Crimes and Punishments* anonymously at first. When it came out in 1764, it caused a massive shock, not just in his native Milan but also around the globe. But it wasn't the shock he expected. Instead of decrying his ideas, the rulers of his time overwhelmingly and publicly hailed them. His work spread east to Russia, where Catherine the Great, then empress, publicly endorsed it and drew on it in issuing her *Nakaz* (Instruction) to Russian legislators, intending for them to create a modern criminal justice system of policing, prosecution, judges, and prisons. And Beccaria's influence spread west to the US, inspiring American revolutionaries Thomas Jefferson, George Washington, and John Adams and their ideas for new laws. After Beccaria's death, his work continued to influence major criminal legal reforms and movements, including France's Napoleonic Penal Code in 1810 and Victor Hugo's campaign to abolish capital punishment in 1848.

Beccaria's argument was radical. He believed that criminal justice was dominated by and unfairly skewed toward the elites, and he argued that the system should be changed to treat all people impersonally and equally. He attacked the common practice of torture and called for the abolition of the death penalty. Instead of gruesome punishments, he argued for punishments that were mild and humane.

Beccaria believed in the power of punishment. Specifically, he believed that punishment was necessary to "dissuade the despotic mentality of every individual from thrusting the laws of society back into a prehistoric chaos."[15] But, in his opinion, the core function of punishment was to *prevent* crime. Any punishment that did not prevent crime he deemed to be contrary to liberal virtues, justice, and the social compact that keeps people bound together in a society. In one of his most famous lines, referring to Montesquieu, he stated, "Every punishment which does not arise from absolute necessity is tyrannical."[16]

Beccaria thus forced his readers to think about the effect of punishment on changing behavior. His focus was on preventing crime, reducing damaging behavior. And as such, he saw punishment not as a form of retribution or compensation for the victims but as a behavioral instrument. For Beccaria, punishment reduced crime by instilling fear in potential offenders. He explained, "Punishments, therefore, and the method of inflicting them, must be chosen, according to the amount needed to make an impression more useful and more lasting on the minds of men, and less to torment the body of the offender."[17]

Today we call this *deterrence*. Punishment ostensibly deters crime because people who experience the punishment, who witness the punishment, or even just hear about the punishment will become so afraid that they do not even think about committing the crime in the first place. This sounds simplistic, but the idea that we refrain from bad behavior because we are afraid of being punished is very similar to Supernanny's naughty corner. It is also very much like what politicians tell us when they appeal to our punitive intuition.

Beccaria developed ideas about what drives our fear of punishment. He articulated three core elements of deterrence. The first is the severity of the punishment. The more severe the punishment, the more likely people will fear it. The second is the certainty of the punishment. The more likely rule breakers are to get caught and punished, the more likely people will fear punishment. And third is the swiftness or promptness of the punishment. The longer the time lag between breaking rules and receiving punishment, the less people will fear punishment and the less it will deter them.

For thinkers like Beccaria, punishment was also a form of pain. Like many people, then and now, Beccaria thought that humans responded to pain and pleasure. The idea was simple: people refrain from action if pain outweighs the pleasure. To prevent someone from violating the law again in the future, punish them harshly the first time they violate the law, so that the painful experience of having been punished will keep them from committing the offense again in the future. This particular form of deterrence is called *specific deterrence.*

Imprisonment is a perfect example of a painful form of punishment. Simply not having freedom is awful enough in and of itself, but modern-day prison conditions in the US are likely to cause real physical pain. Overall, upward of 20 percent of prisoners experience physical violence while incarcerated, and the assault rates on men in prison are almost twenty times higher than on the outside.[18] And prisoners who are victims of assault are placed in solitary confinement, ostensibly for their own protection. Yet to make matters worse, according to the American Psychological Association, solitary confinement is associated with severe and pervasive harm to both physical and mental health, including an increased risk of self-mutilation, suicidal ideation, paranoia, and aggression.[19]

Serving hard time seems like a strong deterrent for re-offending. But is it? Decades of criminological scholarship have analyzed whether there is a relationship between serving time in prison and the probability of re-offending. If specific deterrence works, then the more time people spend in prison, the less they would re-offend. The more painful the punishment, the greater the deterrent, and the less people should commit crimes in the future.

But the evidence seems to be otherwise.[20] Most people who have served time in prison do re-offend. One large study looking at 272,111 people who were released from US prisons across fifteen states found that 68 percent had been arrested again within three years. The numbers were similar for common offenses, such as property crimes (including theft and robbery) and drug-related crimes, for which arrest rates for re-offending were 73.8 percent and 66.7 percent respectively.[21] Three years after release from prisons in the Netherlands, over 60 percent were convicted again.[22] And in the United Kingdom, for those two years post-release, the reconviction rate was 57 percent.[23] And these are just the official rearrest and reconviction rates. They do not reflect the real crime rates. In fact, so much crime goes undetected that criminologists call it the "dark figure of crime." What the dark figure of crime tells us is that if rearrest and reconviction rates hover around 60 percent across these countries, the actual re-offending rates must be shockingly high.

Yet we cannot say that prison fails to deter simply by looking at recidivism rates of those who served time. This would be a flawed reading of the data. Unfortunately, once people begin committing crime, we know they will be more likely to do so again. The question is whether serving hard time reduces such re-offending. Without imprisonment, the recidivism rates of offenders might well have been even higher. So we have to compare convicted offenders who went to prison to those who did not go to prison. The big question here is whether recidivism rates among people who did not go to prison are higher than for those who did. The best empirical studies on the specific deterrent effect of incarceration compare re-offending rates of people who are sentenced to prison time and people who had committed similar crimes (like property offenses or minor drug offenses) but received a sanction they served in their own community.

In 2000, the first major systematic review of this body of work came out.[24] The findings were surprising. Scholars did not find that the experience of imprisonment reduced re-offending. Quite the contrary. Compared to people who had committed similar crimes but who had received community sanctions, those who had been imprisoned re-offended *much more frequently*. Later systematic reviews found the same thing. In fact, the latest review of the available evidence looked at fifty-seven rigorous studies and found not only that imprisonment fails to decrease re-offending but that it actually increases crime. This review concluded that incarceration raises the rate of re-offending to somewhere between 5 and 14 percent.[25]

By and large, studies do not find that incarceration has a specific deterrent effect. In perhaps the most perfectly titled paper, "Prisons Do Not Reduce Recidivism: Ignoring the High Costs of Science," criminologist Francis Cullen and colleagues clearly state that "incarcerating offenders is not a magic bullet with special powers to invoke such dread that offenders refrain from recidivating when released." "If anything," they add, "it appears that imprisonment is a crude strategy that does not address the underlying causes of recidivism and thus that has no, or even criminogenic, effects on offenders."[26]

We have to realize, however, that the existing body of research is not perfect. In large part, this is because there are many challenges in measuring the effect of imprisonment on re-offending. Studies tend to use arrest rates or conviction rates to capture the amount of crimes committed, yet these statistics are incomplete because many offenses are never discovered. That's the "dark figure of crime" problem. The other problem is that it is very hard to isolate the effect of imprisonment on re-offending because there are many other factors simultaneously influencing criminal behavior that are unrelated to punishment, such as socioeconomic conditions, opportunities for crime, and the age, gender, and personality of potential offenders.

Altogether, a conservative view of imprisonment would conclude that, despite our intuitions, there is no evidence that incarceration has a specific deterrent effect. Further, many scholars conclude that incarceration actually creates more crime. Researchers call this the *criminogenic effect* of punishment, meaning that imprisoning individuals promotes more crime.

In 2000, Gary Ewing was caught red-handed. An attentive pro shop employee at a golf course in El Segundo in California noticed a bulge in Ewing's pants as he limped out of the shop. It turned out that Ewing was limping because he was trying to smuggle three golf clubs. Because each club was worth $399, he was charged with and later convicted of felony grand theft. Ewing tried to convince the prosecutor and the judge to reduce the crime classification from a felony to a misdemeanor. Ewing was not just trying to get a lighter sentence by a couple of months or years; he was fighting for his life, or at least a large chunk of it. If convicted of a felony, Ewing would be sentenced under the "three strikes" policy that California had adopted in 1994. And because the golf-club theft would be his third strike, the felony charge meant that he would receive a twenty-five-year sentence.

Clearly, specific deterrence had not worked for Gary Ewing. His first conviction was in 1984, when, at age twenty-two, he received a six-month sentence for theft. Then in 1988 he received a year in prison for grand theft auto. In 1990, he was sentenced to sixty days for petty theft, and in 1992 thirty days for battery. In 1993, he was sentenced to nine years in prison for a string of crimes including burglary, unlawful possession of a firearm, and robbery, the burglary and robbery counting as strikes one and two. And the golf clubs would become strike three.

There have been countless cases like this. Take thirty-three-year-old Curtis Wilkerson, who stole a pair of socks from a department store. Two security guards caught him and decided, after much deliberation, to turn him in to the police rather than let him pay the $2.50 for the socks. Because it was his third strike, Curtis was sentenced to life in prison. Another individual got life for possessing .09 grams of heroin.[27] Can you visualize .09 grams? Let's try it in Splenda packets. Do you know how many Splenda packets that would be? Not even close to one. It would take eleven times that amount to fill a single Splenda packet. Another person got seventy years for stealing a tuna sandwich from Whole Foods, and yet another got life in prison with no parole for fifty years for stealing videotapes from Kmart.[28]

The three strikes policy is a clear example of an attempt to reduce crime through tougher sentences. By mandating that the third strike will result in twenty-five years to life, the policy tries to strike fear in offenders, to deter them from re-offending, at least if they ever get out of prison. But beyond that, perhaps the more important point is to strike fear in everyone else who might be thinking of committing felonies. Criminologists call this *general deterrence*. The core logic here is that punishing one offender will cause many other potential offenders to become fearful and refrain from criminal activity. Beccaria saw this as the core function of punishment, as he wrote, "The purpose, then, is none other than . . . to prevent others from doing the same thing."[29]

General deterrence is far preferred over specific deterrence. Specific deterrence would only work after an offender has already committed a crime and has been punished for it. This would mean that to reduce illegal and damaging behavior, every person that commits a crime must be punished. By its own logic, it also means that people must commit at least one crime before they learn to stop doing so through punishment. But with general deterrence, punishment can achieve a leveraged effect. If just one person is punished, many others who learn of the punishment can be deterred. The question is whether punishment deters other potential offenders.

Just like studying specific deterrence, establishing whether punishment has a general deterrent effect is not easy. Social scientists have spent decades analyzing whether different forms of punishment, such as longer prison sentences, financial sanctions or prison sentences for corporate crime, or capital punishment for highly violent crime, scare off other people from committing similar crimes.

Here a core question has been whether the strictness of punishment matters for general deterrence. A good example are studies looking at how the length of prison sentences affects crime. Scholars conducting such research have used a variety of sophisticated methods and study designs. Many studies use aggregate governmental data on crime rates and rates of imprisonment, and apply complex statistical analyses intended to isolate the effects of imprisonment on crime. There are many confounding variables that can influence crime, so this is no easy feat.

Moreover, there is a fundamental problem with using data in this way. It does not clearly separate cause from effect. It may at first seem logical that imprisonment and crime rates only work together in one direction: namely, that more and longer imprisonment reduces crime. When we think a little deeper, however, we immediately realize that the reverse should then also be true. The amount of crime directly affects how much we punish offenders, and thus the imprisonment rates.[30] Therefore, it has been very difficult to isolate the effect of imprisonment on crime from the effect of crime on imprisonment.[31] Of course, studying the deterrent effect of incarceration using a true experimental design (where all other conditions are controlled and randomly assigned) is impossible. The best method researchers have come up with is to conduct quasi-experiments, in which scientists study crime both before and after actual changes to incarceration policy.

The irony is that cases like golf-club thief Gary Ewing's have provided an ideal quasi-experimental setting to test the effect of general deterrence and stronger punishment. There is a clear "before" and "after." Prior to 1994, California sentences for these cases were substantially lighter than after 1994, when the three strikes laws were enacted. Thus, California, twenty-four other states, and the federal government, which also adopted similar laws, provide excellent test cases.

Do the three strikes laws show us that longer prison sentences deter others from offending? The short answer: not really.

In the 2001 book *Punishment and Democracy*, Berkeley criminologist Frank Zimring and colleagues presented an in-depth study on the deterrent effects of three strikes in California.[32] The study used seven years of data from nine major cities in California to examine crime rates before and after three strikes was introduced. Zimring and colleagues found that crime rates did drop after the policy was introduced. But the problem was that crime rates had already been declining well before the three strikes law was enacted. And, most importantly, they found that the law did not accelerate the decline.

To provide an even more robust test, Zimring and his colleagues focused on criminals with prior convictions. They thought that maybe the three strikes had no effect on first-timers but did have a dramatic deterrent effect on people who already had strikes. After all, these were the people who would lose the most from the new sentence enhancements under the three strikes laws. It was a rational view. But they found that the law had no measurable effect even on second-strike offenders. In fact, they concluded that the deterrent effect of a three strikes law was "between zero and 2%."[33]

Many other scholars have come to the same conclusions. Some researchers use a novel approach of comparing similar counties that have and have not enacted or enforced the three strikes laws. Comparing across counties, one study finds that counties that vigorously and strictly enforce the three strikes law do not experience a decline in any crime category relative to more lenient counties.[34] Another scholar studying similar data reports, "It does not appear that three-strikes in California has had a significant deterrent or incapacitative effect on crime."[35]

Alarmingly, there is some evidence that three strikes may have *increased* crime, especially violent felonies. A study of 188 US cities over a twenty-year period found that three strikes increased crime by 13–14 percent in the short term and 16–24 percent in the long term.[36] In a paper appropriately titled "The Lethal Effects of Three-Strikes Laws," Thomas Marvel and Carlisle Moody, both professors of economics at the College of William & Mary, demonstrated that the three strikes laws have increased homicides between 10 and 12 percent in the short run, and up to 23–29 percent in the long run. They found that "because three-strikes laws call for harsh prison terms for criminals with prior convictions, criminals who fear the laws because they have two strikes would be expected to take extra steps to avoid punishment."[37] People who face a third strike may become particularly violent to avoid getting caught.

The policy may also backfire because two-strikers have nothing to lose once they decide to commit a third offense. Ray Fisman, a professor in behavioral economics at Boston University, explains the predicament persuasively. Suppose you've already decided your only option is to break the law. You have to steal something in order to make some money. The question is, What are you going to rob to give you the best bang for your buck? "Are you going to lift a few golf clubs from the local pro shop? Or are you going to hold up a bank? The potential haul from a bank robbery is obviously much greater, and the penalty is the same: Bank robbery will get you decades in the slammer, but if it's your third offense, so will shoplifting."[38] The example may be extreme, but the logic still stands. You're facing a third strike either way, so why not go for the bigger crime?

Two papers offer some doubt. In the first, Joanna Shepherd, who received her PhD in economics from Emory University where she is now vice dean at the School of Law, used crime data from all fifty-eight California counties in the period between 1983 and 1996 to get a more detailed county-level view of the effects of three strikes policy. Shepherd did find, contrary to some of the other studies, that three strikes has a deterrent effect. Even the first strike is a strong threat: "Fearing initial strikes, potential criminals commit fewer crimes that qualify as initial strikes." However, she did not find a strong deterrent effect for murder and rape, and thus not for the violent crimes for which three strikes laws were instituted in the first place. She explains this finding by the fact that violent criminals simply do not consider the consequences of long imprisonment. "If criminals discount their future as heavily as many believe, stricter sentencing may not substantially increase criminals' perceptions of the prison sentence for murder."[39]

In the second study, two economists also found that three strikes laws do have a deterrent effect.[40] But their study uncovered a different problem. In their calculations, three strikes policy was not cost-effective. The cost of using three strikes to prevent one crime was about $148,000, while the average cost of each crime was only $34,000. Based on this huge discrepancy, this study argued that if the $4.6 billion spent on sentencing and incarcerating criminals under the enhanced penalties of three strikes laws were to have been used on extra police to patrol the streets instead, it would have been astronomically more effective in fighting crime. Instead of reducing an estimated thirty thousand crimes each year through sentencing and punishment under three strikes, using the money on extra police patrols would have reduced one million crimes each year—an effect over thirty times larger.

Overall, we can conclude that existing social scientific knowledge fundamentally questions the deterrent effect of three strikes policies. There simply is no conclusive evidence that the longer sentences of the three strikes laws have had a deterrent effect on crime. Many studies find no deterrent effect, and the few studies that do find such an effect either find it does not deter the violent crimes it seeks to prevent or find that its deterrent effect is far less effective and more expensive than investing in extra policing. But maybe scientists are failing to find evidence supporting deterrence because they aren't looking at the strongest possible punishment: the death penalty.

In 1975, economist Isaac Ehrlich published a paper that he grimly yet appropriately titled "The Deterrent Effect of Capital Punishment: A Matter of Life and Death." Ehrlich employed complicated econometric modeling to study whether executions affect homicide rates. Ehrlich's findings boiled down to a simple and oft-cited conclusion: "An additional execution per year over the period in question may have resulted, on average, in 7 or 8 fewer murders."[41] To Ehrlich, capital punishment has a clear deterrent effect, and about seven or eight murders are prevented each time someone is executed.

Ehrlich's study on the deterrent effect of capital punishment offered a clear answer to a complex question amid a highly polarized debate. The study came at an auspicious moment for the death penalty in the United States. This was a time when, on the one hand, the Supreme Court had put capital punishment on hold,[42] but on the other, just years earlier, President Nixon had been giving speeches wholeheartedly advocating capital punishment. It is no surprise that this study generated much attention. Following its publication, the solicitor general of the United States even used it in an amicus brief filed in the Supreme Court case that ultimately reinstated the death penalty, *Gregg v. Georgia*.[43] Looking back forty years later, one Columbia law professor remarked, "His conclusion had the impact of a sound bite and a bumper sticker rolled into a stick of political dynamite."[44]

There was a problem, however. In the 1970s, just after Ehrlich published his study, academic articles in leading, peer-reviewed journals challenged his methods and conclusions. Scholars pointed to shortcomings in the study's "sample period and/or the variables he chose, and the murder supply equation and the functional form of the equations he estimated." These scholarly critiques even culminated in a study by the National Research Council, the nation's premier source of independent and expert advice on scientific issues. The council is composed of leading scholars who hold varying viewpoints but are collectively charged with advising the federal government, the general public, and the scientific community on the state of the scientific findings. Before being released to the public, its reports undergo extensive review by independent outside experts who also have varied points of view. In 1978, the council published a report laying out a long list of flaws in Ehrlich's study and challenging his findings. This report concluded that "available studies [including Ehrlich's] provide no useful evidence on the deterrent effect of capital punishment." Despite being used so widely during the 1970s, Ehrlich's study fell into disfavor for decades afterwards.[45]

Yet, since the early 2000s, Ehrlich's study has enjoyed a sort of revival. New studies, mostly by economists, similarly conclude that capital punishment can deter crime. One study found that an execution can deter up to thirty-two homicides. Moreover, another paper argued that executions can even deter irrational crimes, such as passion murders. Another economist even concluded that when there is capital punishment, nonlethal sanctions, such as fines and imprisonment, also have an increased deterrent effect. That is, when there are executions, other lesser sanctions begin deterring crime more effectively. As one study summarized this body of "new deterrence" work, "The deterrent effects of capital punishment are apparently indefinite and offer execution as a cure-all for everyday crime."[46]

Just like in the 1970s, the new studies again caused a major stir. Leading magazines and newspapers, including *Business Week*, the *Boston Globe*, and the *Denver Post*, routinely cited one such study that had concluded that each capital punishment prevents five homicides and that pardons and commutations increase murders.[47] Groups supporting capital punishment started spreading these studies like wildfire. And, like in the 1970s, the new deterrence studies were cited again in amicus briefs presented before the courts in death penalty cases.[48] One of the authors of a new deterrence study, Joanna Shepherd, testified before the House Judiciary Committee and stated that "there is sound scientific evidence that each execution deters between three and eighteen murders."[49]

Yet, just like in the 1970s, the new deterrence studies soon were heavily critiqued by leading academics. One scathing study that reviewed the literature found that the studies often relied on "a few outlier states and

years" and "artifactual results from truncated time frames."[50] The studies suffered from the rampant use of inappropriate statistical methods,
frequent omission of key data, and a failure to account for other major
factors that influence murder rates, such as drug epidemics.[51] Perhaps
most importantly, the new deterrence studies did not actually test deterrence.[52] They never directly tested whether potential offenders chose
not to commit murder because they feared capital punishment. New
deterrence proponents never examined whether executing people scared
would-be offenders away from crime. As one critical paper cogently explained, "There is little clarity about the knowledge potential murderers
have concerning the risk of execution: are they influenced by the passage
of a death penalty statute, the number of executions in a state, the pro-
portion of murders in a state that leads to an execution, and details about
the limited types of murders that are potentially susceptible to a sentence
of death?"[53]

   If that wasn't enough, there was evidence that capital punishment
caused *more* crime. Researchers kept finding that capital punishment has
a "brutalization effect" that ends up increasing homicides. The brutality of executions inspires criminals and legitimizes their violence.[54] One
study found, for instance, that immediately following executions, homicide rates against strangers increase.[55] Even Shepherd, the economist who
supported the deterrent effect of capital punishment when she testified
in front of the House Judiciary Committee, subsequently concluded that
executions may cause such brutalization.[56]

   And just like in the 1970s, this again culminated in a National Research Council report. The new NRC report offered an unwelcome and
sobering conclusion: "Research to date on the effect of capital punishment on homicide is not informative about whether capital punishment
decreases, increases, or has no effect on homicide rates."

   What all this shows is how complex the behavioral code is. It is very
difficult to isolate the effects of stricter punishment on crime because
there are many influences on our behavior. And, crucially, all these studies still do not establish the full causal chain necessary to prove that
there truly is general deterrence, namely that potential offenders actually

decide to refrain from crime because they fear the strong punishment they see others receive.[57] This would require very different data, not just on rates of imprisonment and crime but also on the perceptions and decisions of potential criminal actors in the heat of the moment. Moreover, it is very hard to generalize from these studies about all forms of punishment and discipline in every context. There is, for instance, some evidence that initial increases in fines deter traffic violators.[58] Yet there is no scientific evidence that stricter punishment works as a deterrent against corporate offenders.[59]

Altogether, there is no conclusive evidence that stricter punishments do or do not deter criminal behavior. Establishing a link between the deterrent effect of stricter punishment and crime is highly complex and very much context-specific. The causal chain from stricter punishment to criminal decision-making is impossible to establish fully.

We are left with a highly frustrating conclusion that has multiple possible interpretations. One option is that we can say we simply do not know, that science is unable to say whether stricter punishment does or does not deter. The NRC came to this conclusion twice in its reports on the death penalty. The problem with leaving it at this conclusion is that the public debate will then likely move on without the science, without the scientific doubt about the effects of stricter punishment. And all too likely, debates about stricter punishment would revert back to the simplicity of our gut feelings: stricter punishment surely must deter.

The better option is to explain clearly what the lack of conclusive evidence for the general deterrent effect of stricter punishment entails. It means that there is reasonable doubt that issuing stricter punishment will in and of itself have the intended deterrent effect. And such doubt necessitates a very careful deliberation on whether stricter punishment should then be pursued, especially when it concerns life and death or lifelong incarceration. At the very least, it means that societies considering increasing punishments should gather all the evidence they can to carefully evaluate any effects on crime. As Beccaria wrote over 250 years ago, "Every punishment which does not arise from absolute necessity is tyrannical."[60]

The doubt about the positive effects of stricter punishment also means we have to look beyond punishment severity alone. We must assess under what conditions people respond to sanctions.

## GETTING CERTAIN ON CRIME

While there is no conclusive evidence that stricter punishment deters, scientists have come to a strong conclusion about the crucial role certainty of punishment plays in deterring crime. Study after study finds that punishment only deters crime if the punishment is inevitable. The more certain the punishment, the likelier offenders are to get caught, prosecuted, convicted, and made to pay a fine or do the time, the likelier punishment will deter. Daniel Nagin, a leading Carnegie Mellon criminologist who has been involved in over three decades of deterrence research, concludes in his review of the existing research that the "evidence in support of the deterrent effect of various measures of the certainty of punishment is far more convincing and consistent than for the severity of punishment."[61]

Studies show that without a threshold level of certainty, punishment will simply not deter. Criminologists have found that crime increases in places that have lower than a 30 percent arrest rate, and it decreases in places with arrest rates *higher* than 30 percent. Thus, there appears to be a tipping point in the certainty of punishment. Later studies replicated these findings and reported certainty threshold levels ranging between 25 and 40 percent.[62] The same studies also point out that many communities never reach the required tipping-point level of certainty.[63]

If the certainty of being caught matters, law enforcement becomes essential for deterrence. The idea is that people think twice about committing crimes when police are visible in a community. So hiring more officers or simply making police officers more visible in communities can reduce crime.[64] The latter is referred to as the sentinel effect: police presence serves as a sentinel function that deters and prevents crime by making the chances of apprehension extremely high.[65] Studies find that investing in police is a much more efficient way to deter crime than investing in the prison system.[66]

Of course, police cannot be everywhere at all times, but they do not need to be. Criminologists have found that there are "hot spot" crime areas that have a much higher crime rate than average. One study analyzed 323,979 calls to the Minneapolis police over a one-year period and found a clear geographical pattern of high-crime hot spots.[67] Overall, the study found that in Minneapolis, 50 percent of all calls originated from only 3 percent of the city. In particular, the study found that virtually all reported robberies occurred in 2.2 percent of the city, all reported rapes in 1.2 percent of the city, and all reported auto thefts in 2.7 percent of the city. Later studies in other cities, including Jersey City and Seattle, had similar findings.[68]

If crime mainly occurs in particular hot spots, and if police presence can reduce crime by strongly enhancing the certainty of being caught, then it makes sense to concentrate police in such hot spots. Studies support this logically sound proposition, finding that increasing police presence in hot spots can lead to a 6 to 13 percent decrease in crime calls.

You may be wondering whether would-be criminals would just walk a few streets over to where there are fewer police. There are too many cops on Fifth, so I'll just rob the convenience store on Seventh. It doesn't appear that this is the case. Researchers have consistently found that increasing police presence in certain areas of the city did not just displace crime from one area to another.[69] Not only is there no evidence that crime simply gets displaced to the surrounding areas; there is also some evidence that crime actually decreases in the surrounding areas.[70]

Here we must add a word of caution. If the hot-spot policing strategy is executed in the wrong way, in the wrong context, and without ample, ongoing input and supervision from community members, the results can be terrible. A prime example of this is stop-and-frisk policing in New York City. In New York, stops and searches ballooned by 500 percent between 2003 and 2008, but the practice didn't peak until 2011, when in a single year police stopped New Yorkers more than 685,000 times. The idea was that these massive police interventions would help to enhance the detection of drugs and guns and remove them from the streets. However, stop-and-frisk policies disproportionately affect poor and racial minority areas. Particularly in New York, there was a strong racial bias in the way the policies were enacted. Compared to whites, people of Latinx or Hispanic descent were three times more likely to be stopped. In 2016, 82 percent of people stopped were either Black or Latinx. And in 2013, US district court judge Shira A. Scheindlin judged the practice in New York to be unconstitutional.[71] According to data from the New York Civil Liberties Union, stop-and-frisk policy is enormously expensive and counterproductive. Almost 90 percent of stops yield no contraband.[72] But worse perhaps is that this policy erodes trust in law enforcement and the legitimacy of the legal system as a whole, and, as we will discuss later, this can create more crime instead of reducing it.

Enhancing certainty is not easy. Law enforcement will always have limited capacity and not be able to detect all illegal activities, and, even when they do, this does not always result in successful prosecution and conviction. To best understand this, let's look at the corporate world.

In 2014, Eric England had trouble getting an Uber ride as he waited outside the historic Arlene Schnitzer Concert Hall in Portland, Oregon. He kept refreshing the app until finally a driver accepted his request for a ride. England was different from the other concertgoers who were trying to get home on a cold night. He was there to catch Uber in the act of breaking the law.

Uber, the world's leading ride-sharing company, had previously announced that it would launch in Portland, even though it was clearly against local taxi regulations. In fact, Portland's transportation commissioner, Steve Novick, had told an Uber political strategist that they were not welcome. As he put it in no uncertain terms, "Get your fucking company out of our city!"[73] Because Uber had announced that it would be launching in Portland anyway, Novick sent England and many other inspectors to find and fine drivers working for Uber. By posing as a concertgoer, England was hoping to catch Uber in the act. England opened his Uber app, called a car, and waited.

The Uber app indicated that England's driver would arrive in five minutes. It showed him exactly where the car was driving and what route it would follow to pick him up. The minutes and distanced ticked down until suddenly the ride was canceled, and the app showed that the car had driven past him.

England did not know that he had never been in the normal Uber app environment in the first place. Even though he had followed the same procedure that millions of people have followed to download the app and call for an Uber ride, England had never actually ordered a car. Despite the app and the process looking the same, England, as a *New York Times* story would later show, had been "Greyballed."

"Greyball" refers to a secret system in the Uber app that marked people like Eric as a potential threat to the company. Once you are marked, the system relegates the user to a fake version of the app that appears to function as normal but prevents them from ever catching a ride. The cars and drivers that it shows are ghosts that don't exist. In this way, Uber could successfully evade the hefty fines that some cities tried to levy on their drivers.

This was just one of many different methods Uber used to protect itself and its drivers from fines. The company had previously sent drivers instructions on how not to get caught for a variety of different infractions. For instance, drivers got messages like "Keep your Uber phone off your windshield; put it down in your cupholder," and "Use the lanes farthest from the terminal curbside for pickup and dropoff." These are sensible instructions on how to not get caught. And in case that did happen, Uber promised drivers, the company would pay the fines. All drivers needed to do was send a picture of a ticket to an Uber email address.

The Greyball system, though, was different. It was much deeper, as it effectively undermined undercover sting operations that authorities, like those in Portland, had started to use. The big challenge in designing the system had been how to differentiate legitimate customers from potential enforcement threats. Uber engineers came up with many ways to do so. For instance, they used "geofencing," in which they would draw a digital perimeter around police stations and other law enforcement premises and then monitor people in those locations who opened and closed the Uber app. This was considered suspicious behavior and could land a person on Uber's Greyball list. Even more problematic, Uber would also analyze new users' personal data such as credit cards, phone numbers, and addresses to see whether they had any relation to law enforcement.

Uber is not alone in successfully evading detection when breaking the law. Bernie Madoff had for years been able to operate a pyramid scheme that made him billions of dollars and left his investors thinking that their returns were coming from real profits and not from each other. He had been able to do so right under the nose of the Securities Exchange Commission (SEC), which had already raided his offices twice. The problem was that the SEC had raided a building's eighteenth and nineteenth floors, where the legitimate business and investment work was being done, not knowing that the entire seventeenth floor was designated for running Madoff's pyramid scheme.[74] We can also think of the brilliance of the Russian sports federation that successfully evaded doping inspections during the 2014 Winter Olympics in Sochi. When they designed the doping inspections laboratory, the Russians installed a secret opening between room 125, where the doping authorities would collect official urine samples, and room 126, where the Russian medical team would swap dirty samples with clean ones. They even found a way to replace the supposedly unbreakable seals of the doping sample containers.[75]

People have been ingenious in hiding illegal behavior. The Bernie Madoff and the Russian doping cases show that they can do so even while they're under the direct scrutiny and watchful eye of governmental regulators. They can build what sociologist Garry Gray has called Potemkin Villages, after the Russian story that Grigory Potemkin had villages of cardboard constructed to impress Catherine II during her 1787 visit to her new territories that he had been tasked to manage.[76]

With advancing technology, evading detection by the authorities no longer requires creating secret openings in walls or renting out secret floors. All that is needed is a group of smart coders. The more powerful and resourceful the offender, and the more complex the illegal behavior, the harder it will be for law enforcement officials to detect the crime.

The stricter the punishment such offenders face, the more resources they will devote to evading getting caught.[77] And the problem does not just stop with detecting the illegal conduct itself. Consider the challenges prosecutors have in gathering evidence for complex forms of crime. A key problem here is to collect the evidence of rule breaking and then present it in such a way that a jury will convict them. Complex cases that may make this highly challenging are not limited to corporate crimes. Consider this startling statistic from New Zealand: of all cases of sexual violence reported to the authorities, only 11 percent end up in a conviction.[78]

And the problem does not stop with prosecution. Sometimes, especially in corporate cases, even when there is sufficient evidence, authorities have been unable to enforce sentences. A shocking study by Ezra Ross, a law professor at the University of California, Irvine, and Martin Pritikin, the dean of Purdue Global's law school, shows that after corporations are ordered to pay penalties, the actual collection rates are routinely well below 50 percent. In fact, the Department of Justice is only able to get about 4 percent of the fines and penalties it imposes. The Office of Surface Mining, one of the main US mining agencies, does only a little better, with a 5 percent collection rate, and the California Highway Patrol collects about 6.6 percent of its fines. And even the best-performing agencies, such as the SEC, collect only about 45 percent of their outstanding fines and penalties.[79]

The social science conclusively finds that certainty matters more than severity. So, to improve our laws and the operation of the behavioral code, we must invest in good, constitutional, and community-based law enforcement instead of building more prisons. Moreover, we should stop increasing penalties every time we hear of yet another shocking form of rule breaking, and focus instead on ensuring that offenders are caught and punished.

## KNOWING THE PUNISHMENT

Dutch taxpayers have for a long time overestimated law enforcement. When filing their individual income tax returns, the Dutch would think that there was a high chance that should they cheat they would be discovered through audits. Moreover, they thought that when caught, the individual punishment for tax evasion would be severe. In reality, Dutch tax authorities rarely audit individuals for income tax issues, and when they find irregularities they only issue mild sanctions.[80] For tax authorities, such overestimation of risk and deterrence is ideal. Even when there is only limited enforcement, and even when it is very hard to catch violators, there can still be a semblance of deterrence.

However, the opposite may also be true. Even when there is strong law enforcement, people's perception may be that violators have a slim chance of being discovered and punished. The social science shows that deterrence is subjective and entirely depends on the perceptions of the would-be offender. If a potential offender underestimates the certainty and severity, the effect on their behavior will be undermined.

In 2005, a trio of Australian and American political scientists systematically analyzed perceptions of law enforcement held by environmental managers in the chemical industry.[81] Their study examined how hearing about other firms getting punished for illegal pollution then impacted how environmental managers at different companies made decisions about compliance with environmental law. The study found that the environmental managers' knowledge of the frequency and severity of fines was totally inaccurate. As the study summarizes, "Respondents report having heard of far fewer fines than actually occur. For example, the median number of fines against other companies (anywhere in the United States, in the last year or two) that respondents could recall was only eight. Yet in Louisiana alone, in a one-year period (July 2001 through June 2002), thirty-one companies were fined for environmental infractions."[82] Moreover, most respondents remembered the details about the infractions in these cases but not the punishment the polluters received. In fact, the respondents systematically underestimated the certainty and severity of punishment.

The process of the punishment of one actor affecting the perceptions of such punishment among other actors is not clearcut and automatic. Information gets lost and is diffused. This is not a problem if regulated actors, like Dutch taxpayers, overestimate the deterrence threat. However, it is an immense problem when people underestimate the risk of punishment. This means that whatever enforcement efforts are made, and whatever immense costs are spent to enhance the certainty of punishment and improve detection, will not automatically translate into a sufficiently higher risk perception and will not result in as much compliant behavior as might be expected. Detecting and punishing violations is not enough. Equally important is that the enforcement action is properly communicated.

People generally do not have a sound idea of what the expected certainty and severity of punishment are for various crimes. There is a mismatch between public perceptions and the actual certainty and severity of punishment. Criminological studies show that while people can generally discern between what penalties will apply when comparing particular crimes, they do a poor job in knowing the actual probability and severity of punishment for a particular crime. For instance, a study of over fifteen hundred adults from fifty-four large urban counties in the US showed that there was a near-zero correlation between people's perceptions of the severity and certainty of punishment and the actual numbers.[83] In fact, in a 2013 review of existing studies, criminologist Robert Apel summarized: "With few exceptions, the reported correlations between criminal sanctions and individual perceptions are quite weak. Inclusion of even a handful of control variables tends to eliminate any significant correlation—an indication of how tenuous the sanctions-perceptions link might actually be."[84]

We also know that perceptions about deterrence can change with new experiences. Criminologists, for instance, have found that there is a so-called *experiential effect*. People who commit crimes but have not been caught will develop lower risk perceptions of certainty and severity. Essentially, experience in getting away with breaking the law teaches offenders to believe that they can continue to get away with crime.

However, experiencing punishment or seeing others get punished does not always increase people's deterrence perceptions. Most studies find that offenders who get caught and punished tend to develop higher

risk perceptions only if they originally thought the certainty of that was
low. And, problematically, other offenders who get caught and punished
might see lower risks. Criminologists Greg Pogarsky and Alex Piquero
relate this to the "gambler's fallacy," wherein offenders believe that lightning will not strike them twice.[85]

All in all, this body of research shows a key yet often overlooked
aspect of deterrence: for punishment to deter crime, not only must it
be certain; people must also *perceive* it to be so. As Apel concludes in
his overview of this research, "The apparent lack of correspondence
between subjective probabilities and punishment actualities is discourag-
ing for the deterrence doctrine. If people are only vaguely aware of the
criminal punishments in their city, state, or county, then the deterrence
rationale of punishment is seriously undermined."[86] For punishment to
truly deter crime, communication is key. It is not enough to catch and
punish offenders. To achieve a deterrent effect, authorities must take the
next equally important step of communicating enforcement actions to
the general public. The detection and prosecution of crime is but the
first step in successful deterrence; communication to potential offenders
is the crucial second.

RESISTING OUR PUNITIVE INTUITIONS

Since the mid-1990s, David Kennedy, a professor of anthropology at
John Jay College of Criminal Justice in New York City, has successfully
convinced several large US police departments to adopt his science-based
approach to reducing violent gang crime. His strategy has become
known as "focused deterrence." It became famous because of its success,
as Operation Ceasefire, in reducing rampant gang violence that had been
going on for years in Boston.

Kennedy's approach was directly aligned to key scientific insights
about deterrence. First, he moved beyond strictly punishing even the
lightest crimes, which had become popular in the "zero tolerance" and
Strike Hard campaigns that had been deployed against crime across the
country at the time. Instead, he followed Beccaria's ideas and made certainty and swiftness key. In doing so, he sought to ensure that there

would be a threshold level of certainty of punishment without which severe punishment would not work.

Second, he emphasized communication about punishment. Specifically, he used targeted messaging to the most violence-prone gangs and communicated clearly to them what would happen if their gangs did not end the violence. To do so, he asked local authorities to compel gang members out on parole and probation to attend meetings where they would be warned that they and their gangs would face certain, swift, and harsh punishment if they did not end the violence. As such, his approach used the two key insights from the deterrence literature: certainty and changing perceptions.

But beyond deterrence, Kennedy offered gang members employment counseling and life coaching. He also used moral pressure from the local community to convince the youth to alter their violent lives. In doing so, Kennedy connected directly with other social science insights that crime reduction requires socioeconomic opportunities and that people respond to social and moral appeals in their community.

Kennedy's approach was able to reduce gang violence in a community where nothing else had worked. A similar result occurred in Cincinnati. Residents there were overwhelmed by daily reports of murder and were worried about the reputation the city was getting for its extreme violence. As a result, law enforcement had conducted a zero-tolerance campaign for even low-level crimes and minor infractions. Yet even when arrests for minor crimes surged over a three-month period during the zero-tolerance campaign, the campaign backfired; killings in the city increased and reached an all-time high, up to twelve additional murders per day. Nothing seemed to work, until the city police department adopted Kennedy's targeted deterrence approach.

The approach was a success. Not all meetings went smoothly, and not all of the gang-related youth who sought help getting jobs actually ended up securing employment. Nonetheless, the gang-related murder rate declined all over the city. One study that tracked the effects over time found that gang-related homicides declined almost 38 percent in twenty-four months and 41 percent in forty-two months post-implementation in Cincinnati.[87] And such focused deterrence campaigns appear to have had dramatic effects elsewhere too. A review of the empirical evaluations of the effectiveness of this approach across a wide range of cities found that overall it reduces crime.[88] The results have not been as large everywhere, but it does work.

Despite these successes, Kennedy faced an uphill battle in convincing police departments to adopt his approach. His physical appearance may have been an initial obstacle. As John Seabrook reported in the *New Yorker*, police would say things like: "What's some guy who looks like Jesus got to tell us about crime in Cincinnati?" He looked unlike any other academic. As Seabrook wrote: "There was something about him of the High Plains Drifter—the mysterious stranger who blows into town one day and makes the bad guys go away. He wore a grizzled beard and had thick, unbound hair that cascaded halfway down his back."[89]

But the real problem ran deeper. It was one of politics and public perception of what comprises a good approach to bad behavior. Cincinnati mayor Mark Mallory had at first been afraid that Kennedy's approach would be seen as being soft on crime. Following their punitive intuition, people had been calling for tougher policing, longer prison sentences, and even a new jail to house these offenders. These are all things that had been tried again and again but had not stopped the murder rate. Bringing in a social scientist seems like a soft approach, especially when the outside expert offers gang members life coaching and job counseling.

This is the key problem. Our gut feelings, fueled by both our own fears and politicians, tell us that fighting bad behavior is simple: just get tougher and make it public. There is even evidence that humans are biologically hardwired for punishment. One neurological study has found that our brains favor punishment, as the dopamine system is activated when we punish others.[90] So, to fight crime, to fight corporate fraud, or to fight unsafe driving, our intuition tells us that all we need is more and stricter punishment. These sentiments are deeply ingrained. We can find them in major ancient traditions across the globe, from classical thinkers in Greece to the legalist scholars in premodern China and the sacred books of Hinduism, Judaism, Christianity, and Islam. In all we find the same ideas: bad people only respond to pain, punishment is the ideal way to mete out pain to correct bad behavior, and if such punishment occurs in public, all will come to fear it and keep their behavior in check.[91] But this traditional thinking has no contemporary empirical scientific basis. There is no conclusive evidence that stricter punishment, in and of itself, deters.

People tend to let their moral convictions about what is right and wrong shape how they think about what is an effective way to deal with misconduct. It's what psychologists call *moral coherence*. This means that people conflate what they perceive to be morally correct with what is actually effective.[92] If some policy fits with my moral beliefs or intuitions, it must work. People who morally support waterboarding, the "enhanced interrogation" technique some US intelligence officers used in Iraq, automatically think the practice is effective for producing actionable intelligence, which it is not.[93] Unfortunately, we are all susceptible to letting our preferences and intuitions dictate what we think actually works. It's part of being human.

The problem is that all of this undermines how we, the people, as well as our politicians, can use the science. As long as we let our gut feelings about punishment prevail over a rational weighing of the scientific evidence of what works, we will continue to support policies that simply do not work, and thus sometimes make things worse.

Researchers have become highly frustrated that their findings have not shaped public and criminal policy, particularly as the US has watched its prison population grow exponentially. Their despair is practically palpable. In 2011, criminologist Francis Cullen and his colleagues discussed the high costs of ignoring scientific insights. "The era of mass imprisonment has taken over corrections even though nobody has had a firm idea of whether placing offenders behind bars makes them more or less likely to recidivate." Given the high stakes of the costs of imprisonment, they urged, "Without such knowledge, ignorance reigns, and the risk rises that prison policies will needlessly endanger community safety, drain the public treasury, and entrap offenders in a life in crime." They implored those in power to pay attention to the science.[94] We cannot help but agree.

The inconvenient truth is that decades of scientific research have not found that stricter punishment deters wrongdoing, rule violations, or violent crime. In most instances, the threat of strong punishment alone is not enough. We have seen that there is no conclusive evidence that long-term prison sentences prevent recidivism or even that strong punishment deters others from offending, whether it is three strikes policy, the death penalty, or stronger sanctions against corporations.

The certainty of punishment is paramount. This means that rather than focus on meting out longer sentences or higher fines, we should focus on enhancing good, constitutional, and community-driven law enforcement and the chances that would-be offenders are apprehended and punished.

In addition, most people do not even know the probabilities of getting caught and punished or the potential severity of the punishment. It is not enough to enforce the law. For general deterrence to work, people have to learn about what happens to offenders. That means you have to publicize whenever you are punishing the rule breakers.

At worst, stricter punishment can backfire. Serving long terms in prison makes people less able to lead a law-abiding life. Brutal forms of punishment like the death penalty or decades of incarceration in highly unsafe prisons may only cause more brutal criminal responses. And stronger punishment can make people resort to even more violent and extreme ways of avoiding getting caught. Punishment can clearly make people behave worse.

The punishment reflex is deeply ingrained. As conservatives, we may call for getting tough on street crime and may support zero tolerance, three strikes, or capital punishment. And as progressives, we may support stricter punishment against polluting and fraudulent corporations and their CEOs. But there is no scientific support for either approach. And thus we cannot say for sure that stricter punishment will reduce street crime or prevent the next corporate scandal. We all run the danger of letting our moral convictions override scientific evidence of what actually prevents bad behavior.

We have to learn where our own intuitions and biases lie. What assumptions do we have about how to address bad behavior, and what
evidence do we have to back them up? And each time we learn new scientific evidence, even if it shows clear doubt, as it did here, we have to be
aware of how our preexisting assumptions will try to resist insights that
challenge them. Once we do so, we will see that punishment is not the
silver bullet we intuitively believe it is. There is no effective naughty corner against all social evils. Fortunately, punishment is but one of many
interventions to reduce bad behavior.

# CHAPTER 3

# Of Sticks, Carrots, and Elephants

It is a winter morning in 1995 in El Paso, Texas. Around town, phones start ringing just before 7:00 a.m. Families know this can only mean one thing. School is closed once again. As people go outside, they see the culprit: a black haze over their community. This pollution does not originate in their own city, not even from the US. It blows across the Rio Grande from the Mexican city of Juárez, where a few hundred small brick-making kilns emit a thick black smoke.[1] The reason the smoke is black is because these kilns burn scrap fuels like used wood, sawdust, plastics, manure, used motor oil, and even old car tires.

This was nothing new. In the late 1980s, Mexican authorities had started to address the pollution from the brick kilns. At first they had tried to cut brick kiln emissions by banning dirty fuels and forcing the brickmakers to use clean propane instead. But the outright ban was unsuccessful. The kilns operated in the so-called informal sector, where they did not register as a formal business, did not pay taxes, and operated on a day-to-day, low-cost basis. Because there were so many of these small businesses, the understaffed local environmental authorities simply had been unable to carry out regular on-site visits to enforce the law. And because the kiln operators faced stiff competition, they could only survive when they maintained cutthroat low prices. Even then, the kilns were barely breaking even. Operators could not afford to pay extra for burning cleaner fuels. And as you might imagine, making bricks was hard, painful work that provided an income for the poorest and neediest who had nowhere else to turn.

But change was afoot. The Mexican Federation of Private Health and Community Development Associations (known locally under the acronym FEMAP) started the Ciudad Juárez Brickmakers' Project. Rather than rely on the traditional adversarial enforcement focus of governmental authorities, it sought to cooperate with the kiln operators to motivate them to stop using dirty scrap fuels and change to propane. Between 1991 and 1994, the project successfully got many of the brickmakers to switch.

A combination of factors spurred this success. By the late 1980s, elections had pushed Mexican policy to prioritize environmental protection. And the US-Mexican NAFTA trade negotiations provided an extra pressure to go green in Mexico. This gave FEMAP the leverage it needed to push local authorities to take environmental issues more seriously and also to secure funds to support the project. FEMAP built a broad coalition that included brickmakers, local propane companies, and the municipal government, and together they used a carrot-and-stick approach. As a stick, local authorities started to invest in enforcing the ban on scrap fuels in order to end the virtual impunity that had existed. They enlisted help from the local community and asked them to report pollution at the local kilns and issue complaints about kilns still burning scrap fuels. And as a carrot, the brickmakers could not only get free propane equipment that they would never have been able to pay for themselves but also free technical support to help them set up the new equipment.

FEMAP was able to change market conditions. All major brickmakers' unions agreed to sell bricks at a fixed price of 250 pesos per thousand, and construction companies agreed to participate and buy "clean" bricks at this price. The switch to cleaner fuels was further incentivized when PEMEX, the Mexican state-owned petroleum company, began subsidizing propane, which lowered the costs of compliance with the ban on dirty fuels. At its high point, around 1993, about 60 percent of kilns were using propane, which meant that residents of Juárez and nearby El Paso could breathe more easily during the early 1990s.

Unfortunately, soon things went downhill. By 1995, conditions were just as bad as the 1980s. Some brickmakers undercut the price agreement by selling cheaper bricks made with scrap fuels. The municipal government loosened its ban on dirty fuels, started to allow kilns to burn sawdust, and ended enforcement. Construction companies threw away their old agreement to only buy the more expensive but cleaner propane-fired bricks, so the minimum prices were no longer guaranteed. Finally, propane subsidies ended because of economic liberalization policies. As a result, the cost difference between scrap and propane fuels rose from 29 percent in 1992 to 162 percent in 1995. Soon only one brickmaker was still using propane, which is why families in El Paso across the border would wake up to learn that schools were closed due to the black haze enveloping their community.

The initial success and early demise of this Mexican attempt to abate pollution tells an important story. It shows that a legal ban aimed to reduce damaging behavior can successfully change behavior when it gets the incentives right.

The brickmakers face a choice. They can choose to comply with the ban or to violate it. And both choices come with costs and benefits. When brickmakers violate the ban, that means they must pay for scrap fuels as well as run the risk of having to pay penalties should they get caught and punished. At the same time, brickmakers have lower costs and can increase sales by setting a lower price than competitors who follow the rules and sell clean bricks.

The same applies to compliance. The costs of compliance include paying the higher price for propane and the lower quantities of bricks they could sell due to competition from cheaper bricks sold by factories using scrap fuel. The benefits of compliance are the higher prices they get for each brick they do sell. If brickmakers make a rational choice, they will opt for compliance or violation based on whatever has the highest benefits minus the costs.

In Juárez, the costs of compliance went up as propane subsidies ended, and the benefits of compliance went down as clean bricks were outpriced in the market. Meanwhile the benefits of violation went up as there was more demand for cheaper scrap bricks, and the costs of violation went down as both the probability of enforcement and the costs of scrap fuel decreased. All in all, it was a volatile combination for failure.

So it seems that the behavioral code that shapes people's responses to the law consists of incentives, an endless array of sticks and carrots.

## DOES TORT LIABILITY KEEP US SAFE?

In December 2007, *Gawker*, a highly popular blog at the time—with its tagline "Today's gossip is tomorrow's news"—published a post that would cost it dearly.[2] The post's headline read: "Peter Thiel is totally gay, people."

In publicly outing Thiel, the powerhouse venture capitalist and co-founder of PayPal, *Gawker* was true to itself in its disregard for good taste and privacy. But it wasn't the headline or even the text of the post that would eventually bankrupt *Gawker*—it was one comment at the bottom of the post, written by *Gawker*'s founder, Nick Denton, that read: "The only thing that's strange about Thiel's sexuality: why on earth was he so paranoid about its discovery for so long?"[3] According to a book-length analysis of this story, this short comment infuriated Peter Thiel because it questioned his mental health.

Thiel was so angry that he started to refer to *Gawker* as "the MBTO," short for "Manhattan-based terrorist organization." Thiel wanted to go to war with *Gawker*, but there wasn't much that he could do. Was the *Gawker* post distasteful? Yes. Illegal? No. Yet Thiel vowed to bring *Gawker* down, and, being an extraordinarily wealthy venture capitalist and entrepreneur, he set up a shell company that would fund other people who had suffered similar treatment from *Gawker* to help them sue it "into oblivion."[4] All he needed was the perfect plaintiff.

Enter Hulk Hogan, the bandanna-clad and bleached-horseshoe-moustache-sporting former professional wrestling superstar, whose real name is Terry Eugene Bollea. Hogan had had sex with Heather Clem, who was married to radio personality Bubba the Love Sponge. Bubba, who it seems had encouraged his wife to sleep with Hogan, secretly made a thirty-minute sex tape of it, allegedly without Hogan knowing or giving his consent, then put it in his desk drawer. A rival DJ stole the tape and leaked copies in an attempt to get Bubba's popular time slot. Eventually the tape landed at *Gawker*, which published a two-minute clip on its website.

For *Gawker*, this proved to be a mistake. Hogan sued for $100 million in damages for invasion of privacy, infringement of personality rights, and intentional infliction of emotional distress. Backed by Thiel's massive litigation fund, Hogan found himself in a complex legal battle that would produce twenty-five thousand pages of court documents.[5] Hogan refused to settle, the case went to trial, and a massive verdict awarded Hogan $115 million in compensation, of which more than half covered his emotional distress, with another $25 million as punitive damages. *Gawker* founder Nick Denton's twenty-one-word comment about Peter Thiel ended up costing his company $140 million. At about $6.6 million for each word, it must have been the most expensive comment ever made on the Internet.

The *Gawker*-Thiel-Hogan saga is one of revenge and retribution. But the tort liability system that Thiel and Hogan used to get back at *Gawker*—the legal rules that govern how people must pay for damages they cause others—is not about revenge. The key function of tort is to ensure that people get compensation for the damages they suffered. So, in this case, it paid Hogan for the financial and emotional damages he incurred. We can, of course, debate whether his suffering is worth the $115 million awarded. But for some legal scholars and many economists, tort is even more ambitious than being merely restorative; it is also supposed to help prevent damaging behavior in the future. This is the reason why some jurisdictions, like the one in Florida where the Hogan case took place, have punitive damages. Such damages do not serve merely as compensation; they serve to deter damaging parties from engaging in harmful behavior in the future, as well as to deter others from engaging in similar conduct. In that sense, tort liability is not completely different from criminal punishment. In theory at least, the fact that the law holds us liable for causing damages and that we have to pay compensation may create an incentive to refrain from harmful and risky behavior. Don't do it—not because you may get caught and criminally punished but because you may get caught and *financially* punished.

In all of this, there is a central question: Does tort liability actually help to reduce damaging behavior?

Take car insurance as an example. People have car insurance to shield them from full liability. But still, when they cause accidents, their insurance company has to pay more, so the company naturally raises the premiums for people who cause accidents. In some jurisdictions, a different system has been adopted in which liability no longer plays a role. Here, in "no-fault" systems, victims of damages have a direct claim to insurance, which means that each driver's own insurance company pays for their losses, regardless of who is at fault. In effect, the drivers causing the damages are no longer liable. If tort liability serves to make people act more carefully, we would expect that a reform toward a no-fault system would result in more accidents and more traffic-related damages, injuries, and deaths.

However, several studies that have assessed whether this is true have found that unfortunately the picture is unclear and inconsistent. Some find that the reduction of liability due to no-fault insurance resulted in 2 to 15 percent more fatal accidents.[6] Others find no effect.[7] Two reviews of this body of work agree that the findings are inconclusive; we cannot establish whether tort does or does not play a role in reducing unsafe driving.[8]

Scientists have also analyzed the effects of liability for medical errors. When doctors or other caregivers make mistakes, patients have a right to sue for damages. Such medical malpractice liability may help make doctors operate more safely. But when liability for medical errors becomes very high, it may cause negative side effects. Some doctors may opt to leave jurisdictions with high liability or stop doing operations that have higher risk, and thus the supply of medical services may be reduced. And some doctors may order extra yet unnecessary tests just to make sure that they cannot be held liable for negligence. In light of these potential side effects and also because of the broader pressures toward tort reform, some jurisdictions have reduced liability for medical errors. Some have installed caps on the total economic and punitive damages that can be rewarded, some have limited attorney fees, some have reduced liability for plaintiffs when victims are jointly responsible for such damages, and some have instituted shorter statutes of limitations that decrease the time plaintiffs can sue for damages.

Just like with the traffic accidents, we can assess whether lowering liability increases medical errors. If tort liability really reduces damaging behavior, we would expect that when there is lower liability, injuries and fatalities due to medical errors should increase. Again, the evidence is not conclusive. Two major reviews of over one hundred empirical studies find that this picture, too, is blurry. For different types of medical liability, they do not find conclusive evidence that reducing liability increases injuries and fatalities due to medical errors. Instead, the studies have mixed or contrasting findings, and many show no association at all.[9]

Finally, there is also work on whether tort liability helps to reduce other kinds of corporate harm, including unsafe products, environmental degradation, and unsafe work conditions. A review of this work comes to the same conclusion as we have seen for car accidents and medical errors: there is no conclusive evidence that tort helps to reduce misconduct and damaging behavior.[10]

In studies of corporate executives' liability, there is some evidence that tort can help prevent harm. Studies find that when executives face higher liabilities, they make less risky decisions, like restating the earnings of the company, overpaying for corporations the company acquires, or taking the company public when it is not ready.[11] Yet the evidence here is highly circumstantial, and studies assess general risky decisions and not really decisions that directly cause harm.

One study sought to understand what organizations, particularly police departments and hospitals, learn when they get sued for damages.[12] In theory, the study argued, litigation can cause organizations to improve their internal functioning and prevent similar damages from occurring in the future. Whereas hospitals did seek to learn from tort lawsuits and gathered information they could use to improve their operations, police departments were far less likely to do so. So, it may well be that tort can stimulate an organization to be more introspective, but the study concluded that this is only the case when the incentives and the internal capacity to do so are in place, which is clearly not always the case.

Some studies examine the effect of insurance for tort liability, the idea being that insurance companies that provide coverage for tort damages have a stake in ensuring that the people or organizations they insure do not commit the harms that would trigger the liability. One study found some indication that tort insurers have played a positive role, including requiring police departments to adopt policies to reduce damages in high-risk activities such as high-speed vehicle pursuits and use of force.[13] Insurers have also stimulated some police departments to adopt body cameras. Yet the same study expresses doubt about whether adopting such measures truly reduces police misconduct, a question the study does not discuss empirically. That is, merely having a policy may not directly translate to changed behavior.

So, altogether, for many types of liability, including medical malpractice, car accidents, environmental damages, product safety, and worker safety, there is no conclusive evidence that tort liability acts as a disincentive to keep people from engaging in damaging or risky behavior. And while there is some evidence that organizations may learn from tort litigation, and that liability insurers may try to stimulate less risky behavior in their clients, there is no clear data to show that these actually reduce damage. What seems like a very clear disincentive is not so clear after all.

Tort may have the same problems in achieving deterrence as criminal punishment. For tort to deter it must be inevitable, yet achieving a high certainty of being sued and having to pay actual damages is difficult. It means that for every form of damage, there must be plaintiffs who are willing and able to successfully sue for damages. Shareholders are much more in a position to do so than victims of car crashes, medical errors, environmental pollution, unsafe products, or hazardous working conditions. Everyone else would need their own personal Peter Thiel.

For tort to deter, it also means that, for every form of tort, people who may cause damages should be aware of the liability they face. Here it is more likely that corporate executives, with all the legal advice they get on a day-to-day basis, are better informed than most doctors or drivers, for instance. As we will discuss later in the book, most people's legal knowledge is very limited, and that ranges all the way from non-experts to experts.

There is simply no proof that the law's softer stick of liability is effective at preventing harm. Just like with criminal punishment, this means that we cannot assume that simply creating stronger liability will reduce damaging conduct. Scientific insights about behavior could provide a reality check in the high-stakes political battle over tort reform. On one side are corporations, their lawyers, and their lobbyists seeking to reduce liability and lower access to tort litigation, arguing that there are too many frivolous lawsuits that are hurting business. And on the other side are the plaintiff lawyers who have resisted such reforms, arguing that tort is necessary to prevent and reduce damages *caused* by businesses. Both sides have weaponized political lobbying and funding, with corporations typically funding conservatives and plaintiff attorneys funding progressives.

Since the debate about tort has become so political and involves so much funding, each side could easily capture select scientific findings and leverage them. Corporations could draw on these insights to call for more reform by arguing that tort does not serve as a deterrent. But this is a flawed reading of the science. The empirical data do not show conclusively that tort deters harmful behavior. The current state of science is inconclusive as to whether stricter tort liability does or does not deter. What matters here, just like we saw with criminal punishment in the last chapter, is that by incorporating scientific research we start to think about tort in a different way. We should no longer assume that stricter tort in and of itself deters damaging behavior. Rather, for each instance in which we are considering instituting a new tort liability or changing it, we must consider how torts might influence behavior. It is very likely for tort that certainty matters more than severity, just as it does for punishment. Thus, the tort system should be more about ensuring that paying damages becomes inevitable rather than focusing on the size of damages to be paid. This means a refocusing of the current system is necessary, toward easier access for plaintiffs to sue for damages that actually occurred and away from punitive damages.

## REWARDING GOOD CONDUCT

When the stick fails, maybe it is time to bring out the carrot. The idea is very appealing. If we can improve behavior with positive incentives, we need to rely less on the inherent harm of punishment or even the costs of liability. What if we can simply just reward people into behaving?

As a social experiment of using carrots instead of sticks, the city of Richmond, California, definitely put itself on the map.[14] Located in the East Bay of the San Francisco area, this small city's homicide rate was among the highest in all of the United States, with forty-six murders annually per hundred thousand inhabitants—three times more than Chicago. Because of this atrocious statistic, the city's Office of Neighborhood Safety in 2010 invited twenty-five young men to a gathering at city hall, each handpicked because they were collectively responsible for 70 percent of all gun crimes in the city.[15]

When the young men were invited to the meeting, they were apprehensive. Their previous encounters with authorities and government officials definitely didn't include sitting in a conference room and being served lunch, each at a place setting featuring a plaque engraved with their name.[16] DeVone Boggan, who directed the Office of Neighborhood Safety, told the young men how sorry he was that no one in the city had contacted them before. He told them that peace in the city had to "come through them" and that the city would be there for them if they brought peace.[17] As the men were about to leave, Boggan gave each one an envelope with a thousand dollars in cash.

Soon the world learned of the Operation Peacemaker Fellowship. With this project, the city started to provide thousand-dollar monthly cash stipends for high-risk, violent, youthful offenders for making progress toward "life goals." These convicted young offenders could earn more money if they were able to find better housing, end substance abuse, pass their driver's license exam, or pay outstanding tickets.

This is an entirely different approach for dealing with bad behavior. Rather than use the criminal justice system to dole out punishment and threaten them into compliance, Richmond tried to reward good behavior. And it worked. In the seven years since the start of the program, the city's homicide rate dropped by 50 percent—far more than could be explained by overall socioeconomic changes in the area that had helped reduce crime a little in adjacent cities like Oakland.[18]

The program did not rely solely on the cash reward. Its success also originated in providing care and attention that many of the participants had never had, showing them what positive possibilities lie beyond the violence-ridden places they grew up in. That includes taking high-performing participants on coveted trips outside Richmond to places like Washington, DC, Disneyland, and South Africa. The program's central approach to reduce violence was to reward and promote good behavior. It incentivized doing the right thing, without the threat of the stick and without police involvement—and that last aspect was crucial. As one participant explained to a *New York Times* reporter: "When I knew they weren't the police, that's when they gained my trust. I can't be talking to you about stuff that I did and exposing this and that and you're the police. That don't work."[19]

Operation Peacemaker Fellowship showcases an extreme version of the carrot approach to enhance better behavior and reduce lawbreaking, but positive incentives can be used in many contexts and at many scaled levels. Think, for instance, of how teachers use small rewards to keep children in line. Thousands of schools across the US use something called a *positive behavior incentive system*. What this boils down to is giving children rewards for good behavior and taking them away for bad behavior. When children turn in homework, they receive a gold star. If they

help a classmate, they may receive another gold star. But if they misbehave in class, they lose a star. It's simple behavioral coding.

These behavioral incentive systems do have two clear advantages.
First, they reduce misbehavior. Research shows that children, particularly younger children, perform better if incentives are used.[20] And
second, the systems are often very inexpensive. How much time does
it take to give a child a sticker? What's the going rate for a pack of five
hundred stickers?

Despite these advantages, research is beginning to show the downside of using rewards to incentivize better behavior in school. Extrinsic
rewards like money and awards can reduce intrinsic motivation, impede
the development of autonomy and independence, and undermine children's responsibility for regulating themselves.[21] The problem is that
children can learn to simply satisfy the person who has the power to
give them the reward. Rather than be nice to my classmates for the sake
of just being nice to my classmates, I'm nice to my classmates because I
want that sticker.

If used properly, external incentives can promote self-regulation and
intrinsic motivation.[22] The key is to focus on the *behavior*, not simply the
*incentive*. It's one thing to simply give the sticker and say "Good job." It's
far better to also explain *why* the sticker was earned.[23] If we couple incentives with setting goals and inculcating a deeper understanding of why
the behavior matters, we may produce intrinsic motivation and better
behavior among kids. Importantly, this might work for adults too.

There have been several strands of empirical studies of how rewards
affect adult behavior. Much of the research has looked at whether rewards can stimulate more prosocial behavior, such as cooperation and
voting, and pro-environmental conduct, such as recycling and reducing
unnecessary travel.[24] While there is much less empirical work about how
rewards can stimulate compliance with laws, the best and most comprehensive work we have is on tax payment.[25]

Tax authorities and researchers have teamed up to see whether using positive incentives stimulates people to be more honest when they
file their taxes. Authorities have used two kinds of incentives: providing

higher benefits (such as Social Security) for people who report a higher income and offering rewards to people who have been found to have reported their taxes honestly. Most studies use experiments in social science laboratories to see what effect rewards have on tax payment. These experiments let participants play a game where they can earn cash rewards and then ask participants to report their earnings as though they have to pay a tax based on these earnings. And in most studies, there are random audits. Participants who are found to have cheated when reporting their income then have to pay a fine. The idea is to make it as realistic as possible.

These studies find that positive incentives do increase tax compliance overall, both when applied to individuals and in groups.[26] However, the effects of rewards on tax compliance are not straightforward. One laboratory experiment, described in a paper titled "Happy Taxation," found, for instance, a major gender difference: women complied more when they stood to receive a reward, while men did not.[27] An experiment in Switzerland found that people who promised to pay their taxes on time became more compliant when they were also offered a reward—but only when the reward was nonfinancial, like a chance to win a free weekend trip to a wellness spa.[28]

There is also research about whether offering people rewards can help to reduce fare dodging in public transport.[29] In Rimini, a popular beach destination on the Italian Adriatic coast, passengers often ride local buses without paying. They are supposed to get a ticket before boarding the bus, and buses themselves have automated machines where you can purchase a ticket as soon as you hop on. The bus company tried relying on random checks by ticket inspectors who could issue a €65 fine, but this failed to stop the problem. Noncompliance and fare dodging were rampant, so the company turned to researchers for help.

Here is how the scholars set up the experiment. In 54 of the 299 buses that the local company operated, they put up posters advertising that passengers who bought a ticket from the vending machine on the bus would have the chance to win a lottery prize of €500. They then compared whether the "lottery buses" sold more tickets than the normal ones. They found that the reward worked incredibly well; ticket sales increased on the lottery buses by 30 percent. This indicates that there had to have been a substantial reduction in fare dodging. Was it worth it? Kind of. On the one hand, the cost to pay for the lottery prizes was larger than the amount the bus company gained from the increased revenue from the tickets, yet they ended up making money because so many winners failed to claim their prizes.

Positive incentives can also play a role in compliance with environmental regulation. Remember the brickmakers in Juárez? Here, a series of studies analyzed the role propane subsidies played in stimulating compliance with the ban on burning dirty scrap fuels. As we saw, the subsidies promoted compliance.[30] But when the subsidies ended, the effect evaporated and brickmakers went right back to burning the banned, polluting fuels. This shows that even when rewards work, their effects may not last since it may be hard to keep the reward in place indefinitely.

However, the evidence on subsidies is mixed. Take, for instance, the role of subsidies in getting the US trucking industry to reduce diesel fuel emissions. The law did not require trucking companies to replace older polluting trucks, but it sought to incentivize the companies to voluntarily go beyond the existing legal standards, and it helped them pay for new, cleaner trucks. According to one study's calculations, the size of the subsidies was dramatically outweighed by the total investments needed to replace the trucks. Texas had budgeted, for example, only $57 million in such subsidies, while to be effective it would have needed to spend about $1.7 billion to replace all thirty-eight thousand older trucks.[31] Thus, the study shows a major obstacle for rewards in improving behavior: they have to be large enough to work, and that may not always be possible.

Overall, the available empirical evidence is mixed regarding the effect of positive incentives to improve compliance and reduce damaging behavior. We see that there is evidence that positive rewards can work. Yet we also see that rewards can backfire, that at times they are not cost-effective and other times are unsustainable or unaffordable.

There is another potential downside. Rewarding good behavior may undermine the intrinsic motivations that already typically make most of

us behave appropriately. By adding the reward, people's intrinsic motivation to follow rules may become "crowded-out" by extrinsic incentives.
There may even be an "over-justification effect" in which the reward
provides a justification that people already committed to the behavior do
not need. Indeed, some general psychological studies show that external incentives, including rewards, may undermine intrinsic motivation.[32]
Studies have shown crowding-out in general types of behavior, such as
people's willingness to cooperate, to engage in a healthy lifestyle, and to
generally act in prosocial ways. However, a recent review of this body
of work finds that while extrinsic incentives can crowd out intrinsic
motivation, the overall evidence is not conclusive—findings outside laboratory settings offer mixed and limited findings.[33]

When the stick fails, the carrot may improve behavior, but this approach may come with its own limits and risks. Overall, we see that the
incentives our laws use to improve behavior, whether in the form of punishment, liability, or rewards, do not always have the intended effect and
can even make matters worse. Unfortunately, it is hard to predict what
effect incentives might have. To know what liability and rewards will do
to improve behavior requires empirical analysis. But the problem is that
many people who create legal rules do not conduct or read such analyses.
Instead, they rely on what they think the incentives will do. And their
assumptions may well be wrong.

## COGNITION AND RATIONAL CHOICE

Lisa Shu, who teaches at the London Business School, gave her students
some simple puzzles to solve. She paid them for each puzzle they told
her they had solved correctly. Importantly, they knew that no one could
check their answers, so they were well aware that they could lie and get
more money out of the experiment. Not surprisingly, a large number of
these business students cheated.

Shu then had another group of her students sign an honesty pledge
*before* they attempted the puzzles. Pretty much, they just pledged to be
honest. Nothing else changed. The risks of cheating didn't change, nor
did the likelihood of getting caught. And the students were still earning

real money. Yet she found that her students cheated far less if they signed an honesty pledge. Simply signing a pledge made them more honest.

These were remarkable findings. The notion that a simple pledge can make us more honest has enormous implications, so Shu and her colleagues tried to apply this insight to real-world compliance problems. They found a variety of forms and instances where we sign our names and pledge that we completed the form accurately and honestly, like our tax filings or insurance forms. The only problem is that in these real-world forms, people sign their names *after* they have completed them. We do so because we need to attest that what we filled out was the truth, the whole truth, and nothing but the truth.

Think about that for a second. If we have already filled out the form, signing our name at the bottom of the form cannot influence our behavior while we fill out the form. Shu and her colleagues came up with a simple yet brilliant idea: what happens if we have people sign their names at the top of the form instead of at the bottom?

They wanted to test these insights on common forms that we all sign, so they came up with insurance forms. They thought it would be easy to convince insurance companies to let them test whether changing the location of the signature on their forms would decrease dishonest reporting and thus insurance fraud. They weren't asking much of the companies. Moving the signature line is cheap and easy. And if the intervention worked, the companies would receive more honest information about the risks they were insuring, thereby reducing insurance fraud and minimizing their risks. It seemed like a simple win-win situation.

To their surprise, insurance companies were not enthusiastic. Company lawyers first said that the signature at the bottom plays a vital role and cannot be moved to the top. The insurer needs to have a signature that attests that the insured has provided truthful information. So Shu and her colleagues changed their approach. Based on the pushback they received from the companies, they tried to develop a form with two signature lines, one at the top and one at the bottom. The researchers had their line on the top of the form, and the insurance companies had their line on the bottom. This should have pleased everyone.

Yet lawyers in the insurance companies still did not want to proceed. The lawyers thought the two lines were silly. They argued that they were burdensome and would annoy their clients. It was only after a long, difficult search that Shu and her colleagues were finally able to convince one company to allow them to conduct a study on a small insurance policy.[34]

In the ensuing field experiment, they studied a common type of auto insurance in which companies have their employees report their total mileage at the end of each year. When they moved the signature lines, they found something remarkable. On average, people who signed at the top of the form reported a substantially lower amount of mileage than those who signed at the bottom—a difference of more than 10 percent. Top-signers were significantly more honest than bottom-signers.[35]

This field experiment showed quite clearly that merely changing the location of a signature could considerably reduce dishonest reporting. And there's no added cost, no need for increased surveillance, and no need for stricter enforcement.

Shu's finding has enormous implications. Think about an organization of fifty employees that provides car travel reimbursement at a rate $0.57 per mile. This is, in fact, how many universities reimburse their students and faculty for conference travel. Assuming the dishonesty rates Shu and her colleagues found apply here too, having people sign the mileage reports at the top instead of at the bottom would save a fifty-person department about $6,900 each year. Of course, there are many applications far beyond auto-insurance policy. Think about how we currently report our taxes.

Why did top-signing work? How could something as simple as moving where people are supposed to sign make them more honest? Shu and her colleagues argue that what is happening here is quite subtle. By signing up front, we implicitly focus attention on ourselves. And by focusing such attention on ourselves, we become more truthful in what we are about to do. Once we put our name down, the information we provide becomes a reflection of who we are and how we see ourselves.

The core insight from this study is that people do not solely respond to incentives. Those people who signed their insurance form first had exactly the same incentives as those who only signed at the bottom. Yet the behavior was very different. This study clearly shows that human decision-making does not always follow incentives. Behavior is not always the result of conscious, rational choice.

What mattered here was human cognition. The way human brains process information makes us respond in unexpected ways that defy the design of ordinary cost-benefit types of rational, calculated incentives. To understand how our brains work, let's try to solve a simple math problem. Read the three statements below and immediately say out loud what answer comes to mind:

1. A pair of pants and a pair of socks cost $110 in total.
2. The pants cost $100 more than the socks.
3. How much do the socks cost?

Many of us immediately think the socks must have cost $10. But if we do the actual math, we find that we're wrong. The pants have to cost $100 more than the socks. So if the socks cost $10, the pants would have to cost $110. But then the total amount would be $120. So that is clearly wrong.

The correct answer is that the socks cost $5, as then the pants cost $105. And when we add those together, we get the total of $110. This example, adapted from Nobel Prize winner Daniel Kahneman's book *Thinking, Fast and Slow*, shows how our brains can trick us.[36] Summarizing the latest advances in cognitive science, Kahneman explains that our thinking is not as systematic and as reasoned as we may hope. He tells us that the brain uses two systems.[37] System 1 is fast. It is intuitive. It is automatic. We use it for quick, everyday decisions. But because it is so quick, it is very error-prone. System 2, in contrast, is considerably slower, far more deliberate, and requires more effort.

Those of us who immediately responded that the socks cost $10 were using System 1. We thought quickly and intuitively. It sounded good and felt right, so we went with it. In contrast, those who came up with $5 were likely using their System 2. They used more effort to slowly and deliberately calculate the right answer.

System 1 functions largely unconsciously. When we use System 1, we often jump to conclusions. And often we are unaware that System 1 has taken over our decision-making, prohibiting the slower, more deliberate System 2 from helping guide our behavior.

If you're still not convinced, let's play another game. Below is an excerpt of some text. Your mission: count the number of times you see the letter F in the following text:

FINISHED FILES ARE THE RE-
SULT OF YEARS OF SCIENTI-
FIC STUDY COMBINED WITH
THE EXPERIENCE OF YEARS.

So how many did you count? Three? Count again, and this time try a bit harder.

Still three? Don't worry. Most people find only three. Finding four is rare. Yet this is still incorrect. There are actually six F's. Count again and see if you can find them.[38]

If you are annoyed, don't blame us—blame your System 1. The reason most of us fail to find all F's is our brain automatically jumps over the word "of" and skips counting those three F's. We read that word so frequently and so automatically that we may not register it even when we are deliberately trying to slow down and use our System 2.

Psychologist Jonathan Haidt uses the metaphor of a rider on an elephant to help illustrate how we think.[39] System 1 is the elephant. It follows intuitive and automated unconscious cognition. It follows its instinct. Our System 2, on the other hand, is the rider. It uses conscious cognition and can direct the elephant. The issue is that for so many of our behaviors and decisions, our intuitive, automated cognition—our elephant—is in control.[40]

To understand human decision-making, and thus behavior, we must account for the functioning of these two cognitive processes. As humans, we may be very smart and generally pretty rational, but we respond more through our intuition for many decisions and behaviors. Often we never reach the point of consciously analyzing the data in front of us. We have lazy brains that reserve effortful cognition only for complex situations, while relying on the elephant mode the rest of the time. We like quick and easy.

There is an important reason our brains function this way. If all our decisions were deliberate, rational, and slow, and if we always relied on System 2, we would be unable to function. Think about driving. In learning to drive, we clearly use System 2. We locate the brake, the gas pedal, the mirrors, the turn signals, and, in the case of a manual transmission, also the clutch and stick. When we shift into gear, we slowly press on the gas, carefully, fully aware, checking for cars, traffic signs, and our speed. By the end of the first lesson, most people are exhausted. Yet fast-forward a year, and most people are no longer aware of what they are doing when driving; they are able to have conversations, listen to music, and drive for hours on end. By then, they have become able to switch to System 1, allowing them to carry out a complex task with ease and without much conscious thought.

For law and behavior, this has immense implications. When the law seeks to influence human behavior through incentives, it assumes that people weigh these incentives rationally. It assumes that our actions are all thought out, purposeful, and rational. The law assumes that people will weigh the incentives and disincentives we've provided when they decide whether to break the law. The law speaks mostly to the rider and not to the elephant.

Yet cognitive science teaches us that most of the time people follow their automated intuition that is prone to errors. If the law wants to improve our behavior, it must learn how to speak to the automated and error-prone elephant that resides in our brains and directs many of our actions. Recently, scholars have tried to understand how cognition affects the way humans respond to the law's incentives.[41] Most work here has focused on how the biases and shortcuts in automated cognition affect the way people respond to negative incentives, most notably how cognition affects deterrence.

As we saw in the last chapter, deterrence is based on people's perception of the probability of getting caught and punished, as well as the severity of the punishment. Earlier economic models assumed that deterrence was based on rational and deliberate thinking about probability. Yet the work by Daniel Kahneman and his long-time collaborator Amos Tversky has fundamentally altered our understanding of human cognition in decision-making. They have shown that human intuition about statistics, and thus about probability, is easily flawed. Through a series of studies, they have shown that there are several core processes at play that affect the way people overestimate or underestimate probabilities. They call such processes *heuristics* to indicate the shortcuts people's brains make to deal with complex information.

A good example is the "availability heuristic."[42] In a paper titled "Rating the Risks," University of Oregon psychologist Paul Slovic and colleagues sought to understand how people predict uncertain events. They were interested in how our cognition shapes the way we make predictions. They asked respondents, for instance, which of the following events cause the most deaths in the US: tornadoes, strokes, accidents, lightning, botulism, and diabetes. See what you think. Try to rank them in order, from the ones that cause the most deaths to the ones that cause the fewest. Do you think that accidents cause more deaths than strokes? If you did, sorry. That's incorrect. But you aren't alone. About 80 percent of people make the same mistake. In reality, strokes kill twice as many people as all accidents combined. And what about accidents versus diabetes? People generally think that accidental deaths are three hundred times more likely to occur than deaths by diabetes. Yet, in reality, diabetes kills four times more of us than are killed in accidents.[43] Finally, what about death by tornadoes versus death by asthma? Most think death by asthma is less common. But asthma kills twenty times more people than tornadoes do.

People in this study were mistaken because their mind followed a shortcut, the availability heuristic. In estimating these probabilities, people rely on the examples that spring into our thoughts and immediately come to mind. This comes from a variety of sources, the media being one of them. The six o'clock news is far more likely to cover unusual events, like accidental deaths and tornadoes, than they are to cover more common events, like deaths by diseases such as strokes, diabetes, and asthma. Because of the reporting, we are exposed more often to examples of unusual deaths. So, when we try to think quickly about which are more common, we rely on the availability heuristic. Our elephant takes over, and we reach a faulty conclusion.

Recently, criminologists have assessed whether this availability heuristic plays a role in criminal decision-making.[44] In particular, they were interested in examining whether this heuristic affects how much people believe they will be caught and punished for breaking the law. To test this, they conducted an experiment in which half of the participants in the study were asked whether they knew someone who has been punished for breaking the law, and the other half were asked whether they knew someone who had broken the law but didn't get caught. The researchers expected that people who had been primed with knowing someone who had been punished would then themselves report a higher probability of punishment. According to the availability heuristic, that is what they should have found.

The study, however, did not find the expected difference between the two groups. This is not to say that the availability heuristic is not at play in criminal decision-making. If punishment is more salient—for instance, because a famous person has just been punished for a crime—it may affect how people see the overall probability of punishment, even though a single case like that does not affect the overall chances of being caught and punished. The difficult thing here is to find the right study design. It may well be that using a simple question about whether people know anyone who got punished or avoided punishment is not an effective way to measure the availability heuristic.

Another line of inquiry has looked at what Kahneman has dubbed "the affect heuristic."[45] With this he means that people substitute a difficult cognitive question with an easier emotional question. So, when people should weigh complex probabilities, they may instead ask themselves how they feel about option A or B, or which of these they like better. When that happens, people's emotions, their affect, which comes through System 1, shapes and even obstructs their rational and reasoned cognition. Such emotions may impact the way people perceive the risks of sanctions and thus the effect of such sanctions on their behavior.[46]

In one study, Dutch psychologists Jean Louis van Gelder and Reinout de Vries presented participants with short scenarios describing minor forms of criminal behavior that many people may engage in. Think, for example, of things like downloading pirated software or asking for insurance reimbursement for items that may not have been stolen. Participants had to imagine that they were in a situation in which they could engage in these behaviors, were asked whether they would do them, and then were asked how likely it was that they would be caught and punished if they did engage in them. The researchers emotionally primed some of the participants by having them do word puzzles related to feelings. They then compared how emotionally primed participants made decisions to engage in the crimes compared to a control group that was not.

They found that the fear of punishment played much less of a role in the emotionally primed group than it did in the control group. For participants in the former group, what mattered in their decision-making about whether to engage in the crime was how they would feel about committing the crime.[47] This study shows that simply stimulating people to think more of emotions, not even making them more emotional, makes them respond less directly to the potential deterrent effect of punishment.

Another study, by criminologist Greg Pogarsky and colleagues, sought to understand a different aspect of how emotions influence people's perceptions of sanctions. They examined how people's feelings about texting while driving affected the way they estimated the probability of being caught and punished. Study participants were divided in three groups. One group read a negative text ("a new study shows that texting while driving is a leading cause of death among teens"), one a positive text ("couples who text regularly stay together"), and one a neutral unrelated text. The study then compared how participants estimated the chances of being stopped by police when texting while driving. The study found that participants who received the text with negative emotions were more likely to see a higher risk of sanctions.[48]

The application of psychological insights about cognition to understanding how people respond to criminal punishment is quite new. Because the research is still emerging, it cannot offer a robust—or even coherent—understanding of exactly what types of biases and heuristics affect the way people see probabilities of sanctions and how they come to make decisions. But the available work does show that the way humans respond to legal incentives does not occur in fully rational and deliberative ways. It is very likely that the same heuristics and biases also play a role in how people respond to tort liability and rewards.

So the bad news is that legal incentives, which are designed for the deliberate and rational cognition of the rider of System 2, do not work well in the reality of our brains where the elephant of System 1 is also at play. The good news is that there are ways to tap into System 1 and design incentives that also work there. A prime example is how tax authorities have used another idea developed by Tversky and Kahneman: prospect theory.

Imagine you have two options. Which would you prefer to receive: $80 or a lottery ticket with an 80 percent chance of winning $100 and a 20 percent chance of winning $10?[49] Most people prefer to just get the $80.

Now consider the following question about loss. Would you rather lose $80 or run an 80 percent chance of losing $100? With this choice, most people prefer the 80 percent risk of losing $100. They hope for the 20 percent chance that they will not lose anything at all. This example shows us that we have different preferences depending on whether we stand to win or lose money.

Kahneman and Tversky used similar examples to explain what they called *prospect theory.*[50] Their experimental research led them to question the belief in traditional economics that value is objective. That new iPhone costs $1,000, and $1,000 is $1,000. Kahneman and Tversky showed, instead, that value is subjective. It varies from person to person and from situation to situation. The value of $1,000 is different for a billionaire than it is for the average person. And for the average person, the difference between $100 and $200 just feels much larger than the difference between $900 and $1,000, even though the difference in both instances is a nominal $100.

However, and this is vital, as we saw in our different answers to the questions above, we do not assign equal weight to a loss and a gain. We have something called *loss aversion*. This is the notion that we fear losses more than we hope for making gains. The pain of losing $100 affects us more than winning $100. And under such loss aversion, we are more likely to take bigger risks to avoid loss.

Kahneman and Tversky blame our System 1 thinking. Rather than let our elephant rider do the actual math and find out what for each of the choices we make gives us the biggest financial gain, our elephant takes over and inserts subjective and irrational analysis.

Prospect theory has important implications for law and behavior. Take, for instance, tax law. If you found that the IRS owes you money, how would you feel? We're guessing that you would feel happy. And we're guessing you'd finish the paperwork pretty quickly and move on with your day. But if you found out that you owed money to the IRS, we're guessing you would double-check—or even triple-check—to see whether there was anything you could do to reduce the amount you owed. The prospect of losing money may lead people to fudge the numbers, even just a little bit.

Following prospect theory, we are thus more likely to comply with tax law if the tax authorities impose deliberately high automated payments directly taken from our salaries before we even receive them, known as advance tax levies. When we have already paid a tax advancement, filing taxes becomes about getting money back. So filing taxes then becomes about a gain: the better we file, the more we get back. Without paying much in taxes in advance, our filing is all about preventing paying money, and the better we file the less we stand to lose. Following prospect theory, people will take less of a risk, and are less likely to cheat, when they stand to gain something, compared to when they stand to lose.[51]

Behavioral economists and psychologists have indeed found that applying prospect theory can help reduce tax evasion.[52] For instance, one study established that taxpayers who stand to lose money (because they still owe taxes) are more likely to take risks when filing their taxes. The difference was stark: 65 percent of those with a loss perception were willing to take risks, compared to only 25 percent of those with a gains perception.[53] In a study conducted in Belgium, England, the Netherlands, Spain, Sweden, and the US, the findings were clear: "Noncompliance was more likely to occur, occurred on more occasions, and involved larger amounts of money among subjects confronting the prospect of an additional tax payment."[54] A recent study, which looked at actual tax payment data for 3.6 million Swedish taxpayers, confirmed that taxpayers who stood to lose money (because they owed taxes) were 50 percent more likely to file deductions and also to claim larger deductions. The paper concluded that "compliance will increase and auditing costs will be reduced if preliminary taxes are calibrated so that most taxpayers receive refunds."[55]

If we learn to speak to the elephant, we may very well learn to create more effective legal incentives.

A British university's cafeteria had a problem. Students were not cleaning up after themselves. After they ate, they would just leave their lunch trays all over the cafeteria. So a group of researchers came up with an ingenious solution. They decorated the walls of the cafeteria with posters that depicted a pair of flowers, and then replaced those flowers with posters that depicted a pair of eyes. They found that when the cafeteria displayed eyes instead of flowers, students were twice as likely to clean up after themselves.

This simple intervention changed behavior. The researchers did not need to threaten students, nor did they need to post messages pleading with them to obey the rules. In fact, when they added a message to the posters that directly asked students to place their trays in the racks, the message had no added benefit.[56] The eyes, not the message, were what had an effect.

According to the researchers, the eyes made the students feel like other people were watching, overlooking their behavior. They weren't

real guardians of the cafeteria, of course, standing guard and strictly enforcing its rules. Instead, the eyes operated at the unconscious level, giving student diners the illusion of being observed.

The effect here is called *priming.* Priming is a powerful force on human conduct that operates through our System 1, and mostly it operates
without people being aware of it. We have seen it earlier in this chapter
when people who signed their insurance form at the top, instead of at the
bottom, reported more honestly. By signing their name up front, they
filled out the form honestly because they were primed for honesty.

There are many other examples of how priming can reduce misbehavior and enhance compliance. Harvard Business School professors Francesca Gino and Michael Norton, together with Duke business professor
Dan Ariely, for instance, studied how priming can influence cheating. In
one experiment, they randomly assigned participants to put on sunglasses.
Some came from boxes clearly labeled as "Authentic Sunglasses by Chloe"
and some came from a box clearly labeled as "Counterfeit Sunglasses."
Although all sunglasses were real $300 designer sunglasses, half the par-
ticipants in the study were led to believe they were wearing fakes.

Gino and her colleagues then had the students take a math test. Students were told that they would be paid for the number of answers they
reported getting correct. However, the key here was that the students
were told that they were reporting their scores anonymously and were
led to believe that it would be impossible for anyone to check their answers. If no one is checking your answers and you are getting paid per
correct answer, would you report the true, honest-to-goodness number
you actually got correct? Or as a broke college student, would you fudge
it a little bit to cheat your way into squeezing a little more money out
of these ivory-tower professors who were too sloppy or lazy to design a
study where they *knew* how many you got correct?

Gino and her colleagues found that the participants who thought they
were wearing the real designer sunglasses cheated about 30 percent of the
time. But, alarmingly, the students who thought they were wearing fakes
cheated more than twice as often—about 71 percent of the time. Because

the only difference between the two conditions was the sunglasses, the researchers explained that the sunglasses themselves caused the enormous difference in cheating behavior. People who thought they were wearing counterfeits were primed with the very notion of cheating, which then influenced them into cheating.[57] Priming with misbehavior seems to create more misbehavior.

At the same time, it is possible to prime good behavior. Psychologist Jean Louis van Gelder and his colleagues primed people with their "future self." They had participants write a letter to themselves, with a prompt that read, "Think about who you will be 20 years from now, and write about the person you are now, which topics are important and dear to you, and how you see your life." People who wrote these letters to their future self were less inclined to commit minor crimes. In a different experiment, they had participants simply look at a realistic rendition of themselves, in the form of an avatar. One group saw an avatar of themselves just as they were at the time of the study, whereas another group saw a much older version of themselves. The participants then completed a trivia test in which it was very easy to cheat because the researchers had "accidentally" included the answers on the back of the test. (Those sloppy academics!) They found that people who had seen their same-age avatar cheated about 23.5 percent of the time, whereas people who saw their future-self avatar only cheated 6.1 percent of the time.[58] Simply showing people an image of their future self reduced the amount of cheating by about 74 percent.

Sometimes ideas from these priming studies have been applied in practice to improve behavior and compliance with rules. Trains in the Netherlands, like in many other countries, have dedicated silent compartments. If you're in the silent compartment, you aren't allowed to speak or play music. These silent compartments allow people to do work, get some sleep, or just stare off into the countryside and contemplate life silently.

The problem is that not everyone respects the rule of silence. Some talk "quietly" with their friends, and the truly inconsiderate ones play music loudly on their phones. To deal with this problem, consultants trained in behavioral change processes started an experiment. They lined the walls of the silent trains with panoramic photos of library books. From top to bottom, the compartment walls were made to look like library stacks.

The consultants spent a few weeks observing people in silent compartments. Where they had invoked the library setting, they found that not only did fewer people speak; they also spoke less.[59]

Clearly, priming can work remarkably well. Priming is a deliberate, subtle, and often simple way to use our knowledge of cognitive processes to influence behavior. With the eyes, the cafeteria achieved better compliance with its rules. By having people sign an honesty pledge up front, we can reduce fraudulent behavior on insurance forms.

In a variety of ways for a variety of behaviors, psychologists have been able to change behavior on an unconscious level. Primes are thus critically important applications of cognitive knowledge for compliance. When they work, they may improve behavior with very minor costs. They don't require extra law enforcement, nor do they have to rely on social norms or procedural justice. Because they are at the unconscious level, primes do not even require us to know much about the law itself or its associated punishments. And primes might even work well for those with limited self-control, as they are even more prone to follow their subconscious System 1.

Insights from cognitive science can thus help to improve people's behavior. By tapping into people's automated decision-making, existing incentive systems can become more effective. These insights have spurred a whole new field in economics, called *behavioral economics*. Two leading scholars in this field, Nobel Prize–winning economist Richard Thaler at the University of Chicago and law professor Cass Sunstein of Harvard, have drawn on cognitive and behavioral science insights to develop ways to improve existing incentive systems and to sway people to make better decisions and improve their conduct. They use the term "nudge" for such interventions, as people are gently pushed toward better decision-making. As they argue, a proper understanding of cognitive processes can help to develop a choice architecture that guides people toward better behavior. Priming is a good example of such nudging and choice architecture. Other forms of choice architecture are making good behavior easier and thus making it more likely that people (whether they are aware of it or not) choose the better option— for instance, by displaying the healthy food options at eye level in the supermarket or making organ donation an opt-out versus an opt-in process.

Primes do, however, have several limitations. So far, we see that the scope of applicable primes mostly covers minor misbehavior. Similarly, most other examples of nudging and choice are about stimulating pro-social and healthy behavior, like charity donation, collaboration, and healthier eating, or minor forms of rule breaking such as littering or cheating.[60] Sure, it is nice that we can prime people to clean up after themselves. And, yes, it's great to reduce cheating on a laboratory test. But for more major offenses, using primes may be much harder. Whether we can prime major industrial polluters to comply with environmental law or nudge juvenile offenders to adhere to their probationary requirements remains to be seen.

Another question is whether primes would continue to work if they were introduced as a matter of policy. If all cafeterias had eyes on the wallpaper, all forms asked us to sign at the top, or all mirrors showed our future self, maybe we would become so used to this that it would no longer affect us.

Finally, and highly frustratingly, there is the unfortunate fact that some of these experimental studies have not been replicated. In 2020, Lisa Shu and her colleagues published a new paper. In this paper, the authors of the study on the effect of signing at the top of forms to reduce fraud reported that they had failed to replicate their original findings.[61] In other words, they could no longer find evidence that signing at the top makes people more honest. And this is the problem with some of the research about priming: the scientific evidence is far from robust.[62] It provides a potential route forward but not yet one paved in stone.

———————

The law is the domain of legal code and coders. Lawmakers try to change behavior through incentives, leveraging complex systems of sanctions, liabilities, rewards, and subsidies. These legal coders believe that all they have to do to change misbehavior is to get the incentives and disincentives—the carrots and the sticks—right.

Unfortunately, humans do not respond to the legal code as well as computers do to programming code. What may seem like a simple task of pushing the right buttons and applying the proper balance of sticks and carrots proves to be highly complex. We have seen that most of the sticks we apply, whether criminal punishment or torts, often fail to achieve their desired effect. And while the carrots show promise, their effects are uncertain. Creating long-term rewards to improve behavior is often difficult to do and may not be cost-effective. At worst, our law's incentives backfire through eroding intrinsic motivation and making behavior in the long term worse.

Human behavior is the domain of exploration and explorers. The complexity of human behavior and cognition forces us to let go of assumptions about how simple sticks and carrots will work out in practice. Instead, we need to delve deeper into human decision-making. We are at the frontiers of behavioral and cognitive science, especially when we seek to apply it to damaging and rule-breaking behavior. We may know about certain cognitive biases and heuristics but not exactly how to respond to them. We may know how to deploy certain behavioral cues and primes for prosocial behavior, but that does not mean we fully grasp how to apply them to the most pressing compliance problems.

These complexities force us to rethink what incentives mean in our laws. In a sense, they require that legal coders embrace humility and accept that they cannot predict—let alone be absolutely certain—what the effects of a particular legal incentive will be. It means we must reevaluate the ageless assumptions about what "good" laws and legal rules actually are. It requires a different perspective, one that shifts away from the legal code's solitary view of humans as rational computers and instead moves more deeply into the realm of the behavioral code to examine the factors that really shape our everyday conduct.

When we do this, we see that to truly improve the way law shapes human behavior, we must look beyond incentives. The behavioral code is so much richer than just the stick and the carrot, and for that matter, the elephant.

# CHAPTER 4

# The Moral Dimension

A young student comes to the Brussels driving center in Belgium for a driving lesson. In French, the instructor explains that there are new requirements for the driver's license test: "To get your license you have to take the mobile phone test. . . . You have to avoid an obstacle in the road while texting."

The student is shocked: "*Oh putain*" (which loosely translates as "oh fuck"). The instructor calmly explains, pointing to his papers: "I didn't invent this. Look here." The student clicks his seatbelt, shakes his head, and smiles in disbelief, exclaiming, "*Il y en a beaucoup qui vont se crasher, emh, je te dit ça he* (Many are going to crash, I'm telling ya)."

As the instructor takes the student out for the driving lesson on the driving center's enclosed road, he tells him to take out his cell phone. And then he starts telling the student what to text: "*Je vais cherchez des frites* (I am gonna get French fries)." The student holds the wheel in one hand and his phone in the other. He stares intently at his screen as he is trying to type in the text. Immediately, the instructor grabs onto the wheel and exclaims: "Watch where you're going. . . . O la la!"

The test continues, and the student is told to text: "*Nous retrerons en retard ce soir* (We'll be a bit late tonight)." As the student struggles to complete the text, the instructor tells him: "Be careful, I'll correct your spelling."

The instructor checks the student's phone and chides him: "Look, you spelled 'school' wrong." The student gets frustrated: "It's impossible!" And soon the inevitable happens. "Stoooop!" the instructor shouts. The student, busy texting, veers off the road, knocking over orange traffic cones, and then brakes so hard that the instructor, who is not wearing his seatbelt, lurches into the windshield, smashing his head. As the instructor recovers, he looks shocked and a little nauseous. Pointing to the toppled cones, he tells the student: "Imagine there was a child there."

"I can't do it, I can't do it," the student says. "Honestly, I feel like an idiot who can't drive." The student vents his frustration as he waves his phone. "I don't even know what I'm texting!" The instructor tells the student that he will fail his driver's exam because of this. "But it is dangerous what you're asking me to do," the student retorts. "People will die. If this becomes the law, I'll stop driving," says the student. "I can't drive and use my phone at the same time, it is too dangerous."

Cut to a blank screen. The sound of a text message chimes and a green text balloon appears: "We agree." And then another one: "Texting while driving is too dangerous."

These scenes are part of a viral public messaging campaign against texting while driving.[1] In most countries, lawmakers have prohibited texting while driving a car. In the Netherlands, authorities have banned texting while cycling.[2] And some US cities, including Honolulu and Rexburg, Idaho, have even banned "twalking," texting while walking.[3] (Yes, that really is a term that people use.)[4]

The rapid spread of cell phones, especially smartphones, has been proven to be incredibly distracting for drivers, cyclists, and even pedestrians. According to the National Highway Traffic Safety Administration (NHTSA), distracted driving in the United States killed 2,841 people in 2018 and injured an estimated 400,000.[5] NHTSA data show that about 14 percent of the cases of distracted driving accidents involve a cell phone. Cell phones play an especially large role in distracted driving crashes for younger drivers. For people between the ages of fifteen and twenty-nine, about one in five accidents involves using a cell phone.[6]

Because it is so dangerous, most countries have adopted punishments to deter people from using a phone while driving. In the US, each state has its own rules, but in most states texting while driving is a misdemeanor punishable by a fine, ranging from $25 to $500 for a first offense.[7] In the Netherlands, cyclists face a €95 fine for using their cell phone while riding on the country's world-famous bicycle paths. As transport minister Cora van Nieuwenhuizen explained: "I have a clear message for all cyclists: keep your phone, and [keep] your €95 in your pocket."[8] The Honolulu fine for twalking, by the way, is $35.

With the viral video, the Belgian authorities tried a completely different approach. Instead of stating that texting is banned by law or warning that violators will be punished, the video simply shows how catastrophic it would be if we made texting while driving compulsory for teenagers—who, don't forget, are the most text-savvy segment of the population. The result was not only a funny video where viewers see the naïve and flabbergasted responses of students who fail to spell correctly while they drive safely. Viewers also see what actually happens when people text and drive. They see how dangerous it is and hear from youth—who are glued to their phones—that they hope this never becomes the law. Their attention captured by comedy, viewers effectively get the message that texting and driving is dangerous.

This example shows us a different part of the behavioral code. Rather than rely on incentives such as fines or liability, we can efficiently and effectively persuade people to do the right thing. In this case, the video offers a smart moral appeal developed for a young audience.

Such moral appeals are not new or special, nor are they just developed by governments. Consider two videos that American telecom giant AT&T has made about texting while driving. In one, we meet Will Craig, who explains that he hit a tree at 120 miles per hour. The driver of the car he was in had been texting. Instead of braking, she had pressed the accelerator. Will says that she had just started a text: "Where r." "Six letters," Will notes. "It hurts a lot to talk about this." Indeed it hurt: he suffered injury to his cerebral cortex, a collapsed lung, and four broken ribs. "It is by the grace of God that I am walking, talking."[9]

In another AT&T video, we meet Chandler, who seems to be in his early twenties. Seated against a dark background, he tells his story: "You know, the windshield just broke, glass broke, and screeching." The camera zooms out so we see his living room. "You know, I saw, umh, a body come down from off the top of the van." Chandler looks up a little, like he can see it just now. "And I just thought, oh my gosh, what have I done? I sh— What have I done?" He shakes his head. The screen cuts to a black screen with gray letters: "Chandler was texting 'i love you' when he killed three children." Chandler sighs deeply. "There is never, never a day that I wake up and don't think about it." Both ads were part of AT&T's ad campaign "It Can Wait."[10]

By showing what happens to a victim, people can see the damage they may cause. It forces people to confront the morality of handling a cell phone while driving. And by interviewing someone responsible for a lethal accident because of his distracted driving, the ad directly shows what it is like to have to live with the guilt and shame afterward.

All of these ads appeal to people's sense of right and wrong. They appeal to our morality.

## THE MORAL LOGIC OF COMPLIANCE

In the spring of 1984, Tom Tyler, a psychologist who teaches at Yale Law School, organized a massive, groundbreaking study in Chicago to understand why Chicagoans obey the law.[11] His team of researchers contacted 1,575 local residents and interviewed each one for about half an hour. A year later, they interviewed 804 participants from the original study again. That's roughly 1,200 hours of interviews.

Participants in the first wave were asked to indicate how frequently they engaged in illegal behaviors such as speeding, parking illegally, littering, drunk driving, and shoplifting. Tyler also assessed what influenced their illegal behavior. He found that deterrence—the fear of punishment—did not impact why people obey or disobey the law. Instead, he found that people's values and norms mattered. By far the strongest predictor of compliance was whether people held that these laws were in line with their own morals. The more they morally saw that littering was a problem, the more they complied with the littering law. The more they morally rejected drunk driving, the less they engaged in drunk driving.

These findings should not be surprising. It is perfectly logical that people follow their morals, that they do what they deem to be right and just. Also, it makes sense that if people do not morally support a law, they are more likely to break it. In the time of the show *Mad Men*, the 1960s, a smoking ban would have failed miserably in the US because very few people thought smoking was immoral. Yet by the 1980s and 1990s, when most US states had introduced smoking bans, they worked well because the moral and social landscape had completely shifted; people saw smoking as harmful and morally supported antismoking rules.[12]

If the law is in line with their morals, people will be much more likely to obey it, even if there is limited enforcement. Many of our morals are deeply ingrained, learned at an early age from our parents, our schools, or directly from our friends. We learn that it is wrong to steal, to lie or cheat, to hurt or kill people. Much of our legal system has codified these age-old values into formal rules on property and theft, on fraud, and on rape, battery, and murder.

But many laws do not build on deeply ingrained or widely shared morals. Sometimes a law even tries to change existing morals, or at least existing behavior considered to be perfectly acceptable, morally speaking. Think about the rules that ban texting while walking. Very few of us morally oppose twalking, thus only a handful of us would think it needs to be banned or regulated. Or think of all those bureaucratic rules that have crept into organizations that ask for ever more reporting and ever more paperwork; no one really knows why they exist, let alone what their moral basis is. And, of course, there are politically charged disagreements about the morality of many laws. Think of how people in the US disagree about rules regarding coronavirus mask wearing, marijuana, abortion, or guns.

Morals play a major part in the behavioral code. For law to improve behavior it must either align itself with existing morals or take on the task of shaping future morals so that they align with the law. To understand how law can tap into people's sense of morality but often fails to do so, we must delve into the social science of morality and ethics.

In Europe, a woman was near death from a rare kind of cancer. There was one drug that the doctors thought might save her: a form of radium that a pharmacist in the same town had recently discovered. The drug was expensive to make, but the pharmacist was unfairly charging ten times that. He paid $200 for the radium and charged $2,000 for a small dose of the drug. The sick woman's husband, Heinz, went to everyone he knew to borrow the money, but he could only get together about $1,000. He told the pharmacist that his wife was dying and asked him to sell it cheaper or let him pay the second half later. But the pharmacist said: "No, I discovered the drug and I'm going to make money from it." Heinz got desperate and broke into the man's store to steal the drug for his wife.

Here's a question: Do you think Heinz should have broken into the store and stolen the drug to save his wife? Before you keep reading, stop and think about your decision and the reasons why you came to it.

The scenario above is copied almost verbatim from a 1963 study conducted by Lawrence Kohlberg, a psychologist who taught at the University of Chicago and Harvard University. It is one of ten scenarios presented to children ages six, ten, thirteen, and sixteen in Chicago and Boston. The children read about these moral dilemmas, indicated what choice the main actor in the stories should make, and explained their views. Each interview was taped and lasted about two hours, yielding rich data.

Here is how one of the boys (Tommy, age ten) responded to the dilemma above: "His wife was sick and if she didn't get the drug quickly, she might die. Maybe his wife is an important person and runs a store and the man buys stuff from her and can't get it any other place. The police would probably blame the owner that he didn't save the wife. That would be like killing with a gun or knife."[13]

Kohlberg analyzed the data from the interviews to understand the children's moral reasoning. Delving into the rich tapestry of the answers,

he discovered that there were six stages of moral development.[14] Here is
how the six stages are described in his original paper, complete with a
quote from one of the children that illustrates that phase:

> *Stage 1: Punishment and obedience orientation (It's okay to do it if you
> don't get caught)*
>
> "It depends on who he [Heinz] knows on the police force."
>
> *Stage 2: Instrumentalist-relativist orientation (If it feels good, do it)*
>
> "If his wife is nice and pretty, he should do it."
>
> *Stage 3: Good boy, nice girl (Do it for me)*
>
> "He should do it because he loves his wife."
>
> *Stage 4: Law and order orientation (Do your duty)*
>
> "Saving a human life is more important than protecting property."
>
> *Stage 5: Social contract orientation (It's the consensus of thoughtful people)*
>
> "Society has a right to insure its own survival. I couldn't hold my
> head up in public if I let her die."
>
> *Stage 6: Universal ethical principles (What if everybody did that?)*
>
> "Human life has supreme inherent value. I couldn't live with myself
> if I let her die."[15]

The quotes above show how the types of reasoning relate to poor
Heinz's attempt to save his wife. In the first stage of moral reasoning, it
is all about whether Heinz can expect punishment. He should steal the
drug if he will not get punished. In the second stage, Heinz should do it
if it feels good for him. By the third stage, it is about sacrifice for someone
else: because he loves his wife. By the fourth stage it is about a broader
duty, namely a duty to save lives even if it means stealing. At stage five,
it is about the relationship with society and about how one would feel
acting in a way that is not accepted. So Heinz should steal the drug if
society tells him he should feel ashamed for not doing so to save his wife.
And finally, at stage six, it is about general ethical principles that apply to

all humankind. At that level, Heinz should steal to save his wife because of a general respect for human life.

Kohlberg's research suggests that our morals develop sequentially in different stages. In his model, human morality starts as individualistic, based on how people can avoid punishment and pain or serve their own interests. As we progress, we begin to be driven by how we see our own interests and duties. At the highest level, there is a morality that is embedded in society and in abstract general human values.

Kohlberg showed the dynamic nature of human moral judgment. As children mature, their moral judgments evolve. By adulthood, he found, most people have reached stage four, while a few of us reach into stages five and six. Kohlberg's work thus also shows that even in adulthood people may vary in how they make moral decisions. Because human responses to legal rules are deeply rooted in morality, to understand and shape such responses requires an understanding of the types of moral judgments people make. Moral appeals to comply with the law should be very different for people who make judgments at stage two (where appealing to their own interests works) than at stage four (where it is all about duty). Subsequent research provided new insights about human moral decision-making.

Consider the following. A family's dog was killed by a car in front of their house. They had heard that dog meat was delicious, so they cut up the dog's body, cooked it, and ate it for dinner.[16]

What do you think of this family eating their dog?

Is it very wrong, a little bit wrong, or is it perfectly okay?

And can you explain why you think that?

Is anyone hurt by this act?

Would it bother you if you saw this happening, or would you not care?

Participants in a study conducted in the US and Brazil were asked to respond to these questions after reading the exact same scenario. While most people saw no harm to anyone, 23 percent of the participants thought the family might get hurt because of health problems from eating dog meat, whereas 10 percent indicated that others would be harmed by it (without being specific about the identity of such people). And 72 percent of participants said that they would be bothered by witnessing the family eating their deceased pet.

The study sought to understand how people reason about why they think an act is morally wrong. It assessed whether moral reasoning originates in whether people see harm or whether they are just bothered by such an act. The study found that what mattered most for their moral assessment of this case were answers to the question of whether they would be bothered by witnessing it and not whether they thought anyone was hurt by consuming a pet. The study had similar findings for other stories of "harmless" offenses, such as a woman cutting up the national flag she no longer needs, a son failing to keep his promise to his dying mother to visit her grave regularly, a brother and sister kissing when no one can see it, and a man having sex with a chicken carcass he bought in the supermarket.[17]

People in this study came to a moral decision based on whether they were bothered by what was described, not based on whether they thought there was any harm. In a follow-up study that examined how liberal and conservative participants viewed homosexuality, incest, and unusual forms of masturbation, researchers found that participants were often unable to elaborate their moral views.[18] As the paper summarized, "They would stutter, laugh, and express surprise at their inability to find supporting reasons, yet they would not change their initial judgments of condemnation."[19] Participants had suffered from a "moral dumbfounding."[20]

All of this shows that people do not engage in clear reasoning before they come to a moral judgment. Jonathan Haidt, a psychologist at New York University who was the lead author of those studies, concluded that Kohlberg and others who focused on moral reasoning suffered from a fundamental oversight. Kohlberg had looked at how children develop morality through asking them to explain what they thought about moral dilemmas. As Haidt explains: "Kohlberg thought of children as budding moral philosophers." Yet what Kohlberg was studying was the post hoc rationalization of a moral judgment, not the moral intuition that shapes people's moral judgments. Critically, moral reasoning does not cause moral judgment. Rather, Haidt believes, moral reasoning comes after people have made a moral judgment based on their intuition about right and wrong. Thus, there is doubt that moral reasoning can predict moral behavior.

To understand this, we need to return to the elephant in our brain. Our automated System 1 in our brain, with its quick and error-prone decisions, does not only affect our rational weighing of costs and benefits, it also shapes our morality. System 1 engages in moral intuition, which Haidt explains as comprising "fast, automatic, and (usually) affect-laden processes in which an evaluative feeling of good-bad or like-dislike (about the actions or character of a person) appears in consciousness without any awareness of having gone through steps of search, weighing evidence, or inferring a conclusion." Our cool, slow, and deliberative System 2 does moral reasoning, which Haidt defines as a "conscious mental activity that consists of transforming information about people and their actions in order to reach a moral judgment or decision."[21]

Does this mean that people do not engage in deliberative moral reasoning and that all they do is intuitive? Not exactly. System 1 and System 2 operate as a dual system in which we combine fast and automatic responses with slower deliberative cognition. If people really want, they can activate their System 2 to do the hard work of calculating costs and benefits while arresting their instant System 1 responses. They can, in effect, engage in moral reasoning if they can consciously pause their moral intuition.[22]

People's morality plays a major role in how they respond to the law. We now know that, to tap into such morality, people have different ways in which they process issues relying on moral intuition as well as on moral reasoning, especially when they face difficult moral dilemmas. So a successful moral appeal should not just fit the different stages of moral reasoning people may have but also should take into account that they often follow their moral intuition. A whole new field of scholarship has developed promising cutting-edge ideas about how to tap into ethical cognition.

## WHY "GOOD PEOPLE" ACT BADLY

Swedish managers received applications for job openings they had posted without knowing that they were part of an elaborate study. For each job opening, the managers received documents representing four fictitious applicants (two men and two women), each with a photo and almost the same exact typed resume and cover letter. The only difference was that the photos had been digitally manipulated to make two applicants look like they were of an average weight and two look as though they were much heavier. The study then waited to see which of these applicants were invited for a job interview. The study found that the "obese" applicants were significantly less likely to be invited for an interview: 6 percent less likely for men and 8 percent less likely for women.[23]

A few months later, the managers who had made the interview decisions were contacted by the researchers to do an online test. During the test, the managers were asked to pair pictures showing either people of average weight or of plus-sized weight with words like "effective," "productive," "hardworking," "goal-oriented," "ineffective," "incompetent," "slow," and "lazy." The researchers then recorded the managers' response times in choosing whether these words fit the picture best.

The test the researchers used is a so-called implicit association test (IAT). Social scientists developed the IAT to measure implicit biases people may have, for instance about race or gender.[24] Implicit bias can lead someone to discriminate without even being aware of it. And that was the case here. Managers were slower, and we are talking milliseconds, in pairing plus-sized people to words indicating productivity, thus revealing their implicit biases. Not only that, they were also more likely to have discriminated against larger applicants by not inviting them for an interview. This implicit bias was the core explanation for the discriminatory hiring decisions.

The most important finding in this study is that the managers were unaware of their bias against larger body types. When they filled out a questionnaire as a part of the follow-up study, managers were asked to indicate whether they had preferences for slimmer people when making hiring decisions. Statistical analyses of the data revealed that there was no association between how managers answered the questions about their explicit preferences for body type in hiring and their actual decisions not to invite plus-sized applicants for interviews. Probably in their own mind they were acting morally and ethically without any apparent discrimination, while in fact they were clearly discriminating on the basis of people's weight. As such, good people, or people who at least consider themselves to be behaving ethically, can act badly without being aware of it.

This has major consequences for how law can shape human behavior. It shows that even laws that have broad moral support, which we assume a law forbidding discrimination on the basis of race, gender, or looks would have, can still fail to prevent structural and systemic violations. It shows that people can act unethically and badly without doing so intentionally.

Behavioral ethics is a new field dedicated to understanding what drives good people to engage in behavior that even they consider unethical. It draws on insights from psychology that our moral judgment operates in a dual process model combining intuition with reasoning. In their book, *Blind Spots*, Max Bazerman of Harvard Business School and Ann Tenbrunsel from the University of Notre Dame explain this notion with the term "bounded ethicality," which they explain "focuses on the psychological processes that lead even good people to engage in ethically questionable behavior that contradicts their own ethics."[25]

In the most extreme cases, people can be completely unaware that they are being unethical because their unethical behavior operates mostly through their automated System 1. Our subconscious cognition is a double-edged sword. On the one hand, people's basic morality operates through intuition, and thus our intuition can steer us in how we see right and wrong and thus act. On the other hand, our subconscious cognition can make us act in ways counter to what people would typically see as right and just. Our System 1, the elephant, can make us do things that would put the rider, System 2, to shame. So we learn here that the dual process cognition in our brain not only undermines the rational weighing of costs and benefits but can also affect people's ethical thinking and behavior.[26]

Consider a game of dice.[27] Participants in a study conducted in Israel, Spain, the US, and South Korea were asked to roll a die and report what they had rolled. They received a bonus of one dollar for every point they reported from the die roll. So if they rolled a 4, they would receive four dollars. However, participants could lie, as the die was covered by a cup with a small hole so that only they could see what they had rolled. As a twist, researchers randomly assigned the participants to either do the entire experiment in their own native language or in a foreign language. They then compared how honest each of the two groups were by assessing whether, in aggregate, a group of participants reported die rolls that were statistically impossible. It found that participants were more likely to lie when they took the test in their native language than when they used a foreign language. The study's explanation for its findings is that lying for personal gain is an intuitive, System 1 response to a temptation that the study had created. But by doing this test in a second language, participants operated in a more deliberative manner; the second language activated their System 2 more and thus kept their intuitive gut responses in check. Activating System 2 overpowered the System 1 and prevented their cheating behavior.

From this study, we see that not only can System 1 make us more unethical as we respond intuitively to the temptation to cheat, it also shows that there are situations where this is more or less likely to occur. Many other situational studies have found that when people operate more in their System 1, it undermines their ethical behavior. One study discovered, for example, that people who have lost a night's sleep have a lower moral awareness and are less able to determine whether their own or other people's conduct is morally sound.[28] Another study, titled "Honesty on Mondays," found that people are more likely to be dishonest by the end of the workweek, compared to earlier days in the week.[29] And when people are forced to make decisions under time pressure, they become more likely to lie than during situations when they have time to think.[30]

Just like the research about cognition and incentives discussed earlier, these studies are exploring the edges of our knowledge about how our brains function and how that affects ethicality. We have to be aware that the inherent challenges of capturing something so complex as automated ethicality does make it difficult to be sure that these findings also hold true for all situations and can be replicated in the future. Many of these examples we just discussed are singular studies and not robust bodies of work complete with systematic reviews and replications across a wide variety of settings. This line of inquiry is highly promising, as it shows rather simple interventions can help to curb situations with higher risk for unethical behavior, but it may take a while before the scientific evidence provides solid enough footing to directly serve as a basis for policy.

People can also misbehave without being aware that what they did was wrong. Our limited ethical self-awareness makes it easy to commit misconduct. Bazerman and Tenbrunsel provide a useful overview of the different mechanisms that are at play before, during, and after unethical conduct that make people ignorant of their own misbehavior.

A first problem is that people tend to think that they will resist temptation when presented with an unethical opportunity. But in reality people are bad at their own ethical forecasting. One factor is that when we try to predict our behavior in the future, we consciously weigh the ethical pros and cons. But all too often we just follow our gut responses when it is time to act.

People also suffer from "ethical fading." At the moment they face a moral dilemma or an opportunity for bad behavior, their ethics fade to the background, replaced with selfish and hedonistic considerations ("What is best for me?" or "What is best for the business?"). Similarly, when we look back on the past, we perceive ourselves to have been much more ethical than we actually were.[31] A good illustration of ethical fading is a study that found that participants who cheated to get paid more money were more likely to have forgotten the honor code they had signed compared to those who did not cheat, even when they were paid extra to recall the moral rules accurately.[32]

Language euphemisms can play a role here, as people use linguistic metaphors that dampen the ethical implications of their decisions. Here is how psychologists Ann Tenbrunsel and David Messick explain this: "We engage in 'aggressive' accounting practices, not illegal ones. There may be some 'externalities' associated with a strategy, not harmful to others or the environment. We have 'collateral damage' in military campaigns, not civilian deaths."[33]

Incremental processes also matter. People are like live frogs placed in a pot of cold water. When the fire is turned on, the water slowly begins to heat, so slowly that they do not even notice it begin to boil. It is often the same with unethical behavior; a sudden and strong form of unethical conduct will stand out, while gradual and incremental shifts toward more serious misconduct go unnoticed.[34] And as such, people may slide down a slippery slope to where they not only become accustomed to unethical behavior but also actually begin to do things they never thought they would.

Criminologists have also looked at how people live with the guilt and shame they feel after they come to break the law. They have found that people use "neutralization" techniques that help them overcome their own sense of morality in order to engage in crime.[35]

There are several major neutralization techniques.[36] The most basic is that offenders can simply deny responsibility: "It was just an accident." Or: "Everyone does this, it was not just me." Offenders can also neutralize illegal behavior by convincing themselves that the behavior didn't cause any real injury. Vandalism is just "mischief." Stealing a car is just "borrowing."[37] The offender can also reframe the "victim." If they just think of the person they injured as someone who deserved to be injured, the crime itself turns from wrongful to righteous. Rather than an offense it becomes a "rightful retaliation." Everyone knows that the corner-store owner was price-gouging and taking advantage of us, so I was right to spray paint "THIEF" on the store windows. Think of this as Robin Hood neutralization, switching who is seen as victim and offender. Offenders may also say that loyalty is more important than complying with legal or broader social norms. Gang members, for instance, can tell themselves that it is more shameful to betray gang loyalty than it is to commit a crime. Or corporate offenders may argue to themselves that profit matters above all else.[38] Similarly, people may neutralize shame and guilt by turning the blame toward the legal system or those that assign blame to them: "The system is racist and never gave me an opportunity." And there is the so-called metaphor of the ledger: "I have done so many good things already, I am allowed to do this one bad thing."[39] This is also known as moral licensing, where people license themselves to bad behavior because it is compensated by all the good they do.[40]

Albert Bandura, a psychologist who taught at Stanford, developed a related idea that he called *moral disengagement*.[41] Through moral disengagement, people repress their sense of shame and guilt when doing bad things. People may, for instance, use moral justifications for their own immoral and inhumane behavior. Terrorists can point to religion, or gang members to the honor of the group. People may also compare their own wrongdoing to those who acted far worse. Someone speeding on the highway may think about hit-and-run perpetrators as the really immoral drivers. People may also deny that there is harm. Streaming TV series illegally does not really hurt anyone, and these companies and actors all make way too much money anyway. As a last example, people may dehumanize their victims. Selling drugs to addicts is not a problem if one considers them to be less than human.

Bandura argues that, as opposed to focusing on value-based judgments regarding the moral wrongness of certain behaviors, we should be focusing on the cognitive processes that enable these judgments. The more these mechanisms are employed, the greater the individual will disengage from the threats associated with self-sanctioning (such as shame, guilt, or stress), which frees them to commit crime.

Empirical studies of criminal offenders show how these neutralization and moral disengagement techniques play a role in criminal behavior. Interviews with offenders show that neutralizations are often invoked in a wide range of crimes and offenses, including minor offenses, like stealing office supplies, but also in far more serious crimes, even genocide.[42] A recent review comparing results from fifty-three studies finds that the more people use neutralization and moral disengagement techniques, the more likely they will engage in delinquency, aggression, and crime.[43]

There are ways we can overcome neutralization and moral disengagement. We can, in effect, try to "neutralize the neutralizations."[44]

With this approach, people are confronted with the damage their behavior causes, the fact that there are real victims, and that they are to
blame. Think back to the two AT&T ads against texting while driving.
They showed us a very human victim, with very real damage. And they
showed us a highly remorseful driver demonstrating what it feels like to
be responsible for killing three people because of distracted driving.

Another important approach is to confront offenders with victims.
This is the "restorative justice" approach. Criminal law traditionally
seeks to punish the offenders, locking them up or sanctioning them.
Restorative justice is an entirely different way of thinking about justice
and crime that requires offenders to take responsibility for their actions
and the harm that they have caused. It is remarkably difficult because it
challenges the perpetrators of an offense to dig deep into the causes and
consequences of their actions and to commit to a plan of action to show
that they are repairing those harms.

Restorative justice encourages the victim and community to be a part
of the process of enacting justice and repairing harm. By design, offenders
see how their behavior has caused harm and are asked to accept responsibility for their acts. Both are vital elements to counter neutralization
and moral disengagement.[45] And, in fact, research on a wide variety of
restorative justice programs—even for youthful offenders—suggests that
they are markedly effective at repairing harm and reducing recidivism.[46]

All this shows that morality is vital for impacting crime involvement,
both in initiating it and in stopping it. To the extent that we can tap into
someone's morals—particularly the morality they share with the community—we may be able to reduce crime and recidivism. But not all
people who misbehave and break rules share the same moral code.

## ARE SOME PEOPLE SIMPLY IMMORAL?

Joaquín Guzmán, better known as El Chapo, was a leader of the Mexican
Sinaloa Cartel who ran perhaps the largest drug operation of all time in
the United States. During his trial in a Brooklyn courtroom, after he
was finally extradited to the US following an escape from a Mexican
prison, the world heard testimony about the many atrocities he was said

to have been involved in.[47] He was accused of drugging and raping girls as young as thirteen years old. He had one bodyguard beat two people so badly that they looked "like rag dolls" before shooting and burning them. He had his own cousin killed for lying. One witness had seen El Chapo murder at least three men. Overall, El Chapo's cartel was directly responsible for Mexico's bloody drug war, killing 164,000 people between 2007 and 2014, when El Chapo was most active.[48] At his trial, federal judge Brian Cogan said that Guzman was responsible for "overwhelming evil."[49]

Our news is replete with people involved in a wide variety of truly devasting behavior. Bernie Madoff operated a $64.8 billion Ponzi scheme, the largest in history, defrauding 4,800 clients.[50] Larry Nassar sexually assaulted minors under his care as the USA Gymnastics national team doctor and a physician at Michigan State University. He has been accused of assaulting 250 girls and has admitted to 10 of these accusations.[51] Elizabeth Holmes raised over $700 million for her company, Theranos, by fraudulently claiming that the firm could do blood tests using very small amounts of blood, intimidating former employees and journalists who doubted the company's technological claims.[52] Harvey Weinstein abused his power as a Hollywood producer to sexually assault and rape actresses and movie industry employees, while using nondisclosure agreements and intimidation to ensure his abuses did not become public.[53] And then there are the most notorious serial killers, torturers, terrorists, hitmen, and violent dictators. It is clear that some people routinely engage in behavior that virtually everyone else in society would deem deeply immoral. In these cases, there is more at play than some form of ethical fading, neutralization, or implicit bias.

Some people believe there is a fundamental difference between good and bad people. As one of Greece's ancient thinkers, Aristotle, summarized this view: "While the good man, whose life is related to a fine ideal, will listen to reason, the bad one whose object is pleasure must be controlled by pain, like a beast of burden."[54] Following this, bad people simply seek their own pleasure, and because of that they can only be stopped through threats and pain.

Is this really true? Are some people just different, simply less moral or even amoral?

Recall Kohlberg's studies about how children develop moral reasoning. Kohlberg originally suggested that many criminal offenders had a stunted moral development, and this spurred research that led to a large body of work on the morality of convicted offenders.[55] Consider, for instance, a study from 2006 that compared moral reasoning of convicted male and female offenders with a similarly aged and gendered group without recorded offenses. It was found that the offenders, regardless of gender, exhibited significantly less mature moral reasoning than the non-offenders.[56] One review of this work concludes that offenders often do "show immature levels of moral reasoning."[57]

Yet, when delving deeper into the exact types of moral reasoning and types of offending, the relationship between the two is not that clear-cut. One study of sex offenders compared levels of moral reasoning among rapists, incest offenders, and child molesters. It found that their moral development was not similar, as incest offenders had moral reasoning at stages 1 and 2 and similar to those found in studies of general offenders, but rapists and child molesters developed moral reasoning at stages 3 and 4.[58] To further complicate the picture, even if moral development is stunted in offenders, that does not mean that this causes their offending. One study of convicted young male offenders found that while these offenders did have low levels of moral reasoning, it was not at all associated with their offending.[59] The study thus could not show exactly how lower moral reasoning relates to offending, and it argued that maybe the relationship is indirect, as the type of moral reasoning influences other personality aspects that make people more likely to offend.

An entire field in criminology is devoted to personality and crime. One particularly interesting personality measure captures so-called Honesty/Humility. This is defined as "an individual's moral disposition in terms of the tendency to be interpersonally genuine, to be unwilling to take advantage of others, to avoid fraud and corruption, to be uninterested in status and wealth, and to be modest and unassuming."[60] A series of studies has found that people who score lower on this Honesty/

Humility scale are more likely to engage in sexual assault, misconduct at work, occupational crime, and common misdemeanors.[61]

Of course, other personality traits are also associated with harmful and rule-breaking behavior. Three stand out here: narcissism, psychopathy, and Machiavellianism. Together they are known as the Dark Triad.[62] Narcissists have an exaggerated sense of self-importance, a strong sense of entitlement, and a need for superiority and admiration.[63] People with psychopathic traits tend to be more impulsive, selfish, and lacking in empathy and remorse.[64] Finally, Machiavellianism, which was developed in light of the writings of the Italian thinker Niccolò Machiavelli, indicates people who are cold and calculating, who manipulate others, use deception, and use any means necessary to achieve goals that benefit themselves.[65]

As the leading study about the Dark Triad summarized, "The personalities composing the 'Dark Triad' share a number of features. To varying degrees, all three entail a socially malevolent character with behavioral tendencies toward self-promotion, emotional coldness, duplicity, and aggressiveness."[66] And indeed research shows that people who have one or more of these three traits are more likely to engage in bad behavior, such as bullying, deception, deviant sexual behavior, revenge, white-collar crime (such as fraud), academic dishonesty, and violent crime.[67]

People who suffer from personality disorders may also be more prone to engaging in damaging and illegal behavior. Here we are talking about people who suffer from a clinically diagnosed psychiatric disorder that severely affects their everyday functioning. In its main diagnostic handbook, the *DSM-5*, the American Psychiatric Association defines such disorders as "ways of thinking and feeling about oneself and others that significantly and adversely affect how an individual functions in many aspects of life."[68] It lists ten types, such as paranoid, schizoid, antisocial, and borderline personality disorders.

Clearly, not all who suffer from clinically diagnosed psychiatric disorders also engage in crime, nor do all who engage in crime also suffer from psychiatric disorders. Yet a review of the literature has found that people with certain disorders were three times more likely to engage in violent behavior and two to three times more likely to repeat their offense.[69] The review did not find that all disorders in all people are linked with more violent behavior. As it states, the relationship between such disorders and violent conduct varies substantially.[70] Obsessive compulsive and avoidant personality disorders are, for instance, not strongly associated with delinquent conduct, and a recent study found that people with such disorders may even be less likely to engage in violence.[71]

Similarly, developmental psychologists have looked at whether particular traits in children and adolescents make them more inclined toward delinquency and violence. Here they have studied so-called callous-unemotional traits, which are viewed on a scale. Children and teens who exhibit more callous-unemotional traits exhibit an interpersonal style characterized by a lack of empathy, deficient guilt or remorse after misbehavior, and shallow or deficient emotions. There is some evidence that people with more callous-unemotional traits exhibit deficits in seeking out or even just getting pleasure from bonding with others and are less inclined to be moved by threats. It is perhaps unsurprising, then, that studies have found that kids who have more callous-unemotional traits are at increased risk of engaging in illegal behavior.

But what can we do with this information? Can we truly say that there are good people and bad people or, in more neutral terms, that there are people with higher risk or lower risk of committing wrongdoing? Studies show that certain people have traits and disorders that may make them more likely to engage in damaging, violent, or rule-breaking behavior. But we must not forget how complex the data are. The data are likely skewed toward people with personality disorders because they are more likely to get caught and thus show up more often in crime statistics. To make matters worse, the science cannot reliably predict the probability that certain people will engage in crime, let alone state for sure.

Take the case of Dr. James Fallon. A neuroscientist at the University of California, Irvine, Fallon studies anatomical patterns in brains to understand psychopathy. He knows that the brain of a psychopath tends to have decreased activity in areas in the frontal lobe that are linked to empathy and morality. In fact, he knows them so well that he can pick them out from just glancing at an image of a brain scan.

Yet, one day, while doing a different research project on Alzheimer's, he had on his desk a pile of brain scans from a variety of sources—people diagnosed as psychopathic, schizophrenic, and depressive—as well as scans from typical or normal brains from his own family members. When he got to one family member's scan, he was alarmed to see the tell-tale signs of a psychopathic brain. He checked his brain scanner and saw that it was operating fine. So someone in his family had to be a psychopath. As any of us would do, Fallon then looked to see whose brain scan it was. To his surprise, he found out it was his own.

As he later recalled in an interview: "I've never killed anybody, or raped anyone. So, the first thing I thought was that maybe my hypothesis was wrong, and that these brain areas are not reflective of psychopathy or murderous behavior."[72]

Fallon's story shows that we must be careful about using psychological tests as a way of predicting who will become a lifelong, violent criminal. In fact, experts are sounding the alarm about the most commonly used psychopathy checklist as the basis for assessing the risk of repeated violence in capital punishment sentencing cases. In a recent publication, a team of renowned scientists concluded that the psychopathy checklist should "not be used to make predictions that an individual will engage in serious institutional violence with any reasonable degree of precision or accuracy, especially when making high-stakes decisions about legal issues such as capital sentencing."[73] And the other problem is that, for most people, we simply do not know their personality well enough to judge. There is no universally accepted way of using the findings about personality and crime, let alone of forcing everyone to do personality questionnaires, get psychiatric testing, and maybe even charge them hundreds of dollars to scan their brains.

That's not the only concern. When people talk about personality traits and disorders, they often use them to ostracize others—labeling them as remorseless and broken Hannibal Lecters who cannot be changed. But there is accumulating evidence that these traits, including callous-unemotional traits, can be changed through intervention. For instance, one study of 551 families randomly assigned parents of youth displaying serious problem behavior to a variety of different intervention programs. They found convincing evidence that a comprehensive parenting program, which focused on promoting effective parenting skills through twelve weekly sessions, had substantial impacts on youths' callous-unemotional traits.[74] Another study, conducted with about one hundred Italian children, featured a dual-delivery system that focused both on children and on parenting. The child component focused on goal-setting, study skills, identifying different emotions, coping with anger, improving perspective-taking, and coping with peer pressure. The parent component focused on increasing positive attention, rewarding appropriate child behavior, establishing and enforcing appropriate rules and expectations, improving communication within the family, and even reducing their own stress levels. That study found clear evidence that the therapy intervention program reduced children's callous-unemotional traits and their aggressive behavior. Not only that, the families used mental health services less over the entire next year, indicating that the program actually has, in the authors' words, a positive economic implication.[75] In fact, a variety of other studies are also finding that promising intervention programs can reduce callous-unemotional traits and aggressive, violent behavior, showing us that what we previously thought were immutable traits or characteristics that destined somebody to a life of crime are actually surprisingly malleable under the right circumstances.[76] (We will return to this later when we discuss in more depth how different forms of treatment have been remarkably successful at dealing with delinquent and damaging behaviors in both children and adults.)

When it comes to law and morality, social science provides several key takeaways. First, the law's influence on human conduct is not simply a matter of amoral rational choice or even amoral irrational choice. It is deeply ingrained in the way people deliberate about, intuitively respond to, or repress morality. Clearly, people's personal morals, values, and traits directly impact how people respond to the law. As Bar-Ilan University law professor Yuval Feldman explains in his book *The Law of Good People*, for law to improve behavior it must address morality, and to do so the law must make it impossible for people to feel moral when breaking the law.[77]

A second core insight is that the law works best when it is aligned with the morals people already have or when it can convince people that it provides the only moral route forward. Inversely, legal rules that seek to prevent people from engaging in behavior that is widely perceived to be morally acceptable are almost destined to fail.

At the same time, the law must recognize that people have only a limited capacity for ethical reasoning, and that they may not be able to weigh the morality of violating rules, either before or after the fact. To overcome this, authorities must use insights from behavioral ethics to nudge people toward engaging in more deliberate, ethical decision-making.

The final insight concerns people who exhibit serious, clinically diagnosed psychiatric disorders or high levels of callous-unemotional or psychopathic traits. There will always be a small percentage of the population whose morals and traits are so deeply entrenched that there may be little to nothing that we can do to change them. But that is a minuscule percentage of a percentage of people. The research on intervention programming is showing quite clearly that even among those with remarkably high levels of callous-unemotional traits, treatments and interventions not only can work but actually do work. While it is difficult for the law to address people's morals and personal traits, it is entirely possible.

# CHAPTER 5

# Civil Obedience

On April 6, 1930, Mahatma Gandhi made salt. In the village of Dandi, right off the Arabian coast in Western India, he waded into the ocean, took out a lump of mud, and began boiling it with seawater.[1]

Gandhi had come a long way to get to the shore. On March 12, he had set off with seventy-two followers, passing village after village and town after town as they walked the 240 miles from his rural residence at the Sabarmati Ashram to the shore. At each place, more people joined Gandhi's march, until he arrived at the shore with an entourage that spanned two miles behind him. Thousands watched Gandhi break the law by making salt.

Earlier that year, Gandhi had issued his Declaration of the Independence of India. He knew that he needed to incite massive collective action for his words to become reality. He sought to find a rallying point where Indians could come together against the British colonial rulers. He found one in the 1882 India Salt Act. This law mandated that all salt collection and manufacture was under the colonial government's monopoly. This meant that Indian salt producers could only sell their goods through governmental salt depots and had to pay a hefty tax. The law had followed a century of high colonial taxation and restrictions on local salt production, first by the British East India Company, and since 1858 by the British government when it took over colonial rule and established the Raj.

For decades, Indians had resisted the restrictions on salt. The mineral was a readily available source of income to many living in coastal areas. And for all others, salt was vital not just for taste as a seasoning but also as a necessary mineral in the diet of the millions who had to do hard labor in India's hot and humid climate. The smuggling of illegally produced salt became so extensive that authorities ended up erecting a 2,500-mile fence along the western border of the salt-producing Bengal province, made of thorny trees and bushes and guarded by over twelve thousand men. The salt restrictions and taxation also drew widespread criticism. Delegates to India's colonial parliament at the time argued that the system was unjust and should be abolished or fundamentally changed.

Gandhi's 1930 salt march became known as the pinnacle of his nonviolent collective action campaigns. The salt tax epitomized the oppressive colonial rule he was fighting. A crucial element in his approach was civil disobedience. He fought oppression by refusing to follow the unjust rules of the oppressor, creating a model many emulated in later struggles. Nowhere is this clearer than in the US civil rights struggle in the 1950s and 1960s. Like Gandhi, Mrs. Rosa Parks and Dr. Martin Luther King Jr. broke the law to signal the broader injustice of the law and the system that supported it.

Laws that oppress are the exact opposite of what this book is about. We are writing about laws that serve legitimate interests such as reducing pollution, unsafe working conditions, sexual harassment, traffic accidents, and violent crime. Yet, even when laws serve legitimate interests, there is variation in how much people feel obligated to obey them. Some people may think that one should always at least try to follow the law, regardless of whether there is enforcement or whether one agrees with the law. And other people may feel less of an overall duty or obligation to obey the law. They may think, for instance, that it is okay to violate laws if most others do so, if there are no real sanctions, if no one would know, or if there is no harm.

Civil obedience can play a vital role in how law shapes human conduct. It seems logical that people with a higher sense of civil obedience will be more inclined to follow legal rules. When people have a higher sense of civil obedience, it seems that they would follow the law even when there is limited enforcement, even when it comes at great costs, even when most others break it, and even if they do not necessarily agree with the law. They would follow the law because of their sense of obligation. It's the law! And because it is the law, one must follow it.

Civil obedience is a vital part of the behavioral code, a sort of failsafe option the law can rely on when all other mechanisms we have discussed so far are ineffective. Vice versa, civil disobedience is like a canary in the coal mine and may signal that the law has lost its way and no longer serves legitimate interests.

## HOW PEOPLE DEVELOP CIVIL OBEDIENCE

Over the past eight years, we have studied why people feel obligated to obey the law. At first we thought it would be explained by national context. In our cross-national research in the US, Israel, the Netherlands, and China, we expected to find a variety of national differences, especially with China. As China does not have an established democratic rule of law, we assumed that people's duty to obey the law in general would be lower there.

We were wrong. Our research revealed that people in China felt just as obligated to obey the law as people in the US, Israel, and the Netherlands. Instead of national context, certain individual characteristics explain why people felt obligated to obey the law. We found, for instance, that personality mattered: more honest and humble people reported more of a duty to obey the law. We saw that people who were more engaged with moral issues felt more obligated to obey the law, as were people with a more conservative political orientation.[2] Perhaps most illuminating, in a study of adolescents and their parents, we found that when parents felt more of a duty to obey the law, so did their children.[3] From these later findings, we began to see that people's civil obedience, their sense of duty to obey the law, may be something they learn and get socialized into. To make sense of our findings, we dug into the archives and unearthed some incredible studies, almost half a century old, that are virtually unknown.

In the 1970s, researchers began asking kids of all ages, from kindergarten through college, what they thought about laws and rules. The idea was to figure out how our perceptions of rules change as we get older, so the researchers asked a host of wide-ranging questions, like "What is a rule?" or "What would happen if there were no laws?"

A fascinating pattern emerged in the data. The researchers found that younger children tend to see rules as specific no-no's that forbid certain behaviors. Young children obey rules because of their deference to authorities in power and because they simply don't want to be punished. They have what researchers call an *obedience and punishment* orientation to rules. And because younger children are so afraid of being punished, incentives and punishments are crucial for changing their misbehavior. If you want to prevent young children from violating rules, incentives and punishments certainly can help.

But as we age from childhood into adolescence, this orientation starts to change. With cognitive development, social skill development, and experience, we begin to obey rules less and less out of a fear of being punished. Our thinking shifts from an "obedience and punishment" perspective to a "law and order" perspective. Adolescents in particular begin to think that rather than simply prohibit certain behaviors, rules are intended to guide "good" behavior and prevent disorder. To adolescents, compliance with rules becomes fundamental to our joint pursuit of maintaining society; most adolescents think that without rules, there would be chaos. Critically, as we become adults, the vast majority of us comply even less out of a fear of being punished. By college, only 25 percent of people comply with rules simply to avoid negative consequences. As we mature, we largely lose this punishment orientation in favor of a loftier and more sophisticated obligation to obey the law.

These findings tell us that the felt obligation to obey the law changes developmentally, but they also tell us that among adults, there are still individual differences in this sense of duty to follow legal rules. But the findings do not really tell us whether it is possible to increase people's sense of duty. We can't just wait for people to just get older and hope that their felt obligation to obey the law improves. Nor can our laws just rely on adults with a high sense of duty and just address people with an honest and humble personality.

Tom Tyler, a psychologist at Yale Law School, may offer help here. Tyler first assessed how strongly people's sense of duty to obey the law was associated with compliance as compared to other factors, like the threat of punishment (deterrence) or peer approval (injunctive social norms). We might intuit that deterrence and social norms would be the most powerful forces, yet Tyler found that it was this felt obligation that was the most impactful. In other words, people's compliance rests more on whether they feel a duty to obey the law than it does on punishment.

He then analyzed how people's sense of duty to obey the law is related to how people perceive the justice system. He found that people's perceptions of the justice system's fairness and justness shapes their felt obligation to obey the law and thus their compliance. The more people felt the system was fair and just, the more they felt it was legitimate, and the more they felt it was legitimate, the more they felt obligated to obey the law.

Tyler's idea was that people's views of the fairness and justness of the legal system depend less on its outcomes and more on the process, on how legislators, courts, and law enforcement arrive at such outcomes. So even if people lose in court, they might still accept and comply with the ruling and the law moving forward if they think the process has been fair and just. His core idea was that *procedural justice*, the fairness and justness of the process, is vitally important for enhancing people's duty to obey the law and, in turn, compliance.[4] As it turns out, the process matters much more than getting a favorable outcome.[5]

Tyler has analyzed what exactly shapes procedural justice. His first conclusion was that authorities need to allow citizens to have a voice in proceedings and decision-making. Even if our input doesn't change the outcome of our legal proceedings, our participation enhances our perceptions of procedural justice. Second, authorities must treat people honestly and not betray their trust. Third, authorities can enhance procedural justice through treating citizens respectfully. Finally, authorities must maintain neutrality, which requires lawmakers, enforcement officials, and judges to treat citizens equally, impartially, and without being swayed by personal opinions.[6]

When Tyler reported his initial findings in his book *Why People Obey the Law*, he created an entire new field of studies focused on understanding how procedural justice and the felt obligation to obey the law play a role in ensuring compliance. Most work has focused on the criminal justice system. For instance, in one large-scale study of male juvenile offenders known as the Crossroads Study, research teams in California, Louisiana, and Pennsylvania identified over twelve hundred males who had been arrested for the very first time. They tracked them down right after their first arrest and then interviewed them routinely for years, asking them everything about their lives. What they found was that legitimacy was often more important in shaping criminal behavior in these young people than self-control, race, neighborhoods, family, and socioeconomic circumstances.

These are not just isolated studies. Glenn Walters and Colin Bolger, from the Department of Criminal Justice at Kutztown University, have conducted the most up-to-date and systematic review of this body of work.[7] They reviewed sixty-four studies published between 1990 and 2018, including studies conducted in the US, England, the Netherlands, Australia, Israel, Canada, Hungary, Greece, and Nigeria. Their overall conclusion is that across all these different studies, the data overwhelmingly show that the more people perceive their criminal justice institutions to be just and fair, the more they perceive them to be legitimate and feel obligated to obey them, and the less likely they are to break the law.

Scholars in a wide variety of fields have uncovered very similar findings. One study of American soldiers stationed in Iraq and police officers in a large metropolitan department found that the more these soldiers and officers saw their organizations as procedurally fair, the more they saw them as legitimate, the more they felt a duty to obey their rules, and the more likely they were to comply with them.[8] Another study, of Danish farmers, found that as compared to factors like the threat of punishment, awareness of legal rules, capacity to comply, and the costs of compliance, farmers' perceived duty to obey the law was one of the strongest predictors of their compliance with environmental regulations.[9]

Interdisciplinary scholars studying things as diverse as welfare fraud, tax evasion, and even Australian nursing homes come to the same conclusion: the sense of duty to obey the law is a powerful force for enhancing compliance.[10] In fact, when Robert MacCoun, then professor of public policy and law at the University of California, Berkeley, reviewed over seven hundred studies on the topic, he found that procedural justice consistently shaped compliance and cooperation with authorities across a wide array of behaviors.[11]

With all these studies, we see that there is a clear association between civil obedience and compliance. The only problem is that virtually all of these studies are correlational. And as the saying goes, correlation does not equate to causation.[12] Fortunately, some experimental studies offer causal evidence. Take, for instance, the work of Ed Maguire, a criminologist at Arizona State University, and his colleagues, who recorded videos of a simulated traffic stop. They then randomly assigned 266 people to watch one of three versions of the video in which the only variation was how the officer communicated with the driver: positively (procedurally just), negatively (procedurally unjust), or neutrally (neither just nor unjust). Then they asked people how much they would be willing to cooperate with the officer, how much they feel obligated to obey the officer, and how much they trust the officer.

Maguire and his colleagues found clear evidence that the way a police officer treats people during an encounter influences all three outcomes: the extent to which people are willing to cooperate with the officer, feel obligated to obey the officer, and report trusting the officer. When people watched the procedurally just encounter, they were more likely to trust the officer and to both cooperate and obey. That finding suggests that even vicarious experiences, such as watching someone else have a just and fair traffic stop interaction with an officer, impact us.

In another experiment, Elaine Doyle, Kieran Gallery, and Mary Coyle, all tax scholars from Ireland, tried to see what the effect would be of sending reminder letters to Irish taxpayers who were late in filing their taxes.[13] They compared the effect of three different letters. The first was a standard letter, including a message that explained that the taxpayer was late, what they should do, and that they would face prosecution if they did not comply. The second letter was a version of the first letter with more formal language and a stronger emphasis on punishment. And the last letter emphasized procedural justice, especially that the authorities respected the taxpayer (expressing that they believed the taxpayer was honest and also that they may not have known that they had to file their taxes) and provided them with additional insight into how the authorities had come to their decision. They found that all three letters led to more tax returns compared to a group of late filers that had not received a letter. But of the three, the letter signaling the procedural justice message led to the biggest increase in tax returns (30 percent), compared to the standard (25 percent) and deterrent (21 percent) letters.

There we have it. People with a strong sense of civil obedience, a strong sense of duty to obey the law, will be more likely to follow legal rules. They will do so even when there is limited enforcement, even when others break the law, and even when they themselves do not necessarily agree with the law. Procedural fairness is a vital precondition for civil obedience.

But what do we do when legal authorities do not act in a procedurally fair manner?

Derrick Sellers is a veteran of the US Marine Corps. Sellers was in custody at the Iberia Parish Jail in Louisiana when, one evening, jail guards forced him down a deserted hall into a visiting room where a group of guards pinned him to the ground, pepper-sprayed him in the face, and beat him with their hands, feet, knees, and metal objects—all for no known reason.[14] The beating was so brutal that they broke his left cheekbone all the way into his eye socket, and to this day he can no longer see properly and suffers from the headaches and disorientation associated with brain injuries.

Years later, Sellers was granted a settlement with the Iberia Parish
Sheriff's Office for $2.5 million, which constituted the largest such pay-
out so far for the office that has been sued dozens of times for more than
$6 million. (That includes just the publicly disclosed dollar amounts—
the figure is larger since a number of the lawsuits have settled for an
"undisclosed" dollar amount.)

The Iberia Parish Sheriff's Office had become a notoriously corrupt
department, where abuse and law violations by officers were rampant
and officers acted as though they were above the law. For instance, three
officers, including narcotics agent Wade Bergeron, were having an off-
duty party one night when they drunkenly decided to leave the party
to go find some people to beat up. They came across two Black males,
ages sixteen and twenty-one, and beat them up because, as Bergeron
said, "that was the first people we came across." When they later told
the sheriff, Louis Ackal, he shrugged it off and said it just "sounded like
a case of 'n****r knockin'.'" The Sheriff and other superiors allegedly
told them to lie and stick to a cover story about having no involvement
in the beatings.[15]

In all, ten of Sheriff Ackal's deputies have pleaded guilty in federal
court to charges including federal civil rights violations, making false
statements to help cover up assaults, and routinely doctoring incident
reports to justify excessive force. The fallout from these events has been
massive. More than one hundred criminal cases have had to have been
thrown out as a result of the ensuing investigations into the officers, and
more than seven hundred other cases could be affected.[16]

All of this shows a very broken system in which police can for years
commit brutality with impunity. It shows a system in which law enforcement officials, jail wardens, prosecutors, and judges do not offer procedural justice or fairness. Quite the opposite, they have become the very
pillars of injustice. Americans see new videos of police killings and police
brutalities weekly, if not daily. The names of deceased victims have been
etched in the public psyche. And in nearly all cases, brutalizing police
officers face no serious consequences, as hardly any are indicted, let alone
convicted or put in prison.

These events undermine the public's trust in law enforcement and in the justice system as a whole. The harsh reality is that researchers in 2019 found that "about 1 in every 1,000 Black men can expect to be killed by police."[17] Specifically, Black men are about 2.5 times more likely to be killed by police than are white men, Black women about 1.4 times more likely than white women, and American Indian and Alaska Native men and women between 1.2 and 1.7 times (for men) and 1.1 and 2.1 times (for women) more likely than their white counterparts.

It's not surprising that the public at best is skeptical of law enforcement and at worst is fearful of them. Unfortunately, it seems as though this problem is getting worse—even among youth. In one study, Adam leveraged data from the Monitoring the Future study, which surveys about fifty thousand high school seniors every year. What's unique about these data is that the surveys are administered in schools and are done across the country in the forty-eight contiguous United States. Perhaps more importantly, they are completely anonymous, so these teenagers can feel comfortable telling the truth regarding how they feel about law enforcement.[18]

Using data from over a decade, Adam and his colleagues examined whether youths' perceptions of law enforcement have changed in recent years. What we found was depressing but not surprising: youths' perceptions of law enforcement have declined rapidly in recent years, reaching a decades-long low.[19] The sharpest decline happened from 2014 to 2015, which is precisely when, in the span of nine months, the nation was repeatedly shocked and appalled by the deaths of five young Black males at the hands of police: Eric Garner, Michael Brown, Ezell Ford, Walter Scott, and Tamir Rice. What these data reveal is that these police killings ignited widespread criticism of law enforcement and almost certainly undermined the public's trust in law enforcement and thus overall views of procedural justice in America.

The reality is that decades of procedural unfairness within communities leave deep, lasting impacts on people's views of legal authorities and the legal system. Studies find that Hispanic and Latinx youths' perceptions of law enforcement begin declining at age nine, and Black youths' perceptions of law enforcement may begin declining even earlier—as

young as age seven.[20] We know there is continuity, such that if you develop poor perceptions of law enforcement when you are young, you are
more likely to maintain these perceptions as you grow older.

These are not just problems of the police. The US legal system is replete with procedurally unfair practices in how the law is applied. One
immigration law judge in New York grants 6 percent of applications
received while a colleague grants 91 percent.[21] The same problems exist with how judges adjudicate Social Security disability dispute claims:
some judges reverse administrative decisions about entitlements 10 percent of the time and others up to 90 percent of the time.[22] A review of
this body of work finds similar inconsistencies in how US authorities
decide on patent applications, enforce Medicaid standards in nursing
homes, make decisions about removing parental custody over children in
cases of abuse and neglect, and conduct nuclear safety inspections.[23] And
this list goes on and on. Such inconsistencies in these vital legal decisions
can easily undermine people's perception of procedural justice, fairness,
and equality in the legal system.

We can also find Supreme Court cases that promote procedural unfairness. A clear example is *McCleskey v. Kemp*, a 1987 case in which
lawyers for Warren McCleskey, a Black man who had been sentenced
to death for murder, argued that there had been systemic racism in how
judges applied capital punishment.[24] They showed compelling statistical
evidence that defendants convicted of killing a white victim were 4.3
times more likely to receive capital punishment than those convicted of
killing a Black victim.[25] The court not only refused to accept the statistical data as substantial evidence to warrant a reversal, it even argued that
had it accepted the evidence, this would still not be sufficient as it would
not show deliberate and conscious bias of the law in McCleskey's specific
case. Pulitzer Prize–winning *New York Times* columnist Anthony Lewis
stated that the court had "effectively condoned the expression of racism
in a profound aspect of our law."[26] And, by doing so, the Supreme Court
failed to use this clear opportunity to correct ongoing bias and procedural unfairness in the application of the law's gravest punishment: the
death penalty.

Systemic procedural injustice seriously undermines compliance with the law and breeds crime. So where do we go from here?

## BETTER LAW ENFORCEMENT?

In 2015, President Barack Obama convened the Task Force on 21st Century Policing. Cochaired by Charles Ramsey, then the commissioner of the Philadelphia Police Department, and Laurie Robinson, criminology professor at George Mason University, the task force was initiated to strengthen community policing and trust among law enforcement officers and communities. The task force consulted with law enforcement officials, academics, technical advisors, youth and community leaders, and leaders of nongovernmental organizations. Over the course of ninety days, it identified "best policing practices and offered recommendations on how those practices [could] promote effective crime reduction while building public trust."[27]

The task force provided clear guidance on how to improve policing practices, a vital precondition to building trust in the community. It concluded that police should embrace a "guardian" rather than a "warrior" mindset. That means they need to perceive themselves as people who protect citizens through partnerships with the community rather than as crime fighters battling evil.[28]

Kyle McLean and his colleagues surveyed two police departments in remarkably different jurisdictions, one in the Southwest and one in the Southeast of the US, to assess how much officers saw themselves as warriors or guardians.[29] To gauge the officers' perceptions of themselves, they asked them to rate their agreement with nine statements, including these two: "As a police officer, I have a primary responsibility to protect the constitutional rights of residents" (the guardian mindset). "My primary responsibility as a police officer is to fight crime" (the warrior mindset).

What McLean and his colleagues found was fascinating. First, it is entirely possible for officers to be both warriors *and* guardians. Yet the extent to which officers felt aligned with the guardian mindset was critically important. The more they felt as though they were guardians, the

less they supported police misconduct and the more they prioritized procedural justice during interactions with citizens, including doing things
like "explaining [why one has] made contact with the subject," "treating
the subject politely and with dignity," "allowing the subject to explain
his side of the story," and "explaining to the subject the reasons for [the
officer's] decisions." McLean and his colleagues concluded, "The guardian mentality, then, may make officers more likely to treat subjects in a
more procedurally fair manner."[30]

This provides hope that new recruitment strategies and trainings that
focus on the guardian mentality in policing could improve procedural
justice and relationships with the community. We do not yet have experimental evidence to conclusively suggest that recruiting police cadets
who lean more toward the guardian mindset might reduce problematic
policing, nor do we have evidence that changing the culture toward the
guardian mindset may reduce problematic use-of-force incidents. Nonetheless, the findings are promising.


Watts is a Los Angeles neighborhood where residents experience high
levels of gang activity. It is an area that civil rights attorneys have called
"one of the hardest, most violence-entrenched communities."[31] In 2010
and 2011, the Housing Authority of the City of Los Angeles (HACLA),
which operates the public housing developments in Watts, commissioned
the Advancement Project-Urban Peace to engage over nine hundred residents of the community through interviews, surveys, and focus groups
to examine their views of gang violence and the authorities, and how safe
they felt in their own homes. The results were so abysmal that HACLA
recognized that something had to be done immediately to enhance the
safety, security, and welfare of residents and communities.

Chief of the Los Angeles Police Department (LAPD) Charlie Beck,
Connie Rice (a civil rights lawyer who sued the LAPD regularly),
Mayor James Hahn, federal district court judge Gary A. Feess, and a
group of reformers came together to create a solution.[32] They tried to
develop a "relationship-based" model of policing, even though Watts is,

in the words of a civil rights attorney, "a place of historically heightened tension between the community and law enforcement, a dynamic that has persisted for decades."[33] To put it more bluntly, it is a neighborhood with a history of experiencing systemic and rampant racist, biased, and unjust policing.

The group created the LAPD's Community Safety Partnership unit. Recognizing that they were going to be asking "grieving parents . . . to agree to join cops who had jailed or killed their children during the wars on drugs and gangs," members of this new unit began their work with an officer's public apology for past police transgressions. Then, community leaders in Watts began to work with them in the local pilot program. As Chief Beck and Connie Rice wrote in 2016, looking back:

> Call it guardian policing, trust policing, problem-solving policing, relationship-based policing, community policing or partnership polic-ing. The many names share one vision: humane, compassionate, cultur-ally fluent cops who have a mind-set of respect, do not fear black men, and serve long enough to know residents' names, speak their languages and help improve the neighborhood. We believed this approach could reduce bad policing, bolster law enforcement and increase public safety. We went out to prove it, and 15 years later, we think we have.[34]

Uniquely, this unit has worked for years to build up trust and relationships with residents through participating in a wide range of neighborhood activities, including things like starting a farmers' market, implementing one public housing development's first Girl Scout troop, and creating sports leagues for kids, including football teams of nine-to-eleven-years-olds from four housing developments. In few other large cities do officers have the ability to patrol on foot and greet the residents by name. Until the new unit was formed, it was virtually unheard of for a unit's officers to get promoted for demonstrating "impact," not through meeting arrest quotas but by showing how they diverted kids from jail and what they did to increase public trust in them. The core approach was to "avoid traditional suppression strategies that destroy trust."[35]

The results of the program have been impressive. Not only did it create better relations with the community; it also reduced crime. In its first year, the Community Safety Partnership unit had the department's steepest crime reductions, and, remarkably, it has sustained those crime drops ever since. For the two years following the start of the program, the housing projects that had regularly suffered through murder after murder each year did not have a single murder. And in Watts there were no officer-involved shootings for over five years. These are powerful outcomes for a department notorious for a history of racist policies and practices.

The civil rights attorney who had previously sued the department numerous times wrote, "The success has been nothing short of transformative. Not only have violent crimes decreased precipitously, but arrests have gone down by 50%, with ordinary citizens telling visitors that they actually feel safer and know and trust police officers who have become a part of the community's day-to-day landscape."[36] While studies do not yet quantify exactly how much biased or unjust policing has declined in the area, the implication of the numerous qualitative interviews with residents and stakeholders in the area indicate that the LAPD officers who were trained in the program have vastly improved their relationships with minority communities. As civil rights attorney Rice explained, "the residents love it, they want it back, they want it taken to the next level."[37] And independent studies by both the Urban Institute and researchers at the University of California, Los Angeles, found that the program reduced crime and improved policing.[38]

Altogether, we do not yet fully know how to reduce biased and unjust policing on a systemic level, but promising approaches are emerging. University of California, Irvine, criminology professor Emily Owens and colleagues found that a procedural justice training of Seattle police officers had favorable effects. Their randomized controlled study of a program designed to help officers "slow down" their thought processes during citizen encounters found that officers subsequently were about 12 percent less likely to resolve incidents with an arrest, indicating fewer unnecessary arrests overall. Further, officers were also between 16 and 50 percent less likely to be involved in use-of-force incidents as compared with control officers.[39]

There is also evidence from other countries. Lorraine Mazerolle, from the University of Queensland in Australia, conducted the first large-scale randomized controlled trial in the field: sixty planned roadblocks were randomly assigned to be policed using either the procedural justice treatment condition or "business as normal."[40] In all, police pulled over between three hundred and four hundred cars per location. In the experimental condition, the traffic cop used a script that focused on the elements of procedural justice, including encouraging citizen participation and voice, and treating them with dignity and respect. They found that the procedural justice approach led to much better outcomes, including improved perceptions about police and higher levels of satisfaction with police in general.

So far, we have a handful of high-quality studies on how to effectively improve the ways police interact with members of the community. But there is a clear problem: while areas of a city may show promise, bad policing in other areas of the city (or country) still threatens the overall progress. Relatedly, while some officers might improve their behavior, the actions of others can completely undermine any progress. If we return to LAPD's Community Safety Partnership (CSP), we find clear evidence of this. By definition, only some LAPD officers—the ones in the CSP unit—are trained in this community-oriented policing strategy. Community members, residents, and even some of the officers in the unit themselves have reported that the more aggressive policing style of other LAPD units endangers the progress built by the CSP program.[41] This is a major problem with even the most promising police reform efforts. Virtually all are too small in scope and scale, and an unjust incident anywhere threatens procedural justice and legitimacy everywhere. Despite numerous efforts and some promising results, we are only beginning to scratch the surface of addressing what are deeply systemic issues.

There are also ideas on how to improve procedural justice in enforcing other areas of the law outside the purview of the police. Daniel Ho, who teaches at Stanford Law School, studied food safety enforcement practices at restaurants in King County in Washington State. There had been much arbitrariness in food safety inspections there, with some inspectors trying a more accommodative style that sought to persuade and educate businesses into compliance, while others acted more like tough cops.[42] To improve the situation and reduce arbitrary inspections, Ho started an experiment in which he randomly assigned the inspectors into two groups. The first group would serve as a control and carry on inspections as usual. The second group would initiate a form of peer review, in which each inspector would be accompanied by a peer inspector, and both would write their own independent inspection report. Each week, peer group participants were asked to fill out an anonymous survey to explain divergences from their partners' reports and also to indicate what they had learned. And they organized weekly huddle sessions in which peer group inspectors would discuss disagreements in coding and in risk assessment. The experiment worked beautifully; over the course of the fifteen weeks of study, the level of consistency in the peer review group rose significantly—by almost 50 percent.

Improving procedural justice in the legal system is step one in ensuring that our laws can generate civil obedience. This is by far the hardest step. Very often it means dealing both with bad apples—the individual officers who have engaged in or sustained procedural unfairness—as well as the barrels they exist in, the departments and broader contexts sustaining, protecting, or excusing such bad enforcement practices.[43] Everything we have discussed in this book so far can be applied to this complex problem, as we can consider using all the behavioral mechanisms covered to improve the behavior not only of potential lawbreakers but also of law enforcement officials.

But even when those who enforce the law cease brutality, discrimination, and arbitrariness, that does not mean that citizens come to *perceive* the legal system to be operating in a fair and just manner. So once legal institutions improve actual procedural justice, it is time for step two: building trust in legal institutions.

To build trust after decades of abuse is not easy. In some communities, it may be as difficult as the processes war-torn countries go through. Years of institutionalized racism, violent oppression, and struggle left unhealed wounds in South Africa that the freeing of Nelson Mandela and his subsequent rise to the presidency in 1994 could not simply erase. To heal these wounds and build a new society on the ashes of the apartheid state, South Africa engaged in what it called a *truth and reconciliation* process. It established a Truth and Reconciliation Commission that organized public hearings in which victims bore witness to what they had suffered and perpetrators could apply for amnesty if they agreed to acknowledge their deeds;[44] 7,111 perpetrators applied for such amnesty, and 849 were granted it.[45]

While the truth and reconciliation process has not worked perfectly in South Africa, in part because the program has not been effectively combined with punishment for the worst offenders, it has created a model that many have sought to emulate.[46] The model shows that what matters is that there is a process that identifies clearly what abuses have occurred and allows victims to voice their grievances, and that perpetrators acknowledge their role in these abuses. This process ensures that there is clear and open information about the injustices and their underlying causes so they can be addressed in reforms and, for the worst offenses, through prosecution. But the process is also vital for communities to gain back a sense of trust in the authorities.

In such a process, apologies are critical. Whenever an authority uncovers evidence of an egregious wrong, they must make a public mea culpa and communicate widely, openly, and transparently. When agency heads attempt reconciliation with the community through public apologies, they must pair the apology with an acknowledgment of responsibility.[47] To build back trust and confidence, agencies must not deny a problem or shy away from prosecuting the offenders. That would further distance the communities from authorities, likely undermining the obligation to obey the law and promoting noncompliance.

Civil obedience is a key pillar of the behavioral code. When people feel a duty to obey the law, they will do so even when there is limited enforcement, when it comes at a cost to them, and when they see others break the law. We know now that such obedience is directly connected to people's perceptions of the fairness of how the law operates. The fairer the legal system, the more people not only feel obligated to obey the law but actually also comply with it.

This provides a clear win-win situation. We can have more effective laws to protect us from harm while also having fairer and more just laws. In the US, with its endemic forms of procedural injustice, both in its police practices but also in the application of law in everyday life and in the courts, improving procedural justice is a basic necessity for fulfilling the country's promise of rule of law and civil rights protection.

It might seem that no one could be against this idea. Yet there are many who are. Sometimes when officers act as guardians, they get condemned or even formally disciplined in their departments full of officers with the warrior mindset. Such was the case with officer Stephen Mader from Weirton Police Department in West Virginia, who decided not to shoot a drunk man wishing to commit suicide by cop.[48] When courageous police chiefs, like Jeri Williams of the Phoenix Police Department, fire abusive, outright racist, or violent officers, they can face a resistance from the rank and file in the force and from police unions.[49] Under all of this there is a false assumption, that tougher enforcement will lead to less crime. But, as we now know, abusive enforcement undermines people's civil obedience, and it erodes their willingness to obey the law.

Clearly, there is no contradiction between having procedurally fair and effective law enforcement. The concerns of the Black Lives Matter movement should coincide completely with community concerns for crime. There is no zero-sum game situation where we must sacrifice the rights and safety of some people in some communities, especially young people of color, to allegedly protect the rights and safety of others. In fact, it is the complete opposite; such cases end up costing taxpayers millions of dollars, detracting from the total pool of money available for enhancing public safety. Take, for instance, how three hundred people, all victims of unfair and biased policing, have sued the city of Philadelphia, and the city has agreed to pay out more than $2 million in settlements—so far.[50] Or how in another case in Pennsylvania the state had to pay $4.75 million in damages to juvenile defendants because a judge had trampled on their right to have an attorney present during their hearings in his courtroom and had taken kickbacks in return for wrongfully convicting and sending over 2,400 youth to for-profit detention centers.[51]

For law to have a fighting chance to alter deeply ingrained, systemic misbehavior, it must learn to focus on civil obedience and legitimacy. To do so, in both the design and operation of our laws, we must make procedural fairness central.

## CHAPTER 6

# Following the Herd

Daycare programs in the Israeli port city of Haifa had a problem. In each daycare, about ten parents consistently picked up their children late. This was inconvenient for the daycare staff, who, at the end of long days of wrangling toddlers, were forced to stick around and entertain a dozen or so kids until their parents finally arrived. It was such a problem that daycares from across the city teamed up with two behavioral economists, Uri Gneezy and Aldo Rustichini, to see what they could do to reduce the late pickups.[1] The researchers conducted an experiment. In half of the daycares, they introduced a new policy: parents who were more than ten minutes late would have to pay a fine. And then they waited to see whether the fine would work.

To their surprise, they found the exact opposite of what they thought would happen: after daycares added fines for late pickups, *twice as many* parents started to pick up their kids late.

It feels normal to institute punishments whenever we face bad behavior. Instituting a fine to reduce misconduct is fully in line with our punitive intuition, yet it completely backfired in the daycares.

Gneezy and Rustichini were puzzled. From a traditional economic view, they did not make sense. The costs of arriving late went up, yet this did not convince parents to come on time. To understand what was happening here, they realized they had to look beyond financial incentives.

What cost-benefit analyses of such incentives miss is that the social context matters. Before the fine was introduced, parents were expected to come on time. Parents assumed that the daycare center, other parents, and probably even their kids wanted them to avoid being late. Picking up your kids on time was normal. Every day, parents would see that most of the other parents were on time, and those who were late would see that they were the exception. So, before the fine, social conventions drove parents to get to the daycares on time. But all this changed with the fine. Introducing a penalty eroded the social considerations. It translated a social obligation into a market contract. Rather than view the fine as a punishment and a threat to keep them coming on time, parents quickly began to view it as a payment for an extra service. Parents began thinking, "I can be late because I'm paying you for your time." As Gneezy and Rustichini aptly said of the phenomenon, the fine became the price.

Even more surprisingly, after the daycares removed the fine, the number of parents picking up their kids late remained twice as high as before the experiment. By the time they removed the fine, it was too late—the damage was done. Daycare providers had destroyed the old positive social practice of coming on time and inadvertently replaced it with a new, negative social practice, that picking up kids late was normal and acceptable.

People are social creatures who are guided by unwritten rules of behavior that dictate what is—and what is not—acceptable in society. These social practices and conventions are what psychologists call *social norms*. Understanding social norms is key to unlocking human behavior and understanding why people break rules. Social norms form a central component of the behavioral code. For law to become more successful in effectively improving behavior, it must incorporate them.

A leading psychologist at Arizona State University and a world-renowned expert on behavioral influence, Robert Cialdini, took on one of the country's biggest environmental concerns. He tried to reduce energy consumption in American households. Venturing out of the laboratory, his team of researchers headed into the suburbs to hang messages about energy saving on the front doors of almost three hundred houses. Each house randomly received one of four very different messages about energy saving. In a nutshell, these were the four messages: (1) energy conservation helps the environment; (2) it benefits society; (3) it saves money; (4) it is common.[2]

Reread those messages and decide how effective you think each would be. Would appeals to save the environment work? We all like to save money, so what about a message pointing to individual benefits, that reducing energy consumption saves you money? What about a simple statement that reducing energy is common?

Shortly after hanging the signs, Cialdini and his team interviewed residents to ask them what they thought about the message they had received. People who had received the fourth message, the one that said energy saving is common, were the least convinced that this would reduce their energy consumption. Most thought it would be entirely ineffective.

Cialdini's research team then measured each household's energy usage data over the following two weeks and found that ones that had received that fourth message had dramatically reduced energy consumption. Even the most wasteful users reduced energy consumption, and that group of households reduced consumption by an average of 1.22 kilowatt hours a day each, which is a lot—roughly equivalent to unplugging your fridge.[3]

The fourth message triggered a social norm, a *descriptive social norm*, that tells us what other people do. A simple message that the desired behavior is common can trigger even more good behavior. When we hear that others are behaving a certain way, both consciously and subconsciously, that simple yet powerful message compels us to behave the same way.

Cialdini and his colleagues weren't done. In a follow-up study, they gave households information about the average energy consumption in their neighborhood. The idea was to *show* everyone that most people around them were conserving energy.

As the researchers expected, telling people how much energy their neighbors were saving did lead to reduced energy consumption for many people. But unfortunately they found that the effect of these descriptive social norm messages was limited to a particular group of people. Energy use only declined among people who realized that they had been using more than their neighbors. For the energy-savers who had already been using less energy than their neighbors, it showed them that, compared to everyone else, they were overachievers. These energy-savers then started to use *more* energy, an average increase of 0.89 kilowatt hours per household per day—roughly the amount of energy it takes to wash eleven extra pounds of laundry each day.

The researchers realized that simply telling people where they stood in comparison to their neighbors gave overachievers a license to use more energy. To deal with this problem, Cialdini added something new to the energy-use information sheets he was sharing with those in the study group: emojis.

To the people who were using below-average amounts of energy, Cialdini gave happy-faced emojis. Those who were using too much energy received disapproving, sad-faced emojis. This extraordinarily simple and inexpensive treatment worked beautifully. When they received a combined message informing them of the average consumption level as well as an emoji indicating social disapproval of how they were doing, households that had been consuming above the average reduced their energy use dramatically. The emoji indicating social approval or disapproval had a remarkably large effect on behavior.

Psychologists call the motivators in this powerful effect *injunctive social norms*. Whereas descriptive social norms entail our perceptions of what other people are actually doing, injunctive social norms entail our perceptions of what others *think* we should or shouldn't do.[4] In this case, injunctive social norms were telling the energy-savers that other people approved of their behavior and told the energy-wasters that other people disapproved of their misbehavior.

In sum, social norms are very powerful forces to change behavior. When we see others doing the right thing, we will do so as well. But it goes beyond what we see. When we think others disapprove of our bad behavior, we begin to act better to bring ourselves into line with expectations.

If the legal code can tap into the power of social norms it can vastly improve its effectiveness in reducing unwanted and illegal behavior. Consider, for instance, how the state of Montana tried to tap into the power of social norms to reduce drunk driving among young adults.[5] It organized a statewide media campaign targeting people ages twenty-one to thirty-four. One TV commercial showed "a typical Montana ranch family in a barn preparing to ride horses." Viewers hear: "In Montana, our best defense against drinking and driving is each other. Most of us prevent drinking and driving. We take care of our friends, our families, and ourselves. Four out of five Montana young adults don't drink and drive. Thanks for doing your part." Tapping into descriptive social norms, this commercial tried to convince viewers that sober driving is the norm.

Another ad focused on the normalcy of having a designated driver to ensure that those who have been drinking get home safely. Here the setting was another Montana staple: a ski lodge window view with snow falling. The voice-over read: "In Montana there are two things you need to know about snow: how to drive on it and how to ski on it. After a day on the slopes and some time in the lodge, my friends and I all take turns being designated drivers." After this message, the view widened to reveal a message written on the window, "Most of us (4 out of 5) don't drink and drive." A voice then asked, "How are you getting home?"[6] The campaign used two main approaches: it showed how normal sober driving is, and it linked this to core values and common sources of Montanans' pride.

The results of this well-thought-out media campaign were impressive. There was a 13.7 percent reduction of people who reported driving after having two or more drinks and a 15 percent increase in the rate of people reporting they would use a designated driver.[7]

As another example, consider dating violence. Social norms research suggests that most men are uncomfortable with violence against women, seek consent in intimate relationships, and are uncomfortable with language and behavior that objectifies and hurts women. However, they falsely assume that other men do not always seek consent and are comfortable with negative behavior toward women. Consequently, men—

and boys—keep their true feelings to themselves and become bystanders, passive observers of other men's problem behaviors. Further, for the men who do engage in verbal and physical violence against women, they incorrectly interpret this overwhelming silence from other men as approval. Such silence, then, emboldens men to act violently and sexually harass women, even today in the era of #MeToo.

Studies do show, though, that such misconceptions about social norms can be changed. For instance, researchers at James Madison University (JMU) designed a poster with the following three messages:

1. *A man always prevents manipulation.* Three out of four JMU men think it is NOT okay to pressure a date to drink alcohol in order to increase the chances of getting their date to have sex.
2. *A man talks before romance.* Most JMU men believe that talking about sex does not ruin the romance of the moment.
3. *A man respects a woman.* Nine out of ten JMU men stop the first time their date says "no" to sexual activity.

The researchers surveyed students before and after the campaign and found significant improvements in the number of men who said they would stop the first time a date said "no."[8] In fact, a variety of studies have been found to change not only the social norms surrounding perceptions of dating violence but also actual dating violence.[9]

Another prime example of how the power of social norms can enhance compliance is in taxation. Tax authorities have long been masters of the behavioral code. They learned early on that the better they understand why people pay taxes, the more they can improve compliance and ultimately generate government revenue. For tax authorities there is a direct payback from resources spent on understanding the behavioral code. In teaming up with scientists to tap into effective behavioral processes, these scholars, it turns out, turned directly to the power of social norms.

One such tax scholar, Michael Wenzel, who teaches at Flinders University, studied people's attitudes toward paying taxes. In one study, he found that there was a general misunderstanding of the social norms regarding taxes. People would report that in their eyes, most other people were cheating on their taxes. And in the same survey, the same people reported that they did not cheat on their taxes themselves. Can you see what is strange here? It's like the joke in which a Cretan says: "All Cretans are liars." It's impossible.

Wenzel's findings here were in line with other research showing that many people are either unaware of or mistaken about the social norms that are at play. Remember that, in the energy-saving study, people who received the message telling them that energy reduction was common didn't think this would influence their behavior. But in practice this social norm message affected their energy use. A more grave example is research showing that middle school and high school students mistakenly believe there is a peer norm of a code of silence about reporting weapons in their schools. While most students personally thought that they should tell authorities about weapons in school, 37–52 percent of students also mistakenly believed that most other students did *not* support telling authorities.[10]

In Wenzel's case, he used mistaken beliefs about social norms to improve tax payment. He developed an ingenious experiment. Working with the Australian Taxation Office, he first randomly selected 1,500 Australian taxpayers who had filed their own tax returns in the prior year, who had reported income, and who had not been audited. He divided these into two groups: a control group who would not be contacted and a group who would be asked to fill out a survey. The survey first asked respondents to report their own views about whether they thought "one should be honest in one's tax returns." And the survey also asked questions about what respondents thought *others* thought about being honest on their taxes. The results from this survey confirmed there was a "self-other discrepancy" in which people had positive views about themselves and negative views about others. I pay taxes, but most people do not. His findings were very similar to the high schoolers' perceptions about reporting weapons to authorities.

So far, nothing new. But then, three weeks after the survey, Wenzel sent a feedback letter to half of the people who had filled out the questionnaire. The letter explained the discrepancy between the views people had reported about their own tax behavior and that of others. Here is the crucial part of the text that people received: "These results reveal an interesting paradox. The average of all the personal views that we received sums up what most people *actually think*, and this contrasts sharply with what they *think most people think*. Most people actually agree that honesty, responsibility and truthfulness are important when paying our taxes. These results indicate that we tend to think most people accept tax cheating and exaggerations in tax deductions. However, the truth is that most people think we should be honest with our tax statements and claim only those deductions that are allowable."[11]

Through the feedback letter, Wenzel aimed to correct a misconception and show that most people think it is wrong to cheat on taxes. In doing so, he was trying to establish an injunctive social norm that paying taxes is the desired behavior. And he hoped that this would improve tax-paying behavior.

To test whether the intervention had been effective, Wenzel and the tax authorities compared the actual amount of tax deductions that each group claimed, finding that the group that received the feedback letter reported significantly fewer non-work-related expense deductions. The experiment was a success, showing that we can leverage misconceptions about social norms to improve actual behavior—even behavior that literally costs us money.

To tap into the power of social norms and reduce rule violation, we must emphasize that many people are complying with the rules. We have to show that most people approve of the desired behavior and that it is more common than misbehavior. The psychological work on social norms offers several insights into how exactly the law can achieve this most effectively.

Lesson one is to be careful with existing social norms. When social norms support good behavior, we must be careful and leave them intact. In the Israeli daycares, the mistake was instituting a fine, a punishment that eroded the existing social norm. Similarly, we must be careful whenever we introduce rewards for good behaviors people are already doing. When we do so, this can cause an overjustification effect, in which people become reliant on a reward for a behavior that they were already happy to do without any incentive.[12]

Social norms only work when people believe the message and the messenger. Social norms scholars Jessica Nolan and Kenneth Wallen summarize: "Like most persuasive messages, social norms communications will be most effective when the source of the message is perceived to be credible and the information presented is believable. Message sources that are perceived as having a vested interest or that convey false information may arouse doubt, suspicion, or even resistance in the target audience."[13]

Audience also matters. Studies have shown that social norms mostly work within people's own social groups. Nolan and Wallen write, "Behavioral interventions leverage the phenomenon that people are more likely to adhere to the expectations of others like themselves."[14] Scholars point to the influence of social identity, the particular social groups that define part of our identity. As British psychologist Joanne Smith and Australian psychologist Winnifred Louis explain: "When individuals see themselves as belonging to a group and feel that being a group member is important to them, they will bring their behavior in line with the norms and standards of the group."[15] And because of this, people are more likely to adhere to social norms that come from a group or community they strongly identify with and less so to social norms that they consider to be outside their social identity group.[16] Such a group could be a nationality or ethnicity, a sporting team, a neighborhood, a university, a particular hobby, or even a language. Think of the Montana anti-DUI campaign.

Finally, the exact wording of the messages that people receive about social norms matters. Studies have shown that people respond more strongly to messages that have a negative framing (do not litter, do not turn the lights on) instead of a positive one (throw your garbage in the bin, switch the lights off). Also, studies have shown that a combination of descriptive messages (most people don't litter) and normative appeals that invoke injunctive social norms (people think littering is bad) are more effective than either one alone.[17] Remember what happened when the smiley was added to the messages about people's energy usage. Through careful messaging, we can shift the focus to the social norms that support desired behavior.

### THE POWER OF BAD EXAMPLES

Over half a million people visit the Petrified Forest National Park in Arizona each year to see its petrified wood.[18] Over two hundred million years ago, fallen trees were covered by layers and layers of volcanic ash and other sediment. The layers slowed the decaying process, and the minerals pervaded the branches and trunks over the millennia, fossilizing the wood with jewel-like crystals of purple amethyst, yellow citrine, and smoky quartz.

By all accounts, the park is beautiful and the petrified wood irreplaceable. And for decades park authorities had been trying to keep visitors from stealing the fossils. They tried fines. They tried inspections at the park's exits. In a desperate appeal, they even put up large warning signs: "Your heritage is being vandalized every day by theft and losses of petrified wood of 14 tons a year, mostly a small piece at a time."[19] But nothing worked.

Park officials then tried something new. They created what they called "conscience piles." These were essentially large stacks of petrified wood returned by repentant thieves. The piles grew to the size of pick-up trucks. Around these piles, the park officials also posted letters from remorseful thieves. While some simply apologized for having taken the wood, others talked of a curse. One wrote, "Take these miserable rocks and put them back into the rainbow forest, for they have caused pure havoc in my love life and Cheryl's too." Another explained why he returned the wood he had stolen: "The final straw was when I stepped thru the ceiling of our new house. That's when I told my wife. I've had enough. I'm sending it back."[20] Some were even more dramatic. "Believe me, if I would have known the curse went with any of the rocks, I never would have taken these. My life has been totally destroyed since we've been back from vacation. Please take these so my life will get back to normal. Let me start over again. Forgive me for ever taking these."[21]

At this point, the park had tried signs, conscience piles, and displaying remorseful, repentant letters, hoping that, on top of ongoing enforcement, this would alter the behavior.[22] But rampant theft continued.

Social psychologist Robert Cialdini offered to help the park reduce the theft. He created two signs that differed on one key element. One sign portrayed a picture of three people stealing wood. The other sign showed a picture of a lone wood thief. Cialdini put up the signs and then waited to see how much wood was stolen.[23]

The two signs had dramatically different effects. People stole a little bit of wood if the sign showed a single thief. But when the sign showed three thieves, people stole almost five times more wood. Simply changing the number of people on the sign dramatically changed the amount of stealing.

What transpired in Arizona reveals how a subtle change in communication can increase misconduct. The sign depicting three thieves had the effect on park visitors of communicating that stealing petrified wood was almost normal, which triggered a negative social norm and caused even more stealing. Showing just a single thief—perhaps a single bad apple—did not.

There are many ways we can unintentionally trigger such negative social norms. This is easily done, as the Arizona park rangers can attest. Before they brought in the behavioral researchers, the rangers had installed a sign that tried to persuade visitors not to steal by telling them that over fourteen million tons of petrified wood were stolen each year. Though well-intentioned, the sign contained a vital secondary message: such theft happened all the time. Sure, the conscience piles and the letters posted around them showed that some people were remorseful for stealing the fossilized wood, but these also indicated that people were still stealing them. Rangers told park visitors that millions of tons were stolen annually and even allowed the piles of returned wood to reach the size of a pick-up truck. The piles and signs made it clear: some people feel bad when they do it, but the petrified wood can be stolen, is stolen often, and is stolen in large quantities.

For law to successfully change common misbehavior, it must refrain from accidentally sending messages that reinforce the view that the misconduct is normal or commonly accepted. Research tells us that if negative social norms support breaking the law, we must be careful not to draw attention to them. But all too often this is exactly what law enforcement messages do.

When most people are obeying the law, our legal systems can leverage these positive social conventions and only need to be careful about not eroding them. But for law to truly improve behavior, it very often has to deal with behaviors that are common and considered to be acceptable by at least a portion of the population. Sometimes these concern well-ingrained habits, like when we drive above the speed limit. When most drivers speed, many non-speeders automatically begin to drive faster as well. They may do so consciously, as they may think that if everyone else is speeding, the risk of getting singled out and getting a ticket has to be low. But the power of social norms, as we saw, also works unconsciously, and so just by following the traffic, just by following others, we end up speeding.

Adding complexity, quite often such social norms are deeply embedded in culture and societal values, such as notions about honor and respect or religious beliefs about sexuality and marriage.[24] When the legal norm is pitted against such deeply cultural social norms, achieving change will be particularly difficult, and legislators and enforcement officials must develop a deep cultural understanding of the social norms and practices they seek to transform.

Each day, over 5.7 million people cram onto New York City's subway cars and hold on to the metal poles. To protect the subway poles and other passengers, the New York City Metropolitan Transportation Authority (MTA) placed signs: "Poles are for your safety not your latest routine. Hold the pole, not our attention. A subway car is no place for showtime."

This is just one of many new signs the MTA created to guide rider behavior. Another sign addresses "manspreading," men sitting wide-legged and obstructing the already cramped space of their neighbors. The sign reads, "Dude . . . Stop the spread." The MTA's signs rely on quick and funny little phrases, and each sign has a visual schematic: behaviors that are encouraged are shown with a person in green, and behaviors that are prohibited are shown with a person in red. The signs are designed to be easily understood.

Yet after the introduction of the signs, unwanted behavior was still rampant on the city's subway. In a single year, there were almost eighty thousand documented cases of rule breaking on the subway. The *New York Times* reported, "Subway scofflaws are common as rats."[25] Somehow this approach of appealing to people's sense of "do the right thing" did not work here. The question is why not?

The most immediate answer would be that the signs did not affect behavior because they were pitted against powerful negative social norms. If only a few bad apples are violating the rule, adding a sign might be effective. But if most people are routinely violating the rule, adding a sign will do little to change behavior. Manspreading and pole dancing had become regular occurrences in the metro cars, producing powerful negative social norms that made people more likely to continue the practices. What happens when we see a sign against manspreading in a subway car filled with seat-hogging dudes with their legs spread? Will the next guy think, "Hmm, I better keep my knees together?" Or will he think, "Why should I be the only one sitting uncomfortably if everyone's doing it?" Clearly, appeals to passengers to behave better will likely come up short when the behavior they are intended to change is pervasive and highly visible (and for those who continue manspreading, more comfortable).

It is intuitive to put signs where we see violations. But the violations must be cleaned up *first* in these places. Otherwise, a sign simply reminds people a rule is being broken. In effect, the sign can erode the power of the rule. It might remind us of what the rule is, but seeing it widely broken may show us that social norms support violating it, and maybe even that the authorities do not care so much about what we do. By stressing what the law is in an environment where the law is openly and consistently broken, we can inadvertently erode its power, the power of the enforcement, and even the legitimacy of the broader legal system.[26]

All this shows that to improve behavior, communication about social norms is vital. And to communicate effectively about social norms, we need to understand the different audiences, the behaviors involved, the social norms at play, and the social meaning of these norms. Once we understand these, we can craft messages that emphasize what is desired and steer would-be offenders away from misconduct without activating negative social norms that would undermine the functioning of law.

Understanding social norms and our responses to other people presents a critical departure from the individual rational choice model that has mostly informed our current legal systems. It shows us that human behavior is not just an individual affair where people weigh costs and benefits. To truly apply the behavioral science and activate the behavioral code, we need a fundamentally different perspective on law. Our legal system mostly addresses individuals, and to a limited and lesser extent organizations. It is not geared for addressing the broader norms that exist between humans in their everyday interactions, whether as cues they take from each other on the street or complex and deeply ingrained cultural values.[27] Yet to truly tap into the potential of social norms in order to improve behavior requires an anthropological understanding of how people interact and come to share or transmit habits, values, and norms. When we make, communicate, and enforce legal rules, we must carefully consider whether the rules support existing norms or must overcome them. When their creators lack sufficient understanding of the social context of human conduct, our laws can all too easily backfire and strengthen bad habits or erode good ones.

# CHAPTER 7

# Empowering Change

H ello, everyone. Thank you, um, for being here . . . on such short notice." Maria Sharapova, a five-time Grand Slam tennis champion, addressed assembled members of the media in Los Angeles.[1] It was March 7, 2016. Sharapova's voice was clearly emotional. She explained that she was there to come clean: "I wanted to let you know that a few days ago, I received a letter from the ITF [International Tennis Federation] that I had failed a drug test at the Australian Open."

On January 26, 2016, the drug test had found traces of a performance-enhancing substance called meldonium. This medication treats heart disease and ischemia, a condition in which the flow of oxygen to the body's organs is obstructed. By expanding the arteries, meldonium stimulates blood flow and increases the body's flow of oxygen.[2] You don't need to be a scientist to see how that substance gives athletes a wide range of potential advantages, but the US Anti-Doping Agency explains that it banned the drug for use by athletes because it may "increase endurance, improve rehabilitation following exercise, and enhance activations of the central nervous system." The USADA website says: "Meldonium may also provide cognitive advantages."[3]

Just a few weeks before Sharapova's press conference, the World Anti-Doping Authority had added meldonium to its list of banned substances because it had found that during the first-ever European Olympic Games, a tournament of the European Olympic associations organized in Baku,

136

Azerbaijan, in 2015, thirteen medalists had meldonium in their system. Beyond just the medalists, meldonium usage was so widespread that athletes in fifteen of the twenty-one sports at the games tested positive.

Sharapova's press conference was quite special. She was extremely frank in confessing guilt: "I did fail the test, and I take full responsibility for it." She made no attempt to neutralize her shame: "I let my fans down. I let the sport down that I've been playing since the age of four that I love so deeply. I know with this. . . . I face consequences."

In her admission of what she had done, Sharapova stands apart from a long string of drug-using athletes who do everything possible to ensure that they do not test dirty and then, when they do, deny having done anything wrong. With just this one failed test, Sharapova unequivocally fessed up, admitted guilt, and took responsibility. All she wanted was a second chance.

When asking for a second chance, Sharapova made a single argument. She claimed that she did not know that meldonium had been banned. Sharapova explained that for the ten years she had been on the drug, it had not been a banned substance. She simply was not aware that the rules had recently changed. Of course, not knowing the law is said to be no excuse for not following it. But what if Sharapova really had not known that the rules had just changed in January?

All we have seen so far—punishment, incentives, social norms, morals, and our sense of duty—have involved different forms of influences on people's motivations to comply with or break rules. Yet Sharapova's story shows us that people must first have the capacity to do what the law demands. Thus, we must first know whether people know the law and can actually follow it.

## KNOWING THE LAW

"Does anyone know what the Third Amendment is?" Orny Adams, a stand-up comedian, challenges his audience.

Someone replies, "Freedom of assembly."

"No, that's the First Amendment, free speech and freedom of assembly," Adams retorts.

More audience members respond, calling out incorrect answers.

When Adams hears someone state the correct answer, he shouts: "There is always one asshole that knows! What is it? What is it? Yell it out!"

"The protection from being forced to quarter troops in peacetime!" comes the reply.

"How did you know that?" asks Adams.

"I saw you at a previous improv," comes the answer, to great laughter.[4]

With all the pride Americans have in the Constitution, and the vibrant role the Constitution plays in public debates on everything from guns to voting rights, few people know exactly what rights and duties it proclaims. Surely, we do not know the details of rights that do not directly concern our day-to-day lives, like those outlined in the Third Amendment. But people's lack of knowledge about the law is remarkably widespread and concerns many of the most basic rules that govern their everyday lives and behaviors. If we do not know our own rights and duties, how can we effectively respond to laws?

Most US states have adopted a "default rule of employment at will." Under the "at will" rule, employers are given broad discretion in firing an employee as long as they don't violate specific federal statutory exceptions (for instance, based on race, color, religion, gender, or national origin).[5] As long as the action is not grounded in one of those categories, employers in many states can fire anyone for almost any reason—or no reason at all.

Surprisingly, most employees in these states do not know that the law leaves them virtually unprotected. One study by Pauline Kim, a law professor at Washington University School of Law in St. Louis, found that employees were wildly mistaken about what protections the law offered them against being terminated.[6] In Missouri, 82 percent mistakenly thought they could not be fired if the employer just planned to hire someone else at a lower wage. A similar 79 percent wrongly thought that the law offered protection against being fired for reporting theft of company property by another employee or supervisor. And 89 percent wrongly thought the law would protect them against being let go simply because their employer personally did not like them. Moreover, the study found that even when the company informed employees that it "reserve[d] the right to discharge employees at any time, for any reason, with or without cause," over 60 percent *still* believed that the law would protect them. Kim's findings were groundbreaking. She showed that US employees fundamentally misunderstand labor laws. And these are not insignificant laws; they are vital to personal livelihood and job security.

Legal ignorance extends to all aspects of the law. American renters do not know their basic rights or what protections they have or do not have against landlords. And consumers do not know their rights when making purchases or what protections the law gives them against sellers.[7]

There is also ignorance about basic aspects of criminal law. US citizens are ill-informed about what protections suspects have in the criminal justice process. One study of Americans found that 42 percent of adults thought that suspects can be forced to answer questions about their alleged crimes in court.[8] Remember the Bill of Rights? The Fifth Amendment directly protects against that. Another study found that 60 percent of adults mistakenly believe that the "presumption of innocence" means that the accused person has to prove that they are innocent.[9]

If you are feeling smug about that last one, try answering the following questions. In the US, if police believe your child has committed a crime and take her into custody, are they required to contact you before interrogating her? What about once she asks for her parent or guardian? What if you hear she's in custody and demand to be in the room—are they required to let you in? The answer to all three of these questions is no. There is no federal law that requires police to contact parents before interrogating children, regardless of whether a child asks for this, and parents have no constitutional right to be present when police interrogate their children. It may differ by individual jurisdiction, but there are no federal protections.

People also do not know what exactly constitutes a crime. Americans are largely wrong about when a person becomes criminally liable. For instance, imagine someone is planning to rob a store. Most people believe that the legal liability gradually increases as actual preparation and involvement in a crime advance. Yet, under the Model Penal Code that many states have adopted, such liability is immediately very high from the first "substantial step." One is already at risk for criminal punishment even for simply checking out a place in preparation for a robbery. Considering that most Americans do not know this, they underestimate the risk of preparing for (or even talking about) committing a crime.[10]

Even mothers of juvenile offenders—kids who have been arrested, have gone through the system, and are on probation—don't know very much about the law. Researchers gave a few hundred of these families a test of legal knowledge, and mothers' average was about 66 percent correct.[11] These mothers misunderstood much of the law affecting them and their children, including laws regarding the role of public defenders.

Ignorance exists about something so fundamental and personal as marriage law. In a paper entitled "Ignorance Is Bliss," Pascoe Pleasence and Nigel Balmer, both law professors at University College London, reported a widespread lack of knowledge about what legal claims spouses could make in common circumstances, including divorce, spousal inheritance, and rights to decide on medical treatment.[12]

It's not just ordinary people who have trouble knowing the law. Studies show that teachers and school administrators do not have proper knowledge of laws that relate to schools and education.[13] And research shows that doctors do not know the laws relevant to their profession well either.[14] They do not know the rules about doctor-patient privilege well, and, perhaps even more shocking, they are not knowledgeable about the legal rules governing medical malpractice liability. Here one study shows that there is an inverse relation between liability levels and knowledge: in countries like the US where doctors face higher levels of liability, they actually have lower levels of knowledge about it.[15]

With the immense growth of law, can we really be surprised that there is so much legal ignorance? Go into any law school library and look at the giant halls with stacks and stacks of tomes with the primary sources of law, which is the applicable law that we're supposed to know in order to walk around without breaking the law. And it is not just a problem of sheer volume. Law has become a highly complex system. Simply reading a legal text will not tell us exactly what the law expects of us. Most law requires interpretation, and interpretation is covered in decades of case law precedents set by multiple levels of state and federal courts, spanning volumes and volumes. To truly know the law, we must turn to expensive specialist lawyers who have not just studied existing case law but are also able to research and interpret evolving laws. We must hire them to explain what the law requires of us.

Legal knowledge has become a highly protected good. States have restricted legal advice only to registered attorneys who have passed the local bar. Even though all of us should know the law, few of us have the means to hire a lawyer to advise us on all elements of the law that might apply to us. And ethical rules of conflict of interest for lawyers make it hard for ordinary people to directly approach government and law enforcement officials to ask them how they would interpret particular rules. We saw this clearly when the University of California, Irvine, hosted an event together with the Securities and Exchange Commission (SEC) and Department of Justice (DOJ) for Chinese businesses wishing to enter or invest in the US market. Each time a Chinese participant asked a particular question, SEC attorneys and DOJ prosecutors quickly stated that they could not give legal advice and then did not answer the question. They did so because giving such information might lead to a client relationship with the Chinese investor and create a fundamental and prohibited conflict of interest with their governmental work. This means that when you do not know the law, and you try and get information from the government in charge of enforcing the law, they will not inform you of how the law exactly applies to your case.

Some people and organizations can afford to hire specialists, whether they are lawyers or other specialists like health and safety managers, doctors, human resource managers, or accountants who can help them keep track of evolving laws. These specialists can summarize and transmit the law's rules to their clients in a way that is accessible and understandable, or simply make practical adjustments, like changing the medicine for an athlete like Sharapova, to ensure compliance. These "rule intermediaries" play a vital role in how the law shapes behavior, since they not only transmit the law but also transform it by selecting and translating those parts they find most relevant and actionable.[16] Yet, for most, such daily legal advice is just unaffordable and inaccessible.

Our lives are governed by a massive number of rules. Consider all the contracts we enter, each with its own details about our rights and obligations. Few of us take the time to carefully read all the fine print of these contracts, especially now that we frequently encounter this on our phones, where the print is smaller than ever. We scroll to the bottom to press "agree" (or less often "cancel") without reading the full text and thus without fully understanding the contract. Even if we were to take the time to read these contractual rules, we would have trouble understanding them, let alone remembering them.

Most people are part of larger organizations—for instance at work or school—that adopt their own sets of rules. Such organizational rules present another layer of complexity to the already bloated legal code. Consider what happened at the University of California, which operates ten campuses throughout the state that serve over 280,000 students. The UC system entered into a settlement agreement following a major fire at a lab at UCLA, the UC campus in Los Angeles. The agreement sought to impose terms on the university system to help prevent similar accidents. One of the terms in the settlement was that lab personnel had to be well-informed about dangerous substances. So the university developed its own organizational rules, complete with individual protocols for about two hundred dangerous substances. Each of these two hundred individual protocols was about twenty pages long. Health and safety compliance managers were tasked with ensuring that all faculty, lab assistants, and students entering these labs agreed to about four thousand pages of safety protocols. Of course, no one can remember four thousand pages of information about how to handle dangerous substances, let alone conform their behavior to such a ridiculous number of instructions.

What happened here is telling. This massive amount of paper rules is highly unlikely to have much effect in making people act more safely. And maybe that was never the idea anyway. It seems that rather than truly trying to make laboratories safer, the university had a different concern in mind when developing these protocols. The lawyers designing the system probably thought more about what would happen when a future accident occurred. The university could simply say that it had educated researchers and students on how to prevent such risks—in fact, they had produced four thousand pages worth of safety protocols! The university had done its part. Thus, if an accident happened, individuals working with the dangerous substances would likely bear the responsibility. The University of California never developed a system that would reduce risky behavior in the future, an "ex-ante" (before the event) system, but instead had a system that could handle liability afterward in case things went wrong, an "ex-post" (after the event) system.

If we wish to improve compliance, we must recognize that many people simply do not know the law. It is striking that there is so little recognition of this fundamental challenge. There is virtually no sound empirical research on legal knowledge as it relates to compliance. As Princeton professor of psychology John Darley and his colleagues state, "if we examine the ways in which the transmission of knowledge from the halls of the legislature to the heads of the citizens is supposed to take place, we find a puzzling silence."[17]

The relationship between legal knowledge and people's ability to obey the law is not straightforward. Legal ignorance is not simply the lack of legal information. Research shows us that it is more complex. Scholars find that we have individual preferences and intuitions about what the law should be. And what we believe the law should be then influences what we think the law actually is. If we feel or think something is right, we tend to believe it is legal; and when we think something ought to be criminalized, we often assume it is illegal. Therefore, "knowledge" of the law has become a function of attitudes.[18]

This means that, just like deterrence, legal knowledge is subjective. When we are not directly taught about what is in the law, the law becomes what we imagine it to be. Worse, what we believe the law says may obstruct us even after we learn what the law actually says. People resist absorbing legal information that is inconsistent with their folklore.[19]

All of this, of course, makes it harder to reduce legal ignorance. Simply providing more legal information might not work when people are used to intuitively guessing what the law is.

For law to truly become effective in changing future behavior, law itself must change. Our lawmakers and the many rule makers who make contracts and organizational rules must fundamentally alter their approach. Rather than respond to each new risk and ambiguity by creating more and more complex rules, they must realize the limits of this approach. If most of our laws and other rules are not known, knowable, or understandable for most people, how can they then come to play a role in shaping our behavior? A different approach is necessary. We must consider which laws and rules truly are needed and will truly be known, shared, and discussed. Such an approach would shy away from complexity wherever possible and instead use simple and clear language. It would also focus not just on producing rules but also equally, if not more, on disseminating these rules and educating people about them. As Cesare Beccaria wrote: "Would you prevent crimes? Let the laws be clear and simple."[20]

## TREATING CRIME

"There's something deeply satisfying in the feeling of transgression. It tickles down my crooked neural pathways so worn by the ebb of depression and anxiety. The pleasure is not a smugness but a very physical shiver—a deep tickling that's hard to explain or simulate."[21] Meet Patrick Marlborough. Or at least that is the pseudonym he used to tell his story in *Vice*. In an elegantly written self-confession and psychoanalysis, he describes his addiction to petty theft, his kleptomania.

Patrick explains how he steals small objects in public places, preferring airports, shopping malls, bars, restaurants, casinos, and museums. At the Vatican museum, while looking at one of the ancient crucifixion paintings, he sneaks a $34 souvenir into his pocket to join the other items he has stolen that day. He clarifies that he does not do it for the value of the items. As he says about his stolen goods: "To me, they mean nothing. They are just a jumble of pilfered items to add to a collection that has spanned airports, department stores, libraries, and gift shops the world over: pocketable useless goodies that I just can't not pick up."[22]

Patrick is diagnosed with kleptomania, and he has been stealing since he was very young. He used to feel guilty about it, but the shame and guilt gradually faded in puberty. Stealing for him is not about the kick or the rush. It is something compulsive. And indeed, kleptomania has a strong compulsive side for others too. As Peter Klein, a mental health counselor, explains: "Sufferers [of kleptomania] can find it difficult to resist the impulses and feel strong positive emotions after the act which is sometimes followed by guilt."[23] As the *DSM-5* outlines, to diagnose kleptomania several criteria must be present: "recurrent impulses to steal—and instances of stealing—objects that are not needed for personal use or financial gain; feeling increased tension right before the theft; feeling pleasure, gratification, or relief at the time of the theft; thefts . . . not committed in response to delusions or hallucinations, or as expressions of revenge or anger; thefts [not] better explained by Antisocial Personality Disorder, Conduct Disorder, or a manic episode."[24]

Someone suffering from kleptomania will have trouble controlling the urge to steal. And therefore kleptomaniacs have trouble complying with basic criminal rules that outlaw theft. Even if their stealing results in punishment, even when they know that stealing is not socially accepted, even when they personally think it is wrong, and even if it goes against their general sense of duty to obey the law, their disorder simply makes it next to impossible for them to not steal.

Of course, kleptomania is rare, and most people can control their impulses to steal. But kleptomania shows that people's ability to control their urges plays an important role in rule-violating behavior. In fact, one of the leading theories in criminology focuses on the relationship between people's ability to control their urges and their engagement in crime. This theory, promoted and made famous by criminologists Michael Gottfredson, who teaches at the University of California, Irvine, and Travis Hirschi, who taught at the University of Arizona, was published in a 1990 book, *A General Theory of Crime*.[25]

Gottfredson and Hirschi took a different approach to understanding criminal behavior than those who came before them. Rather than find out why it occurs, they flipped the question and asked why people *refrain* from crime.[26] For them, criminal behavior should not be seen as distinct and different from other forms of behavior: "Crime like non-crime satisfies universal human desires. It is[,] in terms of causation, indistinguishable from all other forms of behavior." In their view, crime was normal and not at all shocking. They wrote, "The vast majority of criminal acts are trivial and mundane affairs that result in little loss and little gain." They spoke of the banality of crime and argued that criminal acts "will tend, on the whole, to require little foresight, planning, or effort. Between the thought and the deed, little time will elapse. Thus, the carefully planned and executed crime will be extremely rare."[27]

Gottfredson and Hirschi argued that crime provides criminals with instant gratification. Crime is similar to other undesirable behavior such as excessive drinking, gambling, and promiscuity. People commit crime or engage in such bad behavior to gain pleasure. So their question was, if crime is so gratifying, what keeps us from committing it?[28]

To them, the answer is self-control. Just as self-control keeps us from smoking, overeating, or cheating, it also keeps us from satisfying the urge for immediate gratification by committing crime. Those with low self-control simply cannot resist the urge for immediate gratification.[29] Self-control is what stands between the potential offender and the decision to offend.[30]

The publication of *A General Theory of Crime* started a new field in criminology and spurred a body of empirical work that sought to understand whether crime was indeed related to weak self-control. Following decades of self-control studies, University of Kentucky professor Alexander Vazsonyi and his colleagues did a comprehensive meta-analysis, which is where scholars review a number of studies conducted on the same topic and then use complex statistical methods to calculate an overall, aggregate effect size.[31] Vazsonyi and his colleagues selected ninety-nine high-quality studies for their meta-analysis and examined whether the association between weak self-control and deviant behavior was different for different types of behavior. Here they found the strongest association for deviant behavior in general, at 0.56, which is an effect size rarely found in social science. But there were also remarkably strong effects of weak self-control on crime (0.39), theft (0.34), and physical violence (0.46). Indeed, other reviews of the literature routinely conclude that self-control is one of the strongest correlates of crime.[32]

Self-control helps us understand why we break the law. People with low self-control simply have a harder time regulating their behavior. But what does this mean exactly? And how can we use these insights to address rule breaking and harmful behavior?

The first big question here is what exactly self-control is. A major critique of Gottfredson and Hirschi's theory was that they never clearly defined the concept.[33] Another noted that when they did so, the definition was tautological: weak self-control may be the exact same thing as deviant behavior.[34]

In their 1990 book, Gottfredson and Hirschi described strong self-control by looking at what weak self-control looks like. As they explained: "People who lack self-control will tend to be impulsive, insensitive, physical (as opposed to mental), risk-taking, short-sighted, and nonverbal."[35] The authors did not see these as traits that are determined at birth and then never change. Instead, weak self-control develops during childhood (until the age of ten) and is influenced by parenting. They discussed that the core way parents can enhance self-control is by monitoring, recognizing, and correcting deviant behavior. More recently, Hirschi has added that parental care and warmth are also vital for developing self-control in their children.[36]

Following Gottfredson and Hirschi's ideas, it seems we must address self-control before children grow into puberty. So, to reduce wrongdoing, all parents, and maybe also teachers and other adult authority figures, should receive training on how to promote the development of self-control in young children. A range of studies has shown that there are effective programs that can do so, not only with children but also with teens. Two recent meta-analyses of existing studies (one covering thirty-four and the other forty-one studies) find that self-control improvement programs are effective not only in enhancing self-control but also in reducing delinquent behavior.[37]

One example is the so-called SNAP (Stop Now and Plan) program. SNAP was developed in Canada in 1985, when the age limit for criminal responsibility was raised from seven to twelve, meaning that the justice system no longer had responsibility for children under twelve. The program sought to help deal with deviant behavior in those between six and eleven, offering coping mechanisms for children who were prone to lose self-control or act violently. SNAP targeted their teachers as well as families.[38]

SNAP has a holistic approach that not only treats self-control but also seeks to enhance emotion regulation and problem-solving skills. The way SNAP works is that children learn to see "body cues" and "hard thoughts" (such as unrealistic expectations) that promote bad choices. They are taught to *Stop* when they see such cues or thoughts and take a pause or a breath. Then they learn the *Now* phase—replacing the hard thoughts with thoughts that are realistic and help them cope with the situation. Finally they learn to *Plan* their next action to avoid harm and make them feel good.[39]

Several studies on the SNAP program have found that it can be effective. One study of 252 boys by researchers in Pittsburgh found that SNAP was significantly more effective than standard interventions at reducing aggression, rule breaking, and other conduct problems. Moreover, it found that the program worked best for the children with the greatest self-control problems. Perhaps most importantly, the effects remained stable after one year.[40] Another study of 318 children in Toronto similarly found that SNAP enhanced self-control and reduced both aggressive and rule-breaking behavior.[41]

During puberty and early adolescence, people's ability to regulate their impulses is weak. Fortunately, when the prefrontal cortex, which houses the human capacity for deliberate and complex thought, matures and becomes fully active during the transition into young adulthood, people gain more self-control.[42] Yet even in adulthood some people have lower self-control and are at more risk of deviant and damaging behavior. What helps keep these people from misbehaving?

Wearing a harness with the presidential seal, Sully, an adorable yellow Labrador retriever, sat and looked around at the crowd who had gathered solemnly in the US Capitol Rotunda to pay their last respects to George H. W. Bush, the forty-first president of the United States. Sully had served as Bush's service dog, aiding the elderly former president for the last six months of his life.

Days earlier, the dog had stretched out in front of Bush's casket when it was still in Houston, lying there as if he were ready to continue to serve his master. When Bush had gotten Sully, he had tweeted a picture of himself in a wheelchair, Sully in front of him, joined by a smiling Bill Clinton, sitting together in a homey setting: "A great joy to welcome home the newest member of our family, 'Sully,' a beautiful—and beautifully trained—lab from @AmericasVetDogs." And now, the photo of the dog's sad and loyal look guarding the flag-draped coffin had gone viral. As a Bush spokesperson said about the picture: "Mission complete."[43]

Sully was no ordinary service dog, if there is such a thing. He was part of a program that trained dogs to aid veterans in a wide range of tasks, including fetching certain items and summoning help. What made the program special is that the dog training was done by people serving time in prison, and Sully had been trained at a prison in Hagerstown, Maryland.[44] The inmates received six-week-old puppies and trained them until their first birthday.

For the prisoners, training the puppies brought an immense amount of pride and joy. The puppies depended on them and also offered the men a distraction from the harsher realities of prison life. Herbert Wilson-Bey, a forty-four-year-old interviewed in the *Washington Post*, explained that he had been incarcerated since age seventeen, serving time for robbery and homicide. He had never had a job and had never taken care of anyone else. He did have a son, but the child had just been born when

Wilson-Bey was sent to prison. Training these puppies "had been one of his first responsibilities."

Raising the puppies is a major responsibility. The dogs are with the inmates twenty-four hours a day during the week and only leave them when they stay with families on the outside on weekends. Now training his third service dog, Wilson-Bey learned that raising puppies was not just about teaching them to obey commands; it was also about giving them care and love: "Put the puppy on your chest and let it feel your heart. Let it lick your face, even if you might not like that."

One can imagine what a positive effect raising a puppy can have for people experiencing incarceration. The idea that letting inmates raise puppies helps with their rehabilitation is decades old. The first known program dates back to 1981, at the Washington State Corrections Center for Women. Such programs may have several beneficial effects, including enhancing inmates' self-esteem, empathy, emotional intelligence, and coping skills.[45] There are now hundreds of dog-training programs in US prisons and also many similar programs around the globe.

The puppy training programs also have another important potential benefit: they could enhance the person's self-control. The programs are only open to inmates who have followed the rules and behaved well for a period of time. Even after getting a puppy, they have to stay out of trouble or risk losing their dog. And this has had remarkable effects. As one person told researchers: "One of the reasons I stayed out of trouble was so that I could get a dog."[46] One study found that training the dogs made inmates more willing and able to take responsibility for their actions and to become more patient. As another inmate told a researcher: "I got angry with [my dog] . . . but all I could do was sit down and count to ten, because I refuse to be anything else but loving to him."[47] A study reviewing available evidence concludes that prisoners who trained puppies became more patient "with the demands of imprisonment" and also more willing to comply with their prison's rules.[48] This is a hopeful example and evidence that treatment and training programs may be able to empower people to more effectively control their impulses. What the evidence suggests is that self-control is malleable, able to be shaped and changed.

Here we have an approach to dealing with criminal behavior that differs from our typically punitive criminal justice system. The traditional approach is to try to change behavior through deterrence, through having the negative experience of punishment scare people away from crime. But this reveals that an alternative approach is more effective. Our criminal justice system can offer treatment and support to help people learn to better cope with the problems that led to their criminal conduct and to work on themselves and their own capacities. It can provide them with the opportunity to build real skills that can enable them to get jobs on the outside. This is the idea of rehabilitation.

It is easy to doubt that rehabilitation interventions can be effective, especially when they are carried out in prison systems that are unsafe and where people are very likely to become more deviant because of prison's criminogenic and brutalizing effects. Attempting crime intervention therapies in prison is not ideal. It is far preferable to address root causes when a person is with supportive family, among friends, at work, or in the community, and without the compulsion and negative environment of prison.[49]

One major type of intervention program focuses on "cognitive skills." These programs provide therapy for offenders to teach them to cope with the emotions and thoughts that led them to crime. The best-known example is the "Reasoning and Rehabilitation" program. The idea of this program is that cognition plays a major role in criminal behavior and that people commit crime when they lack cognitive skills, including self-control, critical reasoning, interpersonal problem-solving ability, and empathy.[50] The purpose of the Reasoning and Rehabilitation approach is to teach participants "how to think, not what to think."[51] The therapy consists of thirty-six two-hour group sessions with six to twelve people. During the sessions, participants face their own "egocentric thinking" and learn to take the perspective of others as well as a more critical and reasoned approach to themselves and their own behavior.[52]

This form of cognitive therapy has had a significant effect in reducing crime. A recent meta-analysis found that the approach led to a 14 percent decrease in crime across different national contexts, including Canada, the US, and the UK.[53]

Of course, self-control and other cognitive capacities aren't the only driving forces behind crime. Substance abuse and dependence disorders drive quite a bit of offending. The question is whether treatment programs in these cases are effective. Certainly one size does not fit all, as there are many reasons why individuals turn to substance use. Yet a 2013 review finds that there are a number of successful treatment programs that focus on a wide range of elements, including training in social skills, coping skills, and problem solving; training in stress management; and community reinforcement.[54] These programs can be quite effective. One study found that the re-arrest rate six months after release from prison for people who had completed treatment was 3.1 percent, compared to 15 percent for a comparable group of offenders who had not had treatment.[55] Another study looked at reconviction rates one year after release from prison and found that 16 percent of people who received treatment had been arrested again, compared to 23 percent of those who had not.[56] In all, these programs are up to five times more effective than "treatment as usual" through incarceration.

In 2007, criminologists Mark Lipsey at Vanderbilt University and Francis Cullen at the University of Cincinnati conducted the largest review so far of the available science on rehabilitation. They systematically examined the existing, high-quality reviews of literature on a wide variety of therapies for various offenses and offenders, including both juveniles and adults. Reviews they examined covered anywhere from 13 to 515 studies.

Of the fifty-nine different therapies studied, only one was found to have backfired and caused more re-offending, and two showed no effect. All of the other fifty-six treatments that the meta-analyses reviewed proved to be effective. Educational, vocational, and work programs for adults proved to reduce offending by 6–20 percent. Aggression training for juveniles and adults reduced recidivism by 18 percent. Programs for juvenile and adult sex offenders reduced offending by 12–46 percent. And the program reported to be most successful—behavioral and social-learning treatment for at-risk juveniles and adults—reduced re-offending by 60 percent. As a result, Lipsey and Cullen came to a very strong conclusion: rehabilitation treatment programs have a consistently large effect in reducing re-offending.[57]

Back in the 1970s, there was doubt about the effectiveness of rehabilitation. As the author of the major review of academic studies at the time, Robert Martinson, a professor of sociology at the City College of New York wondered: "Does nothing work?"[58] It seems that more than forty years later we now have many treatments that do work. The trend is unmistakable. Rehabilitation of offenders is not only possible, the programs actually work really well. Of course, treatment does not stop re-offending completely, nor does it work for all offenders or fix the structural, systemic barriers people face. Treatment does not offer a perfect solution. But what is clear is that it offers an important and effective response, one for which the evidence is much more conclusive and positive than for the deterrent effect of punishment.

## THE STRAIN OF SOCIOECONOMIC CONDITIONS

In her groundbreaking book *The New Jim Crow*, law professor Michelle Alexander critically examines the racially discriminatory functioning of the criminal justice system and how such discrimination has moved beyond prison. The result is a new form of segregation where predominantly Black youth become entangled with the law and end up with fewer opportunities for education, housing, and employment. Alexander shows how the punitive nature of our criminal justice system continues to impact the lives of ex-offenders who have already served their time for their crimes.[59]

In discussing employment segregation, Alexander shows that in almost every state, employers are fully free to discriminate on the basis of one's criminal record, regardless of the nature of the job. In many states, even an arrest is enough to refuse someone a job.[60] This severely limits opportunities for people with records.[61] Each time they apply for a job, ex-cons must check a box indicating that they have served time in prison. That's called being "boxed-out." But people with records can also easily get "boxed-in." Since most states make maintaining gainful employment a parole condition, having no job can mean heading straight back to prison.[62]

Finding employment is not only obstructed because employers do not want to hire people with records. People often find jobs through friends and family. Yet after being incarcerated, they often have weaker social ties that may have ordinarily helped them find jobs. Moreover, compared to peers who have not served time, they will inevitably lack job experience and job-related skills and have more transportation challenges.[63] As Richard Freeman, a Harvard professor of economics, summarizes, "Having been in jail is the single most important deterrent to employment."[64]

And people with records do not just face challenges getting employed. Historically, homeowners have been allowed to refuse to rent to people with a criminal record. In 2016, the Obama administration's Department of Housing and Urban Development (HUD) developed guidelines that would no longer allow landlords and home sellers to discriminate against people with a record. As Kristen Clarke, president and executive director of the Lawyers' Committee for Civil Rights Under Law, explained at the time: "Without access to housing opportunities, people with criminal records are placed on a path to failure and unable to take the steps necessary to successfully reintegrate into their communities."[65]

Universities also routinely ask potential students to indicate whether they have a criminal record. Applicants to over seven hundred US colleges have to use the Common Application, which historically included a standard question asking applicants whether they have any misdemeanor or felony convictions. According to one study, 35 percent of universities have denied applicants because they have criminal records.[66] In 2016, sixty-one universities sought to change this form of discrimination through signing the Fair Chance Higher Education Pledge. This pledge, which was launched by the Obama administration and went into effect in 2019, commits these universities to a fair admissions process for applicants with a criminal record.

There is an important idea behind the initiatives to end employment, housing, and educational discrimination against people with records. Not only does it affect racial and ethnic minorities who have been disproportionately arrested and imprisoned but also people convicted of crimes who need access to employment, housing, and education to get their lives back on track and desist from future crime. People need to have the right types of social and economic conditions to support them in leading a law-abiding life. There is, for instance, a clear link between poverty and crime. A 2005 review of 214 studies on the relationship between poverty and crime found overwhelming evidence that more poverty leads to higher levels of crime but also that poverty is one of the strongest macro-level predictors of crime.[67] A 2014 study shifted the focus internationally to look at the relationship between poverty and homicide. In analyzing data from sixty-three countries, it found that poverty rates are consistently associated with homicide, robbery, and burglary, even when controlling for inequality, the level of overall development, economic growth, population density, and population size.[68] This means that, to fight crime, we must address and relieve the root causes of poverty.

There is also clear evidence that education is strongly related to crime. One study, by economists Lance Mochner and Enrico Moretti, looked at how high school graduation for men affects their probability of being arrested and incarcerated.[69] As they summarized their key findings: "A one-year increase in average years of schooling reduces murder and assault by almost 30 percent, motor vehicle theft by 20 percent, arson by 13 percent, and burglary and larceny by about 6 percent." Similarly, Mochner and Moretti reported that "a 10-percentage-point increase in graduation rates would reduce murder and assault arrest rates by about 20 percent, motor vehicle theft by about 13 percent, and arson by 8 percent."[70]

Certainly, not all school experiences are equal. So another study looked at how the quality of middle school and high school education affects crime. It did so by comparing students who had been admitted to higher-quality public schools through a randomly assigned lottery system with those who had not. The study assessed arrest and incarceration rates seven years after the initial school admission. It found that high-risk youth (those most likely to commit crime) were 50 percent less likely to get arrested and imprisoned if they had attended the higher-quality schools.[71] Unfortunately, juvenile detention, with over 130,000 kids detained each year in the US, severely undermines the chances that such children will return to school.[72] Studies show that once youth are placed in juvenile detention facilities, their likelihood of reaching or staying on grade level is severely diminished.[73]

Finally, there has been research about how access to housing is related to crime. With a sample of 390 youth experiencing homelessness in Toronto, one study finds that becoming homeless clearly promotes getting involved in crime.[74] Another study looked at the effects on crime of expanding public housing vouchers that enable folks from poorer neighborhoods to move into richer neighborhoods. You can imagine what the richer, suburban families thought of welcoming poorer folks into their neighborhoods. Yet the effects were not what the rich people expected. Expanding access to better housing had absolutely no impact on the crime rates in the suburban communities.[75] And, extra investment in neighborhoods that already have high crime rates helps to reduce crime. Beyond providing more affordable housing, it also revitalizes the neighborhood and reduces graffiti, abandoned lots, and dilapidated homes.[76]

These studies show that beyond knowledge or self-control, socioeconomic conditions play an important role in rule breaking and harmful behavior. There is also a connection between low self-control and poor socioeconomic conditions. Growing up in deep poverty can impact people's self-control levels.[77] Childhood deprivation can cut deeply into people's personal development and their ability to lead a law-abiding life.

Just because someone is poor, dropped out of school early, or doesn't have access to stable housing doesn't mean they will engage in crime. All people come across hardship. And hardship can have many sources. People may have trouble getting a job, making ends meet, getting housing, or finishing school. They can face conflict and abuse in their family. They can have trouble with their boss or coworkers. Or they can have problems with their neighbors or other folks in the community. Stress is a part of life, and such stress usually has external causes. But some people cope with such stress through breaking the rules. Criminologists call this *strain*, and they have developed a general strain theory that explains how circumstances, including socioeconomic stressors, can pressure people into deviant behavior. The core idea is that different forms of objective or perceived stress can move people to criminal or deviant behavior.

Emory University sociologist Robert Agnew is credited with creating the general strain theory. In his book *Pressured into Crime*, Agnew explains what types of strains push people to deviance.[78] The first set of strains mostly influences juveniles: parental rejection; erratic, excessive, or harsh supervision and discipline; child abuse and neglect; negative experiences in school; and abusive relations with peers. A second set of strains operates mostly on adults: marital problems, unemployment, or unpleasant, low-paid, low-prestige, and unstable work. A third set of strains works on all age groups: desire for thrills; failure to achieve goals, status, or desired money; the experience of being a victim of crime or living in a poor community; homelessness; and discrimination. These strains trigger negative emotions and anger, which people sometimes cope with through engaging in deviant and criminal behavior.[79]

Agnew also analyzes what makes some people cope with strains through crime. He explains that strain is more likely to result in crime when people lack social and problem-solving skills; have limited self-control, less money and lower education than average; and have a low belief in their own capacity to succeed. Agnew also points to the social context, showing that strain more likely leads to crime when people lack social support in promoting their success. He also shows that social bonds matter—for instance, when there are limited emotional bonds with parents or when people live in "disorganized" communities where people do not watch out for one another. Agnew also argues that strain more likely leads to crime if people's peers act criminally or condone such behavior and when there are good opportunities for criminal behavior.

General strain theory is complex and comprehensive. It brings together many aspects of the behavioral code that we have seen matter before. We see that fair treatment matters, just like the findings about procedural justice and crime. We see that social context matters, just like the ideas about social norms, cultural norms, and social learning. We see that opportunities for criminal conduct matter. And we see that self-control and social and economic opportunities matter.

The complexity of general strain theory makes empirically testing it challenging. There are many different forms of strain at play, many negative emotions these can trigger, and many potential personal skills and capacities and social and community characteristics that affect how people deal with strain. Yet a robust body of scholarship began emerging in the 1990s looking at how well basic tenets of general strain theory explain deviant and criminal behavior. A recent review of this body of work has confirmed several core tenets. While the full theory with all its elements has not been fully proven, there is a clear link between strain, developing negative emotions, and engaging in crime. [80]

Following what we learn from the general strain theory, to reduce misconduct we can try to change contexts that induce strain and stress, support people so that they can learn to better cope with strains that may drive them toward crime, or both.

Agnew offers several policy suggestions in his book on strain theory. He proposes, for instance, to fund parent-training programs that enable parents to develop better emotional bonds with their children and prevent kids from growing up with feelings of parental rejection or erratic or excessive discipline, let alone child abuse or neglect. Such programs teach parents how to discipline and how to handle conflicts with or between their children. That would effectively improve the children's self-control too. Another approach is to fund anti-bullying programs in schools so that kids do not grow up with the strains of peer abuse in school that negatively affect their self-esteem and self-efficacy. Another option is to focus on schools more generally and retrain teachers (in how they interact with students), change school disciplinary rules, deploy extracurricular activities for at-risk youth, or provide more academic and counseling programs. Such programs can help ease the strain of negative relations with teachers and low school engagement in general. Agnew also focuses on how to support people so that they can better avoid strain or cope with it. Ideas here include social skills and problem-solving training, anger management programs, training that teaches kids how to set realistic goals, and mentoring programs like Big Brothers Big Sisters or Boys & Girls Clubs that enhance social support.

Agnew also looks at broader political interventions through government support programs. Since, as we have seen, crime often originates in difficult socioeconomic conditions and the strains these produce, it makes perfect sense to address it through providing scholarships, unemployment benefits, health care access, and housing. There could be win-win situations in which expanding health insurance, lowering tuition, or even instituting a basic universal income not only address the primary goals of these programs but could also have the secondary effect of reducing crime.

All of this brings us to the core of this chapter. The law's effect on behavior very much depends on people's abilities to act in a way that the law demands. And, whether we like it or not, people's personal situations and the broader social and economic contexts they live in can undermine their ability to comply.

Maria Sharapova broke doping rules because she did not know them. Patrick Marlborough kept on stealing because he could not control his impulses. The kid in school started to act out and break school rules because of the pressure of racism and because he felt he had to protect his dignity. And the business owner started to cut bad checks because she felt she had to save her business and provide for her family.

In each of these cases, people broke the rules because of the situation they were in. They either lacked a certain capacity, like legal knowledge or self-control, or lived under pressure of a broader context they sought to cope with. Each of these statements can be seen as making an excuse for bad behavior. But we are not excusing it—we are explaining why it happened and why it will continue to happen. Each of these statements shows how the behavioral code is at play. They show that rule-breaking behavior is not just a free decision in which people weigh the costs and benefits or respond to punishment threats. Bad behavior also exists because people lack the capacity, ability, or opportunity to act better and comply with the law.

This is a very different approach to tap into the behavioral code and improve human responses to the law. We have cops and others trying to discipline people into good conduct, economists trying to get the incentives right, people acting as a role models to socially sway better behavior, and others trying to morally convince people that compliance is right. But other roles are necessary—those of the educator, the counselor, and the investor.[81] The educator can teach the people what the laws are, how to comply, and what potential paths lie ahead of them. The counselor can help people strengthen their self-control and empower them to cope with life's challenges in a more positive and less damaging or illegal manner. And the investor can focus on socioeconomic opportunities and ensure that more people can achieve their aspirations and reduce their overall pressures and strains.

None of this is easy. And much of it is uncomfortable. It may feel much better to see rule breakers as bad people who will only respond to pain and punishment. To fully tap into this part of the behavioral code requires a particular mindset, a positive view that believes that most people and misconduct are still malleable. It requires seeing hope in human nature.

# CHAPTER 8

# Speed Bumps for Terrorists

"A s you bomb, you will be bombed; as you kill, you will be killed."[1] The videotaped threats from the two terrorists were clear. These guys were part of a larger group of young men in Walthamstow, a neighborhood in East London, who had become radicalized terrorists.

The terrorist cell was plotting another 9/11, but whereas Osama bin Laden's plot involved four passenger airlines, reports indicated that these men were aiming at a record number of ten planes in a single attack. According to the deputy chief of the London Metropolitan Police, their plot was "mass murder on an unimaginable scale."[2]

These young men were researching new ways to bomb airplanes. Their idea was to smuggle bomb parts through security and assemble them on the plane. Key in this was to use a new liquid form of explosive crafted by mixing hydrogen peroxide with other chemicals. According to the cell's internal emails, the group had amassed a huge stockpile of the chemicals that they code-worded "Calvin Klein aftershave."[3]

The challenge was how to smuggle the chemicals onto a plane. The group thought of a simple solution: put the chemicals in soft drink bottles. Bombs disguised as Coca-Cola. Or, in this case, a sports drink called Lucozade.

The terrorist cell's devices were small enough that they could easily be smuggled and assembled in the confined space of a commercial passenger airplane. Yet, when assembled, they would be the perfect size to blow a hole in the fuselage and crash the plane.

As the two young men recorded their video threat, little did they know that the police were listening to everything they said and watching them. British intelligence had developed an interest in the group's leader, Abdulla Ahmed Ali, because of his contacts with other radicals who advocated violence in Britain. They had been tracking him for a while, and when he returned to London from a trip to Pakistan, officers secretly searched his luggage. They were surprised to find a bottle of Tang, the ultra-sweet and bright-orange powdered drink mix, and a large number of batteries. Intrigued, officers decided to find out more. What followed became one of the largest surveillance operations in UK history.

Two months into the surveillance, and within a day after the two young men had recorded their videotape, Scotland Yard decided it was time to act and shut the terrorist operation down. Officers arrested twenty-one people, and during their raids they found the bomb-making materials, jihadi propaganda, receipts of international money wires, and six terrorist martyr videos.[4]

Soon afterward, Britain's top airline executives received a telephone call. Scotland Yard informed them that, until further notice, all carry-on luggage would be prohibited on commercial passenger airplanes. From that point forward, passengers would only be allowed to bring their wallets and purses. Even pens were banned, as authorities feared that the ink could contain liquid explosives. One of the only exceptions was that mothers were allowed to bring milk for their babies, but they had to drink some first to show that it was safe.[5]

These were drastic steps. Yet British authorities were only trying to make sure that if they had somehow failed to catch all of the would-be terrorists in their crackdown on the terror cell, those uncaught would not be able to carry out planned or retaliatory attacks.

The immediate result of these precautions was a near standstill at London's Heathrow Airport, Europe's busiest airport and the second busiest in the world for international passengers. People became outraged that they could not bring their cell phones on their flights. Many passengers traveling to France and Belgium decided to switch to the Eurostar train service, which uses the underwater tunnel connecting France and England, simply because they did not want to give up their phones. And many who did hand in their phones never got them back because the airlines were not prepared for the logistics of handling so many phones. If that wasn't enough, airplane cargo holds did not have space for all the luggage that would have been carry-on. Within a week, British Airways, the main UK carrier, had to cancel fifteen hundred flights.

It is not surprising that these initial rules that banned virtually all carry-on items on planes did not last. But after the bomb plot was discovered, the way we board planes radically changed worldwide. The direct result of the plot was that passengers are no longer allowed to bring aboard large amounts of liquids, aerosols, and gels (LAGs as they are known to security personnel). And in most airports, passengers must take out their liquids and place them in a transparent plastic bag to be scanned separately from their other carry-on items.

We have these rules because we learned from an averted terrorist attack. We learned that there was a new way to do massive harm. We learned how attackers could achieve such harm. And rather than rely on ramping up punishments or jailing terrorists to prevent similar attacks in the future, we took a different approach. By understanding how the attack was to succeed, we could learn what practical steps we could take to make it harder to attack or, ideally, impossible to do so.

All of this shows a new approach to dealing with misbehavior. Besides trying to use incentives or social norms to motivate people, and besides supporting and helping people lead a law-abiding life, we can also just make it harder or impossible to misbehave in the first place.

## ROUTINE ACTIVITIES AND SITUATIONAL CRIME
Something strange happened in the 1960s in the United States. Generally, the economy was doing very well and many people saw their lives improve. Overall, employment, high school graduation, wages, and general

standards of living increased. Yet, alarmingly, as socioeconomic conditions generally improved in the 1960s and early 1970s, crime rates, particularly for property crime, shot up; according to the FBI Uniform Crime Report, burglary increased by 200 percent between 1960 and 1975.[6]

The combination of these two opposing trends puzzled criminologists Lawrence Cohen and Marcus Felson. The common wisdom at the time was that when there are good socioeconomic opportunities, like education, housing, and employment, crime should decline. But that was the opposite of what was happening, so Cohen and Felson decided to take a deep dive into the data to figure out what was going on.

They first did an in-depth analysis of the crime data. Cohen and Felson looked at what types of people became victims (in terms of age, gender, occupation, marital status), where crimes took place (in the home or elsewhere), and whether victims knew the offenders. That's all routine in good-quality criminological research, but what made their study unique is that they also decided to look much more deeply at data about routine activities during this period. They looked, for instance, at female employment data, the hours that women went to work, and the hours they would be at home. Furthermore, Cohen and Felson also looked closely at consumer data, particularly at the kinds of goods people bought—not just at the value and types of goods but also how large and heavy they were.

Through their deep analysis, Cohen and Felson found patterns that could explain the perhaps counterintuitive link between improved socioeconomic conditions and increased theft. The data showed that during the period of economic prosperity and cultural change in gender roles in the 1960s, more and more women left the house to go to work or school. The female student population rose by 118 percent between 1960 and 1970.[7] And more people started to live alone, an increase of 34 percent in the same period. As a result, US homes were empty more often, especially during the morning.

Also, more and more people left the house to go on vacations and travel out of town, with a 144 percent increase of factory workers who had the right to three weeks of vacation, and a 188 percent increase in overseas travel between 1960 and 1970. In 1972, 81 percent more Americans took vacations than did in 1967.

So there were more empty homes at predictable times.

The data also showed that there were major changes in the goods people bought. Technological advances had reduced the size and weight of electronic devices, such as radios, TVs, and audio equipment. To visualize this, as Cohen and Felson did, let's compare the 1960 Sears catalog descriptions with those in the 1970 one. In the 1960 catalog, the lightest TV on sale weighed thirty-eight pounds. In 1970, the lightest TV was only fifteen pounds, less than half the size. With the lighter weight, not only were the TVs easier to carry, but their value per pound rose, as it did for many products. According to the 1975 Buying Guide issue of *Consumer Reports*, as cited by Cohen and Felson, a Panasonic car tape player was worth $30 per pound and a Philips record player cartridge was valued at a whopping $5,000 per pound.[8] As American incomes rose, people bought more of these valuable consumer electronics.

Together, these two trends stimulated the increase in property theft. Cohen and Felson ingeniously found that burglars were taking advantage of this perfect marriage between empty, unguarded houses full of newly transportable, valuable loot.[9]

Cohen and Felson took their analysis beyond burglary and tried to see whether it applied to other crime as well. To do so, they developed a comprehensive dataset that consisted of the crime rates for five offenses (homicide, rape, aggravated assault, robbery, and burglary) and attempted to connect them to people's daily activities. Their analysis showed that there was a robust relationship between the rates of these five crimes and the level of risk people took in their daily activities.

Cohen and Felson called their idea *routine activity theory*. This is the idea that people's everyday activities—where they live, with whom they live, what they buy, whether they work outside the home, and whether they take vacations—affect crime. The researchers thought that three core elements play a role in how routine activities lead to crime. First, there has to be a motivated offender. Clearly, little crime would occur if people were not motivated to commit it. So, for the spike in burglaries in the 1960s and 1970s, there had to have been people who wanted to steal from other people's homes. Second, there has to be a valuable target. That would have been the houses filled with lightweight valuable goods such as the radios, smaller color TVs, or the tiny but expensive diamond turntable needles. Finally, the target should not be well-guarded. That would have been the case with homes whose owners lived alone more often, were away more frequently, and were out more predictably, leaving their valuables in their houses unguarded.

Since Cohen and Felson's original article in 1979, routine activity theory has spurred a whole new field in criminology. In the decades since, Cohen and Felson's ideas have been tested to explain a wide variety of illegal behaviors, including sex crimes, robbery, medical fraud, and fraud in carbon emissions trading.[10] Susan McNeeley of the Penn State University College of the Liberal Arts and the Minnesota Department of Corrections published a systematic review in 2015 that examined thirty-three articles about routine activity theory.[11] McNeeley reported: "The results show a clear pattern of support that is consistent with hypothesized effects for all four key concepts. Multivariate findings for: (1) guardianship are over 5 times more likely to be protective factors, (2) target attractiveness are 3.33 times more likely to be risk factors, (3) deviant lifestyles are 7.4 times more likely to be risk factors, and (4) exposure to potential offenders are 3.12 times more likely to be risk factors."[12]

Routine activity theory offers a simple framework to analyze crime risk. All we need to do is find out whether valuable (desirable) targets are guarded well enough from potential (motivated) offenders. And just like the restrictions against bringing liquids on airplanes, routine activity theory is all about reducing crime by taking away opportunities for bad behavior.

The idea that we can protect ourselves against crime by reducing easy opportunities is quite intuitive. Every day, when we leave our houses, most of us lock our doors. Some of us activate house alarms. When we park our cars or bicycles, most of us naturally lock them. Most people avoid dark, unlit urban areas when alone at night. And we have all protected our computers against hackers and malware through firewalls and antivirus software (or we trust Apple to do it for us).

Routine activity theory also applies in the online world. Clearly, people can become victims of crime online, as they become suitable and reachable targets for motivated offenders and there is a lack of effective guardianship. Criminologist Travis Pratt and colleagues found that people who make online purchases are 290 percent more likely to become targeted by online fraud schemes.[13] There are countless studies finding similar results. One study found that college students are more likely to become victims of online harassment if they spend more time in chatrooms or even if they hang out with friends who have been involved in online rule-breaking behavior (such as digital piracy or hacking).[14] As anyone who remembers the heydays of BitTorrent, LimeWire, Kazaa, and Napster could attest, another study found that people who use pirated digital media content are more likely to become victims of malware infections.[15] And although this latter finding seems rather obvious, it does show how what we decide to do in our everyday lives can create the opportunity for committed offenders to target us. Once we know what makes people attractive targets, we can help them protect themselves.

Educating people in the risks they are running is a good way to protect them from harm. This is not new. Police departments have long advised people on what alarms, locks, doors, and windows to use to protect themselves against burglary. Software companies have educated us in the use of firewalls and antivirus programs to keep us safe from hacking and cyber-attacks. At work, we regularly get messages about the latest phishing attempts, warnings not to download attachments or click links unless we know for sure that they come from a legitimate source. And we should pay attention to these.

All of this is easy enough. But there is a major problem here; there is an obvious danger of victim-blaming. This is most clearly illustrated in cases of sexual harassment and violence. Women are frequently blamed for sexual assault because of the clothes they were wearing, the beers they were drinking, or the place they were walking. And if we try to reduce the risk of sexual harassment or violence by focusing on what the victims did, we may very well end up blaming the victims for the harm they have suffered. This is an extremely problematic issue that is often raised in discussions of routine activity theory. Fortunately, there is a different approach that focuses less on the victim and more on the practical context where the illegal or damaging behavior takes place. To understand this "situational crime prevention" approach, consider what occurred in 1970s Germany.

In January 1976, West Germany introduced a law that required riders to wear helmets on motorcycles that could go faster than 40 miles per hour. Two years later, it extended these rules to also apply to less powerful bikes that reached up to 25 miles per hour. The laws did not have any fines or penalties at first, but West German lawmakers added fines in 1980.

Wearing a helmet is clearly a good idea and would make riding a motorcycle safer. But the law also had a secondary, unintended effect. After the helmet mandate was introduced, the motorcycle theft rate remained pretty stable, from 1976 to 1979. But after 1980, when the fines were added to the law, motorcycle thefts began declining rapidly.

There seems to have been a connection between the helmet mandate, the introduction of fines for people caught without a helmet, and the declining trends in motorcycle theft. But before we can conclude that there was a link, we must rule out alternative explanations. One factor that could have been at play was a small decline in the West German youth population. Juveniles have less impulse control and are more impacted by their peers than are adults. These developmental influences make them more prone to deviant, criminal, and reckless behavior like stealing motorcycles for joyriding. So a drop in this age group might also explain the drop in motorcycle thefts. But if that is the explanation, then all thefts should have dropped. It's not as though youth steal only motorcycles. Considering that all other forms of theft actually increased in these six years, from 1.86 million cases to 2.26 million cases, that's not a plausible alternative explanation.[16]

Ruling out these and other alternative explanations, Pat Mayhew, a civil servant working for the UK Home Office Research and Planning Unit, concluded with colleagues that the helmet mandates had played an important role in the drop in motorcycle thefts. In the past, a motorcycle thief looked just like any other motorcycle rider. But after the helmet mandate was instituted, stealing a motorcycle and riding off bareheaded drew police attention. So, unless thieves took the step of bringing their own helmet, stealing a motorcycle became harder. Mayhew and colleagues found similar data showing that helmet laws were associated with a 24 percent reduction in motorcycle thefts in London and a 36 percent reduction in the Netherlands.[17]

One of Pat Mayhew's coauthors was Robert Clarke, who served as dean of the School of Criminal Justice at Rutgers University. Clarke drew on the helmet mandate data to develop a new approach to address crime. He called his approach *situational crime prevention*. He argued that crime should not just be addressed by focusing on swaying the motivations of the potential offender. Even if we can establish that offending behavior originates from personal characteristics or broader social structures, such knowledge often offers very limited practical guidance to help reduce offending.[18]

Instead, Clarke focused on the situation that enables illegal behavior right before it occurs.[19] Rule-breaking behavior depends on opportunity. So Clarke looked beyond the victim and target hardening (strengthening security) and focused instead on the contexts and environments where criminal activities can take place. For example, Clarke pointed to data showing that as cities developed better street lighting, crime levels dropped dramatically. A recent systematic review of eight American and five British studies about the effects of streetlights on crime levels confirms this: improving streetlights reduces crime on average by 21 percent.[20]

Recently, Dutch economists applied these insights in an experiment at the Royal Palace in Amsterdam. The palace, which was built in the seventeenth century as the mayor's office and then converted to royal property after Napoleon occupied the Netherlands, stands as a proud symbol of the city's bygone era. Unfortunately, it has also become a popular spot for public urination. Many partying locals and drunken tourists routinely relieve themselves on its walls.

For years, authorities had tried to address the problem. First, they tried extra surveillance and warnings. Then they tried physical barriers, but those didn't work either. Nothing worked. That is, until Robert Dur and Ben Vollaard, two Dutch economists, started their experiment, which, for seven months, required them to analyze video footage of public urination. Over this period, they installed a new lighting system at the palace, and at random intervals they changed the amount of light that shone right on the corners of the building where partyers were prone to pee. They found that by switching the lights on, they could reduce public urination by half.[21]

This sounds like an easier and better solution than what Hamburg, Germany, tried against public urination in St. Pauli, the city's popular nightlife district. Locals used Ultra-Ever Dry, a hydrophobic type of paint that repels liquids. The effect would be that when peed upon, the surface would bounce it right back. And they also warned potential offenders with signs all over the neighborhood: "Wir pinkeln zurück" ("We pee back").[22]

If the physical environment matters and things like lighting affect crime, then we must look more broadly at architecture and urban planning. Here Oscar Newman's work on "defensible space" has been most influential.[23] In 1972, Newman, an architect and city planner, after the publication of an elaborate study of variation in crime and disorder in neighborhoods throughout America, argued that the height and architecture of buildings affects crime. Newman was highly critical of burgeoning high-rise public housing developments, seeing that they had much higher crime rates than low-rise housing communities. In the shorter buildings, he asserted, spaces were more clearly demarcated, and residents could claim space as "their own" and thus bear responsibility for and have control over its safety. Newman also focused on physical aspects in the built environment that could enable or undermine opportunities for surveillance. High-rises simply offered many more obstructions to surveillance: enclosed lobbies, elevators, and stairways, and blocked views to the street.[24]

The situational crime prevention approach is not just about changing the physical environment. It is also about reducing access to items that enable harmful behavior. Clarke pointed to the effects of changing the gas supplied to people's homes on suicide rates. Between 1958 and 1977, 25 percent of suicides in England and Wales involved the use of gas. People killed themselves with carbon monoxide by using their own ovens. However, changes in the way gas was produced in the 1960s reduced the level of carbon monoxide, and when Britain switched to North Sea natural gas, all toxic carbon monoxide was eliminated. Thus, by 1977 only 0.2 percent of suicides involved gas at home. The number of suicides overall dropped from 5,298 in 1958 to 3,944 in 1977. Of course, there surely were more reasons for the drop, but Clarke concluded that when access to the easy and painless killing substance at home was taken away, "many people who would otherwise have killed themselves did not do so."[25]

The idea that we can reduce crime and other damaging behavior by changing access to items that enable the behavior has broad consequences. We can reduce graffiti by restricting who can buy spray paint. We can reduce gun-related shootings by restricting access to guns or ammunition. And we can reduce harm in bar fights by giving customers thicker or shatterproof beer glasses so they can no longer use the broken shards as weapons.[26]

Over the years, Clarke and his coauthors have categorized situational crime prevention strategies into twenty-five types. Many of these have become part and parcel of our everyday lives, as we can see them, if we look, on the streets, in shops, and in our cars. Often, though, we fail to notice these vital elements of the invisible code that are part of our physical spaces and keep us safe from harm. Shops put tags on merchandise that trigger alarms if we exit the store without paying, making it difficult to steal goods undetected; worse, some tags will activate dye that will stain stolen items. On the street, closed-circuit cameras make criminal activity more detectable. We no longer have high-value banknotes like the US thousand-dollar bill, which was taken out of circulation by

President Nixon in 1969, and the five-hundred-euro bill, which will soon cease to exist. In both cases, the reason for their demise is that these high-value banknotes make it easy for criminals to deliver large amounts of cash. One million euros in five-hundred-euro bills weigh just 2.2 kilograms (Americans, that's just under five pounds) and can easily fit in a suitcase.[27] The same value in fifty-euro notes would weigh ten times as much, 22 kilograms (about fifty pounds).[28]

Crime prevention of this sort is not new. Think of the age-old practice of cattle branding, which makes it much harder for rustlers to keep or sell stolen animals. In fact, the situational crime prevention approach has a long and rich history spanning centuries. We can find it in medieval England. In 1285, King Edward I of England adopted a law, the Statute of Winchester, that mandated that landowners remove places potential robbers could hide next to the highway, such as ditches and vegetation. And if they failed to do so, the law made these landowners liable for crimes on those stretches of the highway.

In 2005, the US Congress passed a law mandating that the nasal decongestant pseudoephedrine, found in products like Sudafed, could no longer be sold over the counter without restriction. The law restricted patients to buying 7.5 grams, pharmacies had to track sales, and some states also required individual prescriptions. All of this was not done out of concern for patients. It was done to fight the production of illicit drugs.

Pseudoephedrine, or "pseudo" as people in the drug business call it, is a key substance used in making crystal meth—the addictive crystalline methamphetamine also called "ice," the most potent form of meth. By legally limiting access to pseudo, the Combat Methamphetamine Act followed Clarke's approach. At first, in response, meth producers tried sending kids to get as many single packets of pseudo as they could in as many different localities as possible, a practice that became known as "smurfing." However, the new law made it hard to reach a sufficient scale of production.

As home labs struggled to acquire the key ingredient, meth production plummeted across the US. As one prosecutor looks back: "It was like someone turned off a switch."[29] However, the effect did not last. Mexican cartels moved in to fill the void the law had created. Lacking US home lab competition, the cartels had a massive market all for themselves. And they were able to develop a better-quality product for a far lower price and spread it across the US. The same prosecutor who lauded the law explained to the *New York Times* in 2018, "Where there is a void, someone fills it."[30]

When Mexico tried to follow the American example and restrict access to pseudo, Mexican producers switched to a different cooking process to make meth that did not require pseudo. The cartels' process used phenyl-2-propanone (P2P), which was restricted but could be manufactured quite easily. The result has been a disaster for drug enforcement and meth-related deaths. In 2015, almost six thousand people died because of meth—double the number of deaths in 2005, when the pseudoephedrine law was enacted. By 2016, in Oregon, meth killed twice as many people as heroin. Almost half the car thefts in Portland were committed by meth addicts. In Montana, meth-related arrests increased by 300 percent between 2010 and 2015. The attorney general of South Dakota proclaimed a statewide meth epidemic. In some states, meth has become the number-one drug-related killer, even at the height of the ongoing opioid epidemic.[31] Closing off opportunities to produce meth worked at first but failed in the longer run. In fact, it made things worse.

A big downside to the opportunity approach is that it can create displacement or adaptation. If we add speed bumps to First and Third Streets, we may increase speeding on Second Street. In this approach, the result may be escalation, where offenders use more violent and stronger means. One study found that following the introduction of glass windows between tellers and customers in London post offices, robbers began using more firearms.[32] The introduction of car security alarms reduced ordinary car theft—people breaking into parked cars and speeding away. But it may have also led to an increase in carjacking, in which a driver is forced to hand over one's car at gunpoint.[33]

Part of the problem here is that the opportunity approach might also create inequality in who may fall victim to crime. In Germany, the steering-column lock law reduced car theft, whereas car theft remained about the same in the United States. The difference was that the US mandated that only new cars needed to have the theft prevention device. People who could not afford a new car became the prime—or perhaps the only—targets for car thieves.[34]

Over time, there have been many empirical studies about the potential displacement effects of interventions that reduce opportunities for crime. In one systematic review, criminologists Rob Guerette and Kate Bowers aggregated 102 existing studies and found some type of displacement effect in a little over 25 percent of the cases. However, they found that the crime reduction effects overall dramatically outweighed the displacement effects. By and large, shutting off criminal opportunities prevents more crime than it displaces.[35]

Further, sometimes situational crime prevention has a positive "halo effect" and reduces crime and misconduct beyond its original scope.[36] Houses without security benefit from those in their neighborhood that do.[37] CCTV cameras reduce car crimes not only in parking lots where they are installed but also in those where there are no cameras.

## DO JAILS INCAPACITATE CRIMINALS?

"Get out of the way. Someone's got a knife."[38] Craig Heathcote, a filmmaker, heard someone say as he was walking near London Bridge in the early afternoon on November 29, 2019. Soon people were running for their lives all around him as an attacker, apparently wearing a bomb vest, was charging and slashing people with a knife in Fishmongers' Hall just across the bridge. Brave bystanders tried to stop the attacker. One brandished a fire extinguisher and another charged the attacker with an ornamental whale tusk taken from one of the hall's walls. The attacker was finally stopped when bystanders overpowered him and brought him down to the ground. As one of them recalls: "I stamped on his left wrist while someone else smacked his hand on the ground and then kicked one of the knives away." Luckily, his bomb vest was fake, yet the attack, which was later claimed by terrorist organization ISIS, ended up killing two people and wounding three.

The killer was a twenty-eight-year-old man from Stafford, England. What shocked people around the globe was that he was a known and convicted terrorist who had served time in prison for plotting to bomb the London Stock Exchange by putting explosives in the restrooms. He had been convicted to sixteen years in prison in 2013 but had been released when he had served half of his sentence.

The political response in the UK was intense. Prime Minister Boris Johnson stated that sentences should "toughen up." He added: "I have long argued that it is a mistake to allow serious and violent criminals to come out of prison early." The former head of the UK's National Counter Terrorism Security Office stated: "We're playing Russian roulette with people's lives, letting convicted, known, radicalized jihadi criminals walk about our streets."

This case shows that people believe imprisonment serves a clear purpose: to keep society safe from criminals. In a way, imprisonment is the ultimate form of situational crime prevention. Serving time in prison should take away the opportunity for prisoners to re-offend, or at least their ability to impact society outside the penitentiary. Criminologists have called this the *incapacitation effect*.

Following this logic, punishment can reduce the opportunities for misconduct through incapacitation. And here it is not just imprisonment. Punishment can disbar lawyers caught in malpractice, it can revoke business licenses from highly polluting companies, and it can prevent people from being involved in union activities, as happened famously to Jimmy Hoffa, who was convicted for fraud, bribery, and jury tampering in 1964, though he was later pardoned by President Richard Nixon.

Incapacitation sounds good. Yet the question is "Does it work?" A deeper look at the data about the incapacitating effects of imprisonment shows that its relationship to crime is not as clear-cut as one might think.

Studies about the incapacitating effect of jails and prisons tend to examine what happens to crime when we increase the imprisonment rate by just 1 percent. Does the crime rate decrease? Well, not exactly.

Findings of these studies vary widely. Some estimate up to a 0.4 percent reduction in crime, whereas others find no reduction in crime at all.[39] In reviewing this literature, the US National Research Council concluded in 2014, "We cannot arrive at a precise estimate, or even a modest range of estimates, of the magnitude of the effect of incarceration on crime rates."[40] Despite many studies on the topic, we simply cannot establish to what extent incapacitation actually reduces crime. Yet over the past forty years, the US has increased its prison and jail population by over 500 percent.[41]

Incapacitation is counterfactual. It is based on the implicit—and often explicit—notion that the prison population consists of hardened criminals who would commit crime again and again if they were on the street. What would the criminal have done if he had not been locked away?

The idea behind incapacitation is that people's inclination toward crime is stable. So people will remain as likely to offend the day they were caught as the day they leave prison many years later. In the 1990s, youth offenders were seen as incorrigible "superpredators" incapable of change. At the time, Hillary Clinton warned Americans, "they are not just gangs of kids anymore. They are often the kinds of kids that are called superpredators—no conscience, no empathy."[42]

In many respects, Clinton was parroting some academic researchers of the time, including Princeton political scientist John J. DiIulio Jr., who gained notoriety for his views. He shared his thoughts in a variety of television interviews, scholarly articles, and even at a White House dinner with President Bill Clinton. He infamously proclaimed that kids who commit crime were "kids that have absolutely no respect for human life and no sense of the future. . . . These are stone-cold predators!"[43]

The way politicians and many researchers spoke about juvenile offenders during the 1990s dramatically influenced how the general public thought about youth crime and, consequently, youth punishment. What came out of this era was the idea that the only thing we can do with juvenile offenders is lock them up and throw away the key. If we remove them from society, these "predators" cannot hurt us.

One crucial problem with the superpredator rhetoric is that it is entirely falsifiable by the scientific evidence. Youth who commit crime are *not* destined to become lifelong, career criminals. Inclination toward crime is not stable, let alone permanent.

For a long time, researchers have known that crime peaks during adolescence. Since the 1930s, study after study has shown that both ordinary risk-taking and criminal behavior follow a similar pattern that looks like an inverted "U."[44] Clearly, crime rises during early adolescence.[45] The important part of the picture, however, is that after the teenage years, the propensity to engage in criminal behavior declines rapidly. This is the "age-crime" curve.

In one landmark study, researchers followed over 1,300 adolescent offenders for over seven years from adolescence into adulthood.[46] These were youth who had been arrested and adjudicated for serious, often felony-level offenses. Guess what percentage continued offending. Did you guess 80 percent? Or 60 percent? Or 40 percent? In fact, the vast majority of these serious youth offenders subsequently *desisted* from crime. After seven years, fewer than 9 percent continued to offend at high rates.[47]

Teens who commit crimes—even felonies—are not destined to become lifelong criminals. Crime doesn't peak during adolescence because teens are dangerous superpredators but because teens are still developing their ability to control their behavior, to consider the consequences of their actions, and to resist peer pressure.[48] Teens are not just more impulsive than adults; they are also more likely to focus on the potential rewards in a risky situation than on the potential negative consequences, and they are more sensitive to the heat of the moment. Altogether, adolescents are less "psychosocially mature" than adults, and their developmental disadvantages are especially large when youth are emotionally aroused or are around their peers—or both at the same time.[49] If we think about developmental immaturity, the spike in adolescent crime—not to mention sex, drugs, and rock and roll—makes a lot more sense.

So people's inclination toward crime is not stable. And when we go back to the counterfactual question about incapacitation, namely what the convicted criminal would have done if not imprisoned, the answer changes over time. If a juvenile or young adult is convicted for twenty years, chances are that incarceration might have prevented some limited amount of re-offending in the first couple of years, but after one, three, or maybe five years, most will have aged out of crime. Considering that the vast majority will simply age past and develop out of crime, incarcerating and incapacitating adolescents for years is unnecessary and often counterproductive because of the criminogenic nature of incarceration.[50]

Thus, incapacitation has diminishing returns.[51] The longer the sentences, the less likely they will prevent crime when prisoners grow up or grow old inside. For most convicted criminals, long-term incarceration will at some point fail to offer extra protection to society.

When countries increase their prison populations, it is not necessarily because they are catching more lifelong criminals engaging in heinous acts. Nor is it that they are becoming "tougher" on more heinous crimes. Instead, they often tend to apply longer, more punitive sentences to more *types* of behaviors, which inherently means less serious offenses. When prison populations grow in this way, they inevitably include fewer and fewer truly dangerous individuals. In fact, one study found that precisely when the United States ballooned its prison population, the incapacitating effect of imprisonment steeply declined. The study argued that there are diminishing returns because the prison population includes fewer hardened criminals. "This large decline in the marginal effect of an inmate suggests that the most recent increases in incarceration have been driven by the institutionalization of many inmates who, relative to previous periods, pose less of a threat to society."[52]

The idea of incapacitation also assumes that once a criminal is in prison, the crimes they would otherwise commit will cease. This, however, neglects the fact that, for some crimes and criminals, there may be others who will simply take that person's place, the so-called *replacement effect*. Just think how other Colombian drug cartels, like the Cali Cartel, filled the void left when Medellín Cartel leader Pablo Escobar was imprisoned and later led the life of a fugitive before he was killed in 1993. As one criminological study argues, "The more lucrative criminal

opportunities that the now-incarcerated offenders would have taken become available, raising the net returns per offense for non-incarcerated
persons." It bluntly states, "A higher incarceration rate in a particular
neighborhood may make offending relatively more attractive for remaining residents."[53]

Another problem is that many criminals do not work alone. Simply imprisoning one offender does not incapacitate their accomplices.
Co-offending is especially common in youth and gang-related crime.
One study estimates that, when one accounts for co-offending, the crime
prevention effects of incapacitation would decrease by one-third.[54]

What these studies show is that although incapacitation through imprisonment may appear to be a way to prevent crimes by those who will
otherwise surely recommit them, imprisonment does not generally prevent crime if more people are sentenced for longer times. As such, the use
of prisons to prevent crime by reducing the opportunity for re-offending
in society should be reserved only for the worst cases and not be applied
generally.

## DON'T TOUCH OUR GUNS

Police chief Wilbert Paulissen of the Eastern-Brabant Police Unit in the
Netherlands sounded very proud. His agents had caught 739 drivers illegally using their smartphones on the highway. In an interview with a
popular Dutch newspaper, he reflected on his new method to catch these
reckless drivers. Agents rode in a large coach-type bus, normally used
to transport tourists, so they could stealthily observe people using their
phones behind the wheel. The high vantage point from the bus made
their surveillance work surprisingly easy.[55]

The Dutch initiative is one of many attempts to deter people from
distracted driving. In other instances, authorities have turned to surveillance technology. Australia has even equipped its traffic cameras with
artificial intelligence so they can automatically review millions of hours
of footage for illegal cellphone use.[56]

Authorities have been very creative in trying to catch people in the
act of using their cell phones while driving. They do so in the hopes that

better detection will enhance people's fear of punishment and that this in turn will deter them from using their phones.

But what if there were a much smarter way to deter folks from using their phone that did not require law enforcement? What if we could just make it very hard or impossible to use it while driving? What if people never got to make the decision?

If you have been using the popular Swedish music streaming app Spotify, you may have noticed that it acts differently when you use it in a moving car. The app detects when you are driving and switches to what the company calls *car-view mode*, in which it offers larger controls that make it easier to use the app.[57]

Our smartphones are smart enough to detect that we are in a car, and app makers are clever enough to develop apps that change their functioning while we are driving. The technology has long been there. In 2016, families of victims in a phone-distracted-driver car crash in Texas sued Apple for failing to prevent this known risk. The families pointed to a patent Apple filed in 2008 that covered a new technology that detected when the phone was moving and would then "lock out" functions that would impair the driver, such as texting. In filing the patent, the tech giant even explained why the technology was important: "Texting while driving has become so widespread that it is doubtful that law enforcement will have any significant effect on stopping the practice."[58]

Combined with the Spotify app feature, phones can detect that they are in a car and then can switch to a different mode. So, yes, the technology inside phones is there to automatically keep people from distracted driving. And it is not just technology in the phone. Cellcontrol, a small tech company, sells a $129 device that uses high frequency sound waves to locate phones in a car. When it detects that a phone is in the driver's seat, it can switch off the phone's services that distract safe driving.[59] So there are far better options that never allow drivers to use their phones in the first place and save us the cost of renting a fleet of coach buses or installing AI-operated cameras.

Why don't we use such technology? Why don't our laws mandate that all phones have a safe car mode and that all cars are equipped with something like the Cellcontrol device? Why don't our laws make more use of the opportunity approach to reduce other types of misconduct? The problem here is not victim blaming, crime displacement, or crime replacement effects. It is something more fundamental. To understand this, let us return to the 1970s and people's original refusal to wear seatbelts in their cars.

In 1973, the US National Highway Traffic Administration (NHTA) mandated that all new cars without airbags had to have a system that prevented the car from being started if the front-seat passengers did not have their seatbelt on.[60] This ignition lock effectively meant that you could not drive without first putting on your seatbelt.

The mandate could have completely changed American seatbelt habits. It didn't matter if there was a law requiring people to wear them. It also didn't matter if the police actually enforced this law. And it didn't matter if people saw others clicking their seatbelts. If a car wouldn't start without seatbelts first being engaged, people would have no choice. The ignition lock would have completely obviated the decision to buckle up simply by taking away the choice.

When the American public learned of the mandate, they became outraged. Never mind safety. The rule directly limited their freedom as drivers and car owners. It was bad enough that federal law had already mandated that seatbelts be installed in cars. But it was their own business whether they would actually use them. Congress responded swiftly to the public outrage. It adopted a new law that banned the National Highway Traffic Administration from mandating the ignition lock for seatbelts. But Congress didn't stop there.

You know the annoying seatbelt alarm systems that chime when you don't put your seatbelt on fast enough? Congress stipulated that the NHTA could not require alarms to sound for longer than eight seconds. Subsequent studies have found, ironically, that only alarms that last longer than eight seconds actually increase seatbelt usage.[61]

The seatbelt example shows us that there is a political and even a moral side to using the opportunity approach. The seatbelt effort failed because of a combination of distrust in government and a fear of direct infringement on personal freedom. And this is justified. The strategy of reducing opportunities for illegal behavior does inherently reduce free choice. Do we want the government to reduce our opportunities for bad behavior? Do we want our governments to reduce our freedoms? The danger of authoritarianism lurks.

In no area is this issue clearer than in mass shootings and gun-related deaths. In August 1996, a man in Australia used a Colt AR-15 SP1 light-weight semi-automatic rifle to kill thirty-five people in a café, gift shop, and parking lot in Port Arthur, Tasmania. The Australian legislative response was clear and swift: all states, under federal coordination, severely restricted ownership of self-loading rifles and shotguns. The government also initiated a scheme to buy back guns already in circulation, ultimately involving about 643,000 weapons at a cost of $350 million USD. Clearly, Australia saw that in order to reduce mass shootings, it would have to take an opportunity approach and restrict access to the key enabling component: the guns.

The US, under President Clinton, adopted a federal ban on assault rifles in 1994. The ban was enacted, similar to the one Australia, after a series of mass shootings, including one in 1989 in Stockton, California, killing thirty-four schoolchildren and their teacher; one in Killeen, Texas, killing twenty-seven people in a cafeteria in 1991; and a 1993 rampage in San Francisco where the killer brandished two TEC-9 semi-automatic weapons with special "Hell-Fire" triggers that allowed for full-automatic firing speeds. However, the law expired in 2004. And since then America has witnessed shooting after shooting, massacre after massacre. The names are etched in the national psyche: Sandy Hook, Parkland, Virginia Tech, Pulse Orlando, Paradise Las Vegas. None of the ten deadliest shootings in the US occurred during the ban on assault rifles. Three occurred before the assault rifle ban started in 1994 and the other seven—including the top five—all occurred after the ban lapsed.

With each new massacre, the United States seems to be split in two. All Americans agree that the carnage must end. But one part of the population sees the solution in reducing the opportunities for these senseless killings. These people support gun restrictions and controls. They very much view the problem as originating in easy access to highly dangerous weapons and high-caliber ammunition. Their proposals thus range from overall bans on all guns to restricting certain weapons (like the 1994 restrictions on assault rifles); banning certain technologies that make weapons more dangerous (like the bump stocks that the 2017 Las Vegas shooter, who killed 58 people and wounded 413, used to modify his semi-automatic to reach full automatic speeds); or limiting access for certain people (with criminal records, documented domestic abuse, diagnosed mental health disorders, or below a certain age). This follows an opportunity approach to mass shootings. It looks at how mass shootings take place and takes out key elements that allow offenders to kill on a mass scale.

Another part of the population has a very different view. For them, the weapon is not the problem. The killer is the problem. As one person wrote in a letter to the editor of a local newspaper after the Parkland shooting in Florida that killed fourteen teenagers and three high school staff members: "It is easy to blame the gun in a shooting. However, it was a person who carried, operated and pointed it."[62] As the letter continues: "The high school shooter in Florida was known well in advance. The FBI was notified of this individual, the local law agency was aware of him, and they did nothing." So the argument here is, let's not focus on what enabled the shooting but instead focus on how we can deal with the shooter. The focus here is on law enforcement and early detection. The argument often comes out of a deeper fear. As this letter explains: "Are we now going to hold automakers accountable for drive-by shootings, drunk drivers and hit and runs?" There is a fear that once we approach crime and harmful behavior through reducing opportunities, people will lose freedom. Those with this viewpoint ask: What freedom is stronger than owning a gun? And what is more fear-inspiring than a government that wants to restrict gun ownership or even take your guns? These Americans will often frame this under the Second Amendment, the core sentiment being one of freedom and protection against the power of a tyrannical government.

So even if there are effective ways to reduce crime and harmful behavior, for law to promote these, there needs to be a political mandate.

And the more the interventions are seen to restrict people's freedom, the less likely the law can adopt them. "Don't come for my guns." "Don't interfere in my car." "Stay out of my phone."

This is a one-sided view of the opportunity approach to crime and misconduct. Surely, this approach restricts freedom. But so does the alternative. When law leaves us opportunities to do harm, it will develop other ways to try to keep us from using these opportunities. When we are technically able to use our cell phones in our cars, law enforcement will use invasive surveillance followed by sanctions to keep us from doing so. And when any citizen can access any type of gun, law enforcement needs extra electronic oversight to ensure that it can keep people who develop plans for mass shootings from executing them. Even worse, police may fear more for their own safety and become more likely to violate other constitutional rights, including using deadly force, when handling suspects.[63] This is not only costlier economically and squanders our tax dollars but also restricts our freedom in serious ways, often more seriously than the freedom lost because of opportunity interventions.

All of this plays out in the public sphere where ultimately politics must balance these interests between different forms of freedom and the prevention of harm. Without public support, the opportunity approach to crime and misconduct will never come to pass. And this is where the true problem lies. How will the public know how to pick one policy intervention over another if it is not well-informed, if it doesn't know about their comparative costs and benefits?

Part of the problem is that people are not well informed about the opportunity approach. In debates about reckless use of cell phones, the practical and technological interventions hardly ever feature. And Americans who want to know whether gun restrictions would reduce mass shootings and homicides in general would find that there is only limited research. The political forces that fear gun restrictions have been so strong that Congress for decades restricted funding to the Centers for Disease Control and Prevention (CDC) to block them and serious scientists from doing research about the relationship between homicide and gun ownership. They did so after the National Rifle Association complained about a study funded by the CDC and published in the *New England Journal of Medicine* that found that the risk of homicide in the home is almost tripled when there are firearms in the house.[64] In 2015, just after another massacre, one in San Bernardino, California, where a couple shot and killed fourteen people, Congress decided to continue to ban the CDC from studying the relationship between gun ownership and homicide.

People have different preferences when it comes to using the opportunity approach. It is widely supported in preventing burglary in our homes, where we use locks and security systems. It is normal in our computers, where we use firewalls and malware protection software. And, of course it is one of our main responses against suicide bombers and terrorist attacks, not just in banning large bottles of liquids on planes but also in installing heavy concrete barriers in public places to prevent attacks using buses and trucks. But the divide is abundantly clear when the opportunity approach is proposed to reduce distracted driving or gun-related deaths.

# CHAPTER 9

# Eating Systems
# for Breakfast

I n November 2006, Siemens AG, the German engineering giant
known for its home appliances, was caught red-handed in a massive corruption scheme.[1] To win a major mobile phone deal, it had paid
$5 million USD to the son of the Bangladeshi prime minister and sev-
eral local officials. It had paid another $13 million in bribes in Nigeria,
$14 million in China, $16 million in Venezuela, $20 million in Israel,
and a whopping $100 million in Argentina, which won Siemens a con-
tract worth $1 billion USD for national identity cards.[2] Siemens had even
bribed Saddam Hussein when he was still in power in Iraq.[3]

Over the course of seven years, the company had funneled an estimated total of $1.4 billion.[4] It had done this through fake consultancy
contracts, fabricated bills, and shell companies.[5] The graft involved hundreds of Siemens employees, from local operators at lower levels to senior
executives.[6] It had been systematic, intentional, and widespread throughout at least six of the company's main divisions. As a spokesperson for the
German association of federal criminal investigators stated: "Bribery was
Siemens's business model. Siemens had institutionalized corruption."[7]

Siemens settled with the American and German authorities, agreeing
to pay $1.6 billion in fines, and three higher-level Siemens executives

were sentenced to fines and probation.[8] Yet the strongest criminal punishment was not for a Siemens employee. Shi Wanzhong, an executive at a state-owned telecom company in China, received a death sentence in a Chinese court with a two-year reprieve (which effectively means life imprisonment) for taking $5.3 million in kickbacks.[9]

In its 2008 sentencing memo submitted to a federal district court as part of the settlement deal with Siemens, the US Department of Justice (DOJ) applauded the company and its new management for immediately taking steps to remediate existing practices and prevent future bribery. The sentencing memo highlighted how Siemens completely overhauled its compliance management program. Siemens expanded its compliance personnel, growing it to five hundred full-time staff positions across its global operations. It also vested all responsibility and authority for compliance with a chief compliance officer who reported directly to the company's general counsel and CEO.

In this memo, the DOJ explained that Siemens had developed new "anti-corruption compliance policies" complete with a new "anti-corruption handbook, sophisticated web-based tools for due diligence and compliance, a confidential communications channel for employees to report irregular business practices, and a corporate disciplinary committee." The memo also detailed how Siemens had collaborated with the firm PricewaterhouseCoopers (PwC) to develop a "step-by-step guide on the new compliance program and improved financial controls known as the 'Anti-Corruption Toolkit.'"[10] Siemens hired 150 staff members, half of whom were PwC consultants, to implement the "Toolkit" at 162 of its entities. All of this cost Siemens over $150 million.

Siemens went from corruption villain to compliance hero. The DOJ argued to the federal district court that because Siemens had so completely overhauled its compliance management operations, it should receive a more lenient sentence.

The Siemens corruption saga shows that human misconduct is not just individual. Much of our behavior occurs inside organizations. And organizations can become structural rule breakers causing massive amounts of damage. There are countless other examples. Widespread sexual harassment and abuse continued for decades in the Catholic Church, major Hollywood studios, and in college and professional sports teams. Corporations like BP and Volkswagen caused environmental damage and created safety hazards. And in the wake of yet another police shooting of a Black or brown person in America, it is clear to all that many police departments have been unable to end the structural racism and violence that have occurred in their departments for decades—if not centuries. Sure, there are bad apples, but organizations that create, promote, and protect the bad apples ruin the entire barrel.[11]

If law is to keep us safe from harm, it must look beyond individuals and address organizational behavior. The most common response when major scandals in organizations erupt is to try to discipline the individuals who directly caused the damages. Often, law enforcement and prosecutors attempt to hold the highest officials in the organization responsible. This may be justified because it is unfair that executives go free for abuses that cause harm to millions if not billions of people while street crime offenders serve hard time. At the same time, there is no conclusive evidence that harsher punishments for corporate executives or for corporations as a whole will reduce their criminal activities.[12] This is an inconvenient truth about punishment.

When an organization like Siemens commits massive offenses and the case ends in a settlement, it does not feel like justice was served. But the core question for us here is not whether justice is served. It is how law can prevent future injustice and keep us safe from harm. Of course, people in organizations should be held accountable. But an even bigger question is what else should be done to address organizational misconduct and prevent it from happening in the future. This forces us to look beyond the bad apples, to looking at the barrel and maybe even the orchard itself.

During the Siemens sentencing hearing, DOJ prosecutors were following US federal law. Their pleas for mercy were couched in the Federal Sentencing Guidelines for Organizations of 1991. These guidelines sought to incentivize organizations to adopt an "effective compliance and ethics program." In cases where organizations are prosecuted for federal offenses, the guidelines state that organizations with such programs should receive a reduced sentence.[13]

The guidelines explain that compliance and ethics programs are "designed to prevent and deter criminal conduct."[14] These guidelines recognize that preventing corporate wrongdoing and damages requires more than punishing corporations or executives. Organizations must have their own proactive programs that enable them to know who is breaking the law inside their organization and that help them prevent this from happening in the first place.

The guidelines generally state that the programs must "exercise due diligence to prevent and detect criminal conduct" and that they must promote an organizational culture that stimulates ethical conduct and compliance. The guidelines then provide further details about what this means exactly, listing seven elements: (1) there must be rules and procedures for preventing and detecting illegal behavior; (2) top-level leaders must have knowledge and oversight of the compliance and ethics program; (3) organizations must have a dedicated high-level officer in charge of the program; (4) they must organize training to disseminate the program; (5) they should have effective monitoring and evaluation of the program's effectiveness; (6) they must have a whistleblower protection program so that employees can report illegal behavior without retaliation; and (7) they must have incentives aligned with the program and adapt the program in case illegal behavior occurs.

There are other incentives for companies to develop compliance and ethics programs. For instance, organizations with compliance management systems may have the benefit of receiving less governmental oversight. In the US, several regulators, including the Occupational Safety and Health Agency, the Environmental Protection Agency, and the Department of Agriculture, carry out fewer inspections or even cut all inspections at firms that have adopted compliance management systems.[15] And some laws simply mandate that organizations have compliance management programs. One example is the 2002 Sarbanes-Oxley Act, which Congress adopted in the wake of the Enron and WorldCom scandals.[16]

Another is the 2012 Dodd-Frank Wall Street Reform and Consumer Protection Act (Dodd-Frank), adopted after the 2008 financial crisis that spurred the Great Recession.[17] All companies that want to be listed on the New York Stock Exchange must have a compliance management program.[18] All of this has spurred a whole new industry and profession of compliance managers and consultants who help organizations establish and operate such programs.

But does all this work? And if it does work, what elements and conditions are most important in its success?

The existing body of empirical work has mixed findings. On the one hand, several studies show that compliance management and ethics programs can be effective in reducing unethical and illegal behavior. But they show that their effectiveness is limited.[19] One study looked at whether companies that have adopted the ISO 14000 environmental management system, which is a specialized system to manage environmental risks, are more likely to be in compliance. It found that most firms that had adopted the ISO system improved compliance. However, the improvement was tiny. The ISO-certified firms on average had only a 2 percent increase in compliance.[20]

Another study compared firms that had to adopt a compliance management system under the Sarbanes-Oxley Act with those that did not. This study came to a similar conclusion; firms with the compliance management system performed better in their financial reporting obligations, but the overall difference was only 3.5 percent.[21] Furthermore, two recent meta-analyses found that firms with ethical codes did slightly better than those without.[22] All in all, compliance and ethics programs can be effective, but their effects are minimal.

What aspects of these programs are effective? Perhaps we can identify the mechanisms and then tweak those so that the programs emphasize the core elements that are working, ramping them up to reduce misbehavior. One study of 999 large Australian firms found that the vast majority of compliance management system elements—fifteen of the twenty-one—actually had no impact on compliance efforts with competition and consumer protection laws.[23] These included having a hotline for complaints about compliance, using a compliance manual, using a computer-based training program for compliance, having written policies to protect internal whistleblowers, and requiring managers to frequently report on compliance and internal employee discipline for noncompliance.[24] These essentially worthless elements are many of the same elements that the DOJ had applauded Siemens for introducing following its massive fraud scandal.

The six elements that were effective in improving compliance efforts included having a written compliance policy and systems for handling compliance failures complaints from customers or clients.[25] On that front, the research is fairly promising, at least in identifying what might stimulate greater efforts to improve compliance. There is one catch, though. It should be noted that the study did not assess actual compliance, only compliance efforts, but the findings are nonetheless illustrative.

Some research makes a distinction between programs that focus on instilling values of integrity and ethicality (which we can call *values-oriented*) and programs that focus on rules, procedures, and incentives (which we can call *incentives-oriented*). Such studies find that values-oriented programs are better at motivating people than are incentives-oriented programs.[26] Programs that introduce ethics and compliance procedures and practices without really convincing employees of the underlying values will backfire. Worker voice or empowerment in the adoption of such programs is also key for effectiveness. In alignment with the work on procedural justice, one study finds, for instance, that the more employees are involved in decision-making about compliance, the more they are motivated to refrain from rule breaking.[27] These findings cast doubt about whether the types of systems that Siemens adopted, and that the DOJ has promoted, may be effective, since values and worker empowerment were not central.

Other scholars are more skeptical that compliance and ethics programs can even be effective. One study found, for instance, that the effect of ethics training wears off after two years.[28] Training creates an immediate boost in ethical values, but that fades over time. Another study found that ethical compliance programs have no impact at all on improving compliance and reducing occupational health and safety violations.[29] Several studies of formal ethics training found that this either does not impact ethical behavior in organizations or that the effects are at best only temporary.[30] A review of the effectiveness of ethical codes revealed that in 33 percent of studies, these codes had no effect on reducing unethical behavior.[31]

Some scholars argue that compliance and ethics programs may have sometimes made matters worse. Studies indicate that the more firms incorporated ethical compliance into their operations, the *more* likely they were to have "willful and repeat" violations.[32] This body of literature suggests that compliance management programs may backfire through undermining employees' trust in the ethical commitment of their leaders. Compliance programs may send mixed messages to employees. On the one hand, they see that their firm has publicly adopted a lofty ethics and compliance system; on the other hand, they see that the firm does not "follow through" in everyday working practices. Linda Treviño, who teaches at Penn State University, and Gary Weaver, who teaches at the University of Delaware, argue that such a mismatch may damage employee expectations of procedural and retributive justice.[33] As Treviño summarizes: "What hurts the most is . . . the perception that the ethics or compliance program exists only to protect top management from blame."[34]

This is the worst case scenario, when compliance and ethics programs serve only as window dressing to avoid liability.[35] All we get then is "cosmetic compliance," not the real thing.[36] One study of compliance management in about one thousand American companies finds that "the vast majority of firms have committed to the low cost, possibly symbolic side of ethics management (e.g., adoption of ethics codes and policies, etc.)."[37] When the compliance management programs shield the corporation from liability, such a program becomes a perverse incentive, as the firm cares less about preventing the illegal behavior they are now less liable for.[38]

Part of the problem is that it is hard to know what comprises a good and effective compliance management program.[39] As Duke School of Law professor Kim Krawiec explains, "The indicia of an effective compliance system are easily mimicked and true effectiveness is difficult for courts and regulators to determine."[40] Because of this, she explains, there will be more window-dressing and cosmetics.

There is ambiguity not just about what compliance and ethics programs may work, but also about what the law requires corporations to do. In her study about employment discrimination compliance programs, Lauren Edelman, a law professor from the University of California, Berkeley, shows that organizations are caught in a dilemma, as they must appear to care about the law while also keeping costs at a minimum. Because the law is often unclear about what exactly it requires, organizations can overcome the dilemma simply by creating compliance management processes and "symbolic structures" such as special affirmative action officers and anti-discrimination codes. These then "serve as visible efforts to comply with law" without effectively achieving the substantive goals of the law, such as reducing employment discrimination.[41]

Thus, addressing compliance and ethics can become mere optics of serving the vague letter of the law rather than its original spirit. When that happens, implementing a compliance program in an organization becomes a hollow exercise. As Hui Chen, a compliance consultant and former compliance expert at the DOJ, and Eugene Soltes, a Harvard Business School professor, have argued, all too often compliance becomes just another burden, "a series of box-checking routines and mindless training exercises" that have nothing to do with the real work in the organization.[42]

At best, these programs are able to help prevent some unethical and illegal conduct. But even in the most positive studies, we find hesitation. Even when corporate compliance management systems do improve corporate behavior, it seems their effects are often quite limited or temporary.

The law, most notably the Federal Sentencing Guidelines, has incentivized companies to adopt systems whose effectiveness is backed by very little evidence. It is clear that compliance and ethics programs alone are not enough and that they only work under particular conditions. There must be independent oversight, corporate leadership must be committed to compliance and ethics, and the organizational climate and culture must be ethical.[43] Just let that sink in. The chief reason to have compliance and ethics programs is because some or all of these conditions are missing. This brings us to a startling conclusion: compliance and ethics programs only really work exactly where they are not really needed.

West Point graduate John Kopchinski had to lose first to win the jackpot later.[44] He lost his cushy $125,000 per year job at Pfizer, the American pharmaceutical behemoth. For years afterward, he was forced to live off the funds he had reserved for his retirement, which he depleted quickly. But after six years, he finally struck gold. He won a massive $51.5 million by being a whistleblower and telling on his former employer.

Kopchinski had been a long-time Pfizer employee, joining the company directly after serving in the military as a platoon leader during the Gulf War. His job as a sales rep was to ensure that doctors would prescribe Pfizer drugs—the more, the better. One such drug was Bextra, a nonsteroidal anti-inflammatory approved in the early 2000s for arthritis and menstrual pain.

Kopchinski was pushed to get doctors to prescribe Bextra not just for its approved use but also for pain more generally. He would, for instance, get a fifty-dollar bonus each time he got a doctor to make Bextra part of a patient's standard pain relief plan before and after surgery. The FDA had never approved such general usage because Bextra was also known to have cardiovascular risks. Yet Pfizer sales reps were pushed hard to get doctors to prescribe higher doses—eight times higher than the approved standard of ten milligrams daily.

Pfizer provided its reps with scripts to help them convince doctors to prescribe Bextra, and it set high sales targets that reps could only meet by pushing the drug beyond its approved usage and dosage. It also created strong social pressure among the sales reps. As Kopchinski recalls: "If you don't aggressively sell your products . . . you're labeled a non-team player."[45]

Kopchinski at first tried to alert his superiors that he was worried about these practices, but to no avail. He felt that "the ethical line kept moving."[46] At some point, he had finally had enough. "You have to live with yourself when you look at yourself in the mirror." As he explained in another interview: "In the Army I was expected to protect people at all costs. At Pfizer I was expected to increase profits at all costs, even when sales meant endangering lives."[47]

Kopchinski decided to file a whistleblower complaint. To do so, he started what is referred to as a qui tam suit under the US False Claims Act. This act, also known as Lincoln's Law, was adopted during the Civil War to fight fraudulent companies selling low-quality war materials for the troops, like wool, gunpowder, and horses. To ensure that the law would actually catch such fraudsters, it regulated that whistleblowers would get 50 percent of the amount recovered by the government.[48] This was later lowered to between 15 and 25 percent.[49] Nearly 150 years later, this same law made Kopchinski a multimillionaire as he received his due percentage (having to share with five other whistleblowers) from the overall $2.3 billion settlement Pfizer entered into in order to end civil and criminal suits it faced for its Bextra marketing campaign.

Whistle-blower provisions are an important strategy to address organizational misconduct and rule breaking. In a sense, such provisions enlist people in organizations to perform a vital regulatory role, namely, to detect illegal behavior from within the organization. Whistleblowers can solve two key problems in the legal regulation of organizational wrongdoing. First, they help to get information from inside the organization that outside inspectors simply cannot get. Second, such whistleblowers add inspection capacity to government authorities who often do not have the means or staff to carry out necessary inspections. As a financial regulator explained to Henry Pontell, a professor of criminology at the John Jay College of Criminal Justice, and his colleagues, "There aren't enough [law enforcement] employees and investigators in the world to ferret out every single person who was involved, and even if you could ferret them out, you can't wait the three years it takes."[50]

The questions are whether whistleblower programs detect and reduce illegal behavior. When whistleblowers come forward, does this reduce illegal behavior in their own and other organizations?

The downside is that whistleblowers who come forward do so at great costs and great risk. Sure, a range of laws nowadays protects whistleblowers by making retaliation a criminal offense. Yet there is clear evidence that, despite the protections, many whistleblowers get demoted, fired, or "quit under duress."[51] Consider, for instance, how a highly trained and skilled nuclear physicist who blew the whistle was subsequently moved to a broom closet, then lost his computer, and finally was put to work in the mailroom.[52] Another particularly sinister approach employers use against whistleblowers is forcing them to undergo "psychiatric fitness-for-duty examinations."[53] And once whistleblowers are fired or forced to resign, they are labeled as troublemakers to future employers.[54] Meanwhile, whistleblowers face tremendous financial costs, including loss of income and having to pay insurmountable legal fees.[55] The latter is likely if their employer sues them, as happens in about one-fourth of all cases.[56] And then there are the personal costs of stress that often result in divorce and substance abuse or both.[57]

Whistleblowing is not for the faint-hearted. For every Kopchinski, there are thousands or maybe tens or even hundreds of thousands who never see justice, let alone compensation for their costs. Yet there are many reasons why people step up. Some whistleblowers may simply speak out because they want to avoid prosecution for the behavior at work they had been involved in. Some do so because they have just been fired or fear this is about to happen.[58] Other whistleblowing cases have more altruistic and moral purposes. Some people simply want to speak out, to *do the right thing*.[59]

Whistleblowing does not automatically mean that the illegal or damaging behavior being called out will stop in an organization, let alone in other organizations in the future. Before Kopchinski reported on the illegal marketing of Bextra, another whistleblower had already filed a qui tam suit against a Pfizer subsidiary for similar illegal practices regarding another drug, Neurontin.[60] And both suits did not prevent an even larger case against Pfizer competitor GlaxoSmithKline that ended in a $3 billion settlement and a $250 million reward for the whistleblowers. As a whistleblower who won a $22 million reward for informing the SEC about accounting violations at Monsanto, the major chemicals and agricultural firm, explained to the *New York Times*, winning these whistleblower rewards does not mean that things will actually change. As he explained: "The company got fined and some money changed hands, but that's not the answer. Management not being held accountable, that still bothers me. I went into this to get that fixed, and that didn't get fixed."[61]

Internal organizational rules and structures can stifle whistleblowers before they can be heard. One study assessed the effect of the whistleblower protections in the Sarbanes-Oxley Act on preventing corporate misconduct. It concluded that whistleblowers did not significantly help uncover the massive corporate fraud that resulted in the 2008 financial crisis and Great Recession.[62] Because of internal codes of ethics procedures, employees are strongly encouraged to report the misconduct to their supervisors, whose positions give them immense power to "block and filter the reports."[63] Relatedly, a series of studies on which conditions empower whistleblowers to get their organizations to take true remedial action found that whistleblowing will fail when a weak whistleblower makes a complaint with a weak complaint manager about a powerful wrongdoer, and when there is insufficient internal support for compliance and external oversight.[64]

Just as with compliance management systems, we see that there are formidable obstacles to effective whistleblowing, and that whistleblowing works best where we need it the least. Namely, it works when non-anonymous higher-level employees report on misconduct of their subordinates (rather than the reverse), when there is sufficient organizational support to take action, and if there is external oversight to ensure that problems are addressed effectively. Yet the worst cases, those where we need whistleblowers the most, will often involve misconduct by higher-level employees, will occur when there is limited internal support for taking action (and maybe even outright resistance), and when there is an absence of effective external oversight.

Altogether, compliance management systems and whistleblower protections do not really offer much protection. They can work under certain conditions, but all too often those conditions are not present. In all of this, there is a massive elephant in the room. A consistent conclusion in studies about compliance management and whistleblower protection is that such systems only work when there is commitment inside the organization to comply with the law.[65] And this is not just a matter of having the right leaders, ethical leaders. It is about the structures, values, and practices of the organization as a whole. It is about its organizational culture. As one study so clearly summarizes it, "Culture can indeed 'eat systems for breakfast.'"[66]

In sum, all roads lead to organizational culture. We learn about culture in news stories following every major corporate scandal. Boeing's "culture of arrogance" supposedly led to the two crashes of its 737 Max, killing 346 people.[67] A "culture of silence" at Penn State reportedly allowed Jerry Sandusky to sexually abuse ten boys over a span of thirteen years while dozens of people at the university knew about his crimes.[68] A "culture of fear" is thought to have led Japan's steel giant Kobe to illegally fabricate data about the composition of its steel, aluminum, and copper, allegedly enabling it to sell lower-quality products to leading car manufacturers, including Toyota, Nissan, and Honda.[69]

## TOXIC ORGANIZATIONAL CULTURE

In the late 1950s, cockfights were immensely popular on the beautiful island of Bali in Indonesia. The government had tried to end the rooster fights by making them illegal, but they continued nevertheless. Most people would assume that these fights were all about gambling, because spectators did bet on which bird would win the fight. But there was much more behind these fights.

Clifford Geertz, an anthropologist from the Princeton Institute for Advanced Study, set out to study the cockfights by becoming deeply embedded in a Balinese community. As Geertz writes about his initial reception in the village: "We were intruders, professional ones, and the villagers dealt with us as Balinese seem always to deal with people not part of their life who yet press themselves upon them: as though we were not there. For them, and to a degree for ourselves, we were nonpersons, specters, invisible men."[70]

In one instance, Geertz and his wife joined a few hundred other people to watch an organized cockfight in the village's main square. A match had just started when suddenly people started to shout "Pulisi! Pulisi!" As cops entered the square with their weapons drawn, people scattered. Geertz describes what happened next: "People raced down the road, disappeared head first over walls, scrambled under platforms, folded themselves behind wicker screens, scuttled up coconut trees. Cocks armed with steel spurs sharp enough to cut off a finger or run a hole through a foot were running wildly around. Everything was dust and panic."[71]

Geertz and his wife decided to get out as quickly as possible, and they ended up following a complete stranger into his house and sitting down for tea, acting as if that was what they had been doing all along when the police came inside to question them. After this escapade, the villagers no longer saw the Geertzes as strangers. Once people learned that they had fled the police like the rest of the community, that they had shown their solidarity, the whole village opened up to them.

Through his prolonged fieldwork in the village, meticulously recording details about fifty-seven fights, Geertz learned that what was at stake was not so much money as status. In the main fights, those where the pillars of the community matched their roosters, prestige was central. Almost all of such fights were between different kin groups, and people would bet with their own kin group, or, if they were not part of the match, an allied kin group. And when there were roosters from another village, they all bet against them. Based on his study of these main fights, Geertz concluded that they helped make up the fabric of the community, binding community members into "a symbolic structure in which, over and over again, the reality of their inner affiliation can be intelligibly felt."[72]

Geertz fundamentally altered how we understand and study culture. Through his work in Bali he came to see culture as a form of shared interpretation in a particular community. Rather than using preconceived notions of culture, Geertz showed that culture is deeply embedded in a community's own rituals, hierarchies, and values and that a culture consists of the shared understanding a community has of the world around them.[73]

Geertz's work teaches us that a culture is not something we can grasp easily from the outside. It requires an in-depth local understanding of how a community develops shared meanings that come to shape its common values and practices. So, if we want to understand an organizational culture, and analyze what cultural elements breed illegal behavior, we have to try to grasp how people in the organization develop and transmit shared understandings.

To understand an organizational culture and how it can come to sustain rule breaking and damaging behavior, we must analyze the rituals, symbols, practices, and values of an organization. Edgar Schein, who taught at the MIT Sloan School of Management, has shown that to do so we must look at three levels.[74] The first consists of what he calls "artifacts." These are the tangible aspects of an organization's culture consisting both of the "visible and feelable structures and processes" as well as of "observed behavior." Artifacts are at the surface of an organization's culture; they are how the organization manifests its culture. They are the visible products of an organization that may include its physical environment and architecture, its technology, its creations, its style, and its stories and myths. Moreover, artifacts also include the published documents that cover the values, operations, rituals, and organizational charts.

The second level includes what Schein calls *the espoused beliefs and values*, which encompass the shared ideals, goals, values, and aspirations among individuals within an organization. These can come in the form of shared ideologies and also rationalizations for what the organization does. These espoused beliefs and values are deeper in the organization and cannot be directly observed; they must be learned by talking with organizational members.

The third level of an organizational culture is what Schein calls the *basic underlying assumptions*. These are most deeply embedded in the organization and operate unconsciously through organization members. They concern taken-for-granted beliefs and values that can "determine behavior perception, thought and feeling." It is this last level, where the deeper understanding that is implicit and tacitly acknowledged by everyone in an organization, that is hardest to grasp yet is most vital in shaping the way systems and values impact behavior. This is what Clifford Geertz, based on his study of the Balinese cock fights, called the *deep game.*

Capturing an organization's culture requires a complex form of research. It requires doing an in-depth case study that includes the structures, values, and practices of an organization. And at each of these levels, we have to assess what elements come to sustain misconduct and illegal behavior. In other words, in doing a cultural diagnosis, we must look for toxic elements. Ideally, we should do a *forensic ethnography*, in which we conduct an anthropological analysis of the culture in organizations that have been found to have structural rule breaking and damaging behavior. We need to do an autopsy of the organization and assess the structures, values, and practices that were at play in the organization's structural deviance and misconduct.

Ideally, we would hire researchers like Geertz to do a prolonged ethnography in the organizations and conduct participant observation of the structures, values, and practices. For the most part, this is practically impossible, as organizations are too closed-off and also too large to capture their culture in this manner. Fortunately, we can still get a good picture about what is wrong in an organizational culture through publicly available documentation of major scandals. Investigative journalism and court records can shed light on how structures, values, and practices sustain wrongdoing.

On April 20, 2010, an explosion and fire at a Deepwater Horizon drilling rig resulted in a massive crude oil leak in the Gulf of Mexico.[75] On that day, BP, the British oil company that operated the rig, became responsible for the largest oil spill in US history.[76] The spill caused tremendous economic, ecological, and health effects around the Gulf Coast, and eleven employees died in the explosion.

This was not the first time BP operations had caused a major disaster in the US. Five years earlier, an explosion at a BP refinery in Texas City had killed 15 people and injured 170 more. And even after this major explosion in 2005, BP's major safety problems had continued. In the three years following the explosion, and after BP paid $20 million in fines to OSHA and was forced to do a $1 billion upgrade to its facilities, four more people were killed at the refinery and two others were killed at another BP refinery in Washington State. And in March 2006, a leaking BP pipeline led to the largest spill ever on Alaska's North Slope: 267,000 gallons of crude oil spilled on the freezing tundra, remaining undetected for five days.

The issues at BP were not just the product of individual decisions but were also part of broader patterns in the company. These problems were endemic to the culture at BP. Indeed, William Reilly, cochair of the presidential investigation commission on the Gulf of Mexico oil disaster, concluded that BP had been operating under a "culture of complacency."[77]

Of course, BP is not alone. In 2014, American researchers started to suspect that German carmaker Volkswagen (VW) was using a cheating device that would lower its vehicles' emissions specifically during laboratory testing.[78] The device made the vehicle appear cleaner during lab testing, while the nitrogen oxide (NOx) emissions under actual driving conditions would be about forty times higher. Investigations uncovered that VW had installed this cheat device in over eleven million vehicles.

At Volkswagen, this type of illegal behavior was nothing new. The company had used defeat devices all the way back to 1973, when it was first caught and ordered to pay a $120,000 fine to the EPA. Dating back to 1999, the company had been installing cheating devices in its Audi engines that would reduce pollution when it recognized the car was being tested. Later, in 2005, VW had to pay a $1.1 million fine to the EPA for emissions cheating in Golfs, Jettas, and New Beetles.

After a West Virginia University research report discovered the discrepancy between laboratory and real driving emissions, and California regulators later confirmed this, VW reacted by stalling the investigations, questioning the investigative methods, and even modifying the cheat device to make it still more effective. Finally, under pressure from the California Air Resource Board (CARB), which threatened to block VW from selling cars in California in 2016, the company admitted its cheating.

Between 2009 and 2016, Wells Fargo had fraudulently opened 3.5 million accounts without authorization from their customers.[79] Moreover, the bank had enrolled 528,000 customers for online bill payment services without their authorization. Recent evaluations suggest that the fraudulent practices had been occurring for about fifteen years.[80] However, the offenses had for a long time been treated as individual offenses of local bank employees, who, if found to have created unauthorized or fake accounts, would simply be fired. Yet these sales practices had become endemic in the bank, occurring across its local branches and even in its San Francisco headquarters. As early as 2002, it was discovered that a whole Colorado branch had been opening unauthorized and fake accounts simply to reach sales targets. And all of this was well-known inside the bank.

When the media broke the scandal in 2016, Wells Fargo blamed and fired 5,300 local employees for being involved in the practices. However, it soon became clear that these were not simply the actions of bad individuals in a particular locale but rather the result of corporate incentives within the firm, pushing employees to continually increase their sales and sell customers as many products as possible. In a 2017 report of the Independent Directors of the Board of Wells Fargo, the bank itself admitted that what happened was an organizational problem, not just an individual one.

These three companies—BP, VW, and Wells Fargo—caused massive damages, driven by something amiss in their organizational cultures. To understand the issues with their corporate cultures, we can read the research commission reports, listen to the public hearings in Congress and

access the court records, and dive into book-length exposés by investigative journalists and newspaper articles with firsthand accounts from in-
siders. Using these records, we find seven elements that produced a toxic
cocktail that sustained the damaging and illegal behavior over the years.

1. *Just get it done.*

All three companies adopted a core value to *just get it done, no
matter what the costs.* The three companies were once underdogs
with big dreams. When John Browne took over BP in 1995, he
wanted the company to close its gap with the largest petroleum
giants and become one of the most successful oil companies
in the world. When Ferdinand Piëch, grandson of Ferdinand
Porsche who had designed the original Beetle for Hitler, took
over as CEO of Volkswagen in 1993, he declared that the German carmaker would become the largest in the world. And when
Richard Kovacevich became CEO of Wells Fargo, he wanted to
guide the bank to the top by outselling all competitors.

The problem was that all three companies adopted highly
risky and unfeasible ways to pursue their goals. BP laid off
many engineers and cut investments necessary for safety and
maintenance, while also pursuing high-risk offshore oil exploration that needed the exact engineers it was laying off. VW
sought to compete in the US market, and to do so it bet on
so-called clean diesel and hoped that it could produce the vehicles at a reasonable price. But engineers had simply been unable
to deliver. Wells Fargo set an unprecedented sales target of eight
products (like bank accounts, savings accounts, credit cards, or
insurance) per client, which was a rate more than four times
that of other banks. Wells Fargo employees found to be lag-
ging risked demotion or dismissal. As one recalled: "We were
constantly told we would end up working for McDonald's if we
did not make the sales quotas."[81] All three companies exerted
immense pressure on employees to achieve unrealistic, if not
impossible, goals.

2. *Do not speak out . . . or else.*

Employees learned that they should not provide critical feedback about the problems caused by the unrealistic strategies, goals, and pressures. An investigative report following the 2010 Deepwater Horizon spill found that BP had "a pattern of intimidating workers who raised safety or environmental concerns."[82] Employees of Wells Fargo were forced to resign after voicing critique and later found out they could not get a job elsewhere because Wells Fargo had put a red flag on their U5 document, which serves as a report card for bankers.[83] At VW, intimidation occurred at the highest levels as CEO Martin Winterkorn would mercilessly criticize at the notorious Tuesday meetings any executive who had failed to meet targets. And he would let his executives find out they had been demoted or fired by leaking this to the press.

The few times employees or lower managers did speak out, their concerns were ignored and no action was taken. At BP, for instance, in 1999, a group of seventy-seven workers at the Alaskan operations—where a major spill would occur—wrote a desperate letter to CEO John Browne trying to sway him from cuts they feared would undermine the already appalling safety conditions. Browne did not reply and instead, a month later, announced another $4 billion budget cut. In each case this further established a corporate culture in which open discussion was not possible. With such organizational secrecy, keeping silent becomes a core value and practice, and critique is difficult, useless, and even dangerous.

3. *It's okay to break the rules.*

In all three companies, employees came to understand that it was okay to break the rules. At Volkswagen, cheating on emission standards had been going on since 1973. Years of structural health and safety violations at BP became a normal part of working at the company, embedded in the strategy of cost cutting and high-risk exploration. Real change did not even come when BP's

new CEO, Tony Hayward, promised a "new BP" and announced
the company would hire one thousand engineers and improve
safety in all of BP's global operations. Hayward never took full
accountability for how BP's cost cutting had led to the major
accidents that had occurred before his tenure. At Wells Fargo,
branch managers went as far as aiding employees in their fraudulent sales practices. A former Wells Fargo employee explained:
"It's all manipulation. We are taught exactly how to sell multiple
accounts."[84] Or, as another former employee explained, "Training in questionable sales practices was required or you were to be
fired."[85] Wells Fargo did not just normalize deviance; it made it
mandatory.

4. *It's okay to hide violations.*

The companies were not transparent about their violations, and
they sometimes took action to hide them. Following the deadly
Texas refinery explosion in 2005, BP locked down the facilities for eight days in a clear attempt to control the facts on the
ground. Similarly, BP would at first not release its live video feed
from the Deepwater Horizon spill, as it was trying to hide how
much crude oil was gushing into the ocean. When Wells Fargo
CEO John Stumpf was questioned by Congress in the wake of
the fraudulent and unauthorized accounts scandal, he indicated
that these practices had only occurred in the Community Banking Division, while the *New York Times* reported that at the time
the bank had already known that similar practices had been going
on in its auto insurance division.[86]

Volkswagen was perhaps the most brazen. From the moment
Volkswagen learned of the West Virginia study comparing emissions between laboratory and road tests, it knew the writing was
on the wall. Yet it stalled environmental regulators for over a year
and claimed that the study was flawed, that subsequent tests by
regulators were wrong, and that the outside temperature affected
the results. The company even updated the software to reduce

the difference between road and laboratory emissions, and it improved the software so it could better detect whether it was in the laboratory. To install these newly improved cheating software packages, it organized a recall, telling car dealerships and owners that the cars needed servicing because of an electrical problem.

5. *It's you, not us.*

Once the scandals became widely known by the public, all three companies tried to deflect blame toward lower-level employees. For Wells Fargo, it was a group of rogue bankers in branch offices. Volkswagen executives claimed they did not know about the emissions cheating software in their cars, as the new CEO, Matthias Müller, who replaced Winterkorn in the wake of the scandal exclaimed in an interview with a German newspaper: "Do you really think that a chief executive had time for the inner functioning of engine software?"[87]

BP went even further, at times blaming the specific individual employees and managers who had spoken out about the safety issues. BP also tried to deflect blame onto subcontractors. With the Deepwater Horizon disaster, BP tried to hide behind its ownership structure, claiming that their subcontractor Transocean owned the rig, even though Transocean operated under direct BP instructions with regard to drilling and safety. Such blame shifting shows that the company itself did not want to take responsibility and would not protect its own. Above all, the company made it clear that it cared about protecting itself and its profits, not ensuring that this sort of accident would not happen again.

6. *There is no harm.*

Even after they had been caught, the companies tried to deny that there had been damages or harm—a classic form of neutralization. Volkswagen, once it had been forced to admit responsibility for the emissions scandal, sought to prove that the damages were limited. It even tried to refute that NOx was harmful. In a statement issued in late 2016, VW said: "A reliable determination of morbidity or even fatalities for certain demographic groups based on our level of knowledge is not possible from a scientific point of view."

In the wake of the Deepwater Horizon explosion, BP publicly disputed how many barrels of crude were leaking into the gulf. At first, BP had stated that that oil was leaking at one thousand barrels a day, a relatively "modest" spill. A little later, BP raised that figure to five thousand barrels a day. Oceanographers from Florida used satellite imaging data and found that the size of the leak was actually substantially larger at thirty thousand barrels a day, meaning that the leak at that rate would surpass the Valdez spill in only two weeks. It ended up spilling nineteen times more oil into the ocean.[88]

7. *Do not believe what we say.*

None of the companies officially stated that it was okay to cut corners, that one should not speak out, that breaking rules would be tolerated or even supported, or that the company would never take responsibility. Yet employees saw a large disconnect between the company's official policies and messages about compliance and ethics, on one hand, and the everyday practices, values, and incentives they actually operated in, on the other. Employees simply learned that whatever the official line was, the actual expectation of them was different.

We can see the disconnect most clearly at Volkswagen and BP, which marketed themselves as environmentally responsible companies. BP adopted a "beyond petrol" slogan and was the first major oil company to acknowledge that climate change is related to fossil fuel emissions. Volkswagen paid for a range of TV ads with a cute grandmother bragging how clean her new diesel Beetle was, in one ad even putting her white handkerchief behind the exhaust pipe.[89]

When there is a disconnect between official and practiced values, employees lose trust in leadership. When new leaders tell them that this time it is different and that change must come, the employees are often already too jaded to change deeply ingrained values and practices. In that sense, this seventh toxic element is perhaps the most damaging since it directly opposes change.

In combination, these seven elements of toxicity formed a powerful negative culture that bred and sustained wrongdoing at VW, BP, and Wells Fargo. These seven elements activated many of the behavioral mechanisms that promote bad behavior detailed throughout this book. Unrealistic targets cause strain. Staff inability to speak openly makes it easier to break the rules without getting caught. Normalization of rule breaking sets a strong negative social norm. Hiding violations from inspectors breeds more opportunity for crime and undermines the certainty of punishment. Shifting blame to others and denying harm are classic forms of neutralization that help executives overcome their sense of shame and guilt surrounding their misconduct. And the dissonance between the tone at the top and daily ongoing misconduct pits negative descriptive social norms against positive injunctive social norms.

Every organization is at risk of developing a toxic culture. The exact aspects of the culture may differ, but they likely include many of the seven elements of toxicity. Once such a culture sets in, change is remarkably difficult, especially when trust in leadership has eroded. So the first and most important takeaway is that all organizations must become better at assessing the risk of toxicity in their culture at an early stage and address it before it fully blossoms.

In the worst cases, where a full-blown toxic culture is uncovered in the aftermath of a major scandal, our response should change. We must look beyond the individual executive and corporate leader, and beyond just changing the incentives or the compliance management system. We have to address the cultural values and practices that were at play. And that is very difficult. Each time something bad happens in an organization, we tend to want to have the person directly responsible or the highest leader in the organization fired and punished. But when we face a cultural, systemic problem, just addressing such an individual will be ineffective. It may lull us into a false comfort that the problem has been addressed, while it is in fact still there.

To address a toxic culture once it has developed, fear must be taken out of the equation. All people should feel safe to speak out and share their view of the problems inside the organization. This can only be done once the most directly responsible persons have been held accountable. Just like the truth and reconciliation processes in post-apartheid South Africa, once that is done, there should be a process that fosters transparency and honesty, and where people feel safe to share information and concerns without fear of consequences. It is only under such conditions that a full analysis can be made of the pockets of toxicity that exist in the organizational culture. Here forensic ethnography is essential to move forward. This means that organizations should be required to hire anthropologists and cultural criminologists to conduct fieldwork inside their organization to assess the deeper cultural origins of their transgressions. Unless the organization knows in full detail what structures, values, and practices had been sustaining illegal and damaging behavior, it cannot address them.

Once an organization has conducted such a postmortem of its toxic culture, the hard work begins. Management science has developed some ideas, but its focus has been on how to create cultures that foster productivity and cooperation, not how to alter cultures that foster illegal behavior and wrongdoing.[90] What we do know is that change starts with a big shock, where new leaders try to unfreeze the cultural patterns that have deeply set in. New leaders can use a scandal as a new awakening moment.[91] Here the most difficult opposition comes in cultures where employees have seen and heard it all before, where they have not witnessed any true follow-through or real changes following grandiose speeches by new executives. So new leaders in these cases must address all issues found from the forensic ethnography to show that this is not just words, that this time they will address the specific, deeper underlying causes.

Of course they should not just change the tone at the top but also the "smell at the bottom," as a major accountancy firm in the Netherlands calls it. This means setting different targets, alleviating pressure, responding to complaints and protecting complainants, taking full responsibility for structural issues, responding directly to violations, being honest and open about such violations, and showing that they mean it, day in and day out.[92]

# CHAPTER 10

# Behavioral Jurisprudence

There's no magic bullet. There's no magic vaccine or therapy. It's just behaviors." Deborah Birx, who was charged with coordinating the US response to the COVID-19 coronavirus pandemic, stated on April 1, 2020, just weeks into the country's fight against the pandemic.[1] And she was right, of course. People needed to wash their hands more frequently, wear a mask, keep a safe distance from each other, quarantine themselves if they had symptoms, and stay at home when ordered to do so. Mitigating the pandemic meant that governments worldwide had to fundamentally alter human conduct.

Early in the twentieth century, the world experienced an influenza pandemic caused by the H1N1 virus, better known as the Spanish flu, which killed millions, and it faced similar challenges when countries tried to get people to change their behavior. In the immediate aftermath of that earlier pandemic, an editorial in *Science* summarized how hard changing behavior had been: "It does not lie in human nature for a man who thinks he has only a slight cold to shut himself up in rigid isolation as a means of protecting others on the bare chance that his cold may turn out to be a really dangerous infection."[2]

Yet in late March and early April 2020, something remarkable happened. Governments in the US and Europe adopted strict mitigation measures that asked people to stay at home and keep a safe distance from people outside their household. And for a while it really worked quite well. People followed the rules. Through Google's location-tracking data, we can see just how much daily activities changed. In the US, in the period between March 21 and April 11, people went to retail and recreation locations 45 percent less often, 49 percent less to transit stations, and 38 percent less to workplaces. Across Northern America and Europe, the high compliance with the mitigation measures created a Bizarro World. There were unprecedented pictures of Venetian squares emptied of tourists. Stranger still, at some point the price of crude oil became negative (below zero dollars a barrel), as demand dried up completely when people stopped driving and using public transportation.

It is remarkable what governments were asking of people. The mitigation measures asked people to go against normal social behavior. People had to stay at home, children had to stay indoors, and when meeting people outside the household, they had to maintain an unnatural physical distance from each other. At no time before had so many governments adopted similar rules that required people to completely change their most basic behavior.

Obeying the social distancing directives did not come cheaply. Many people lost their income. Employment tanked, with tens of millions of layoffs in the US alone. And everyone lost freedom. Still, in the early days of the pandemic, people generally complied. The success of these early mitigation measures may have been the greatest feat of compliance in human history.

We sought to understand how the measures were shaping human conduct. In early April 2020, we studied thousands of people in multiple countries, including the US, the UK, and the Netherlands, to examine how much people were complying with the stay-at-home orders and social distancing measures, and also why. We comprehensively assessed a range of potential influences such as deterrence, the costs of compliance, support for the mitigation measures, social norms, sense of duty to obey rules, procedural justice, impulsivity, and negative emotions. Through the study, we wanted to see which parts of the behavioral code were influencing behavior.

The data we collected in early April showed that compliance with the mitigation measures was generally quite high; most people either always or almost always followed the rules.[3] Yet this massive behavioral change did not originate from a fear of punishment or a calculation of financial costs and benefits. Compliance here was more moral and social. In the Netherlands, people who were more worried about the health threats the virus posed for themselves and others were more likely to comply. In the US, people who morally supported the mitigation measures were more likely to comply, as were those who thought others were adhering to the stay-at-home orders and social distancing measures. And Israelis who felt more of a duty to obey the law generally also were more likely to adhere to COVID-19 measures.

Moreover, in all the countries we studied, compliance also very much depended on the situation people were in. People who were more able to work from their home and who could stay at a safe distance from people outside their household did so. We also found that people who had less opportunity to break the rules—for instance, because they could no longer go to their office building or workplace or because people outside their household would not let them get physically closer than restrictions allowed—were more likely to follow the rules. Finally, people's personal characteristics mattered. In the US and the Netherlands, for instance, people with lower self-control were more likely to violate the measures.

By early May 2020, when we were writing our first papers on the data, it was clear that the first wave of lockdowns was going to end but that social distancing was going to have to continue. We were wondering how authorities would be able to ensure that people would stay a safe distance away from each other. In a sense, we expected compliance was going to be like a New Year's resolution to live healthier. Unfortunately, we found that the very forces that sustained compliance in early April were eroding by May. People were less afraid of the disease as the number of cases declined. We also saw political polarization as some people openly questioned and even protested against the mitigation measures, which undermined the overwhelming support for the opportunity-based policies that had existed earlier in April. But, most importantly, with the easing of the lockdown, people became able to leave their homes again, and, with businesses and venues opening, they now had somewhere to go. And before we knew it, compliance levels declined, the virus returned, and a new round of lockdowns in the US and in Europe became necessary. Policymakers had been unable to sustain their initial behavior success.

The pandemic made the behavioral code visible. There were punishment threats, with the most severe example being the hefty €25,000 fines adopted by German authorities. There were also moral appeals. In California, Governor Gavin Newsom explained that twenty-five million people would be affected, and he appealed to people's sense of duty: "There's a social contract here, people I think recognize the need to do more to meet this situation."[4] Prime Minister Mark Rutte in the Netherlands asked people for solidarity, and he specifically addressed younger people who thought they were less at risk. Explicitly, he said: "Maybe not for yourself, but you do not live for yourself only, we are with 17 million people in this country, do this for the elderly, people with poor health, who do run a risk when you infect them."[5] In the UK, Prime Minister Boris Johnson, who had just recovered from a serious bout of COVID-19 himself, tweeted on April 4: "In this fine weather, please don't be tempted to break the regulations. I urge everyone to stay at home, protect the NHS and save lives."[6]

Authorities also turned to social norms, trying to show how normal it was to follow the rules. This was clearest in the Netherlands where Prime Minister Rutte explained: "Most of us comply with the measures, almost all do so. . . . When you see the empty streets, the empty offices, the empty highways, the empty train platforms, I think the message has landed with many people in the country, and many comply with the measures."[7]

The response to the pandemic also revealed the invisible code in the physical environment. Posters and signs reminded us of the rules: keep a safe distance, sneeze in your elbow, wash your hands, stay safe! Equally if not more important, local authorities and businesses took many opportunity-based measures to make it harder for too many people to get too close: they closed public park benches, took away hoops from basketball courts in New York City's Central Park, removed seats in restaurants, and limited the amount of customers allowed inside supermarkets.

## THE BEHAVIORAL CODE IN SIX STEPS

Compliance with COVID-19 measures shows us that the behavioral code does not operate through one singular mechanism. We must have an integrated view of how rules shape behavior. Of course, that is difficult since so many different of mechanisms are at work. But let's take a helicopter view here.

Overall, we see that the behavioral code works through two broad types of mechanisms: *motivations* and *situations*. If people are both motivated to comply and in a situation where they can comply, then they are very likely to comply. And vice versa—when people are motivated to break rules and are placed in a situation where they can make that choice, they are very likely to violate the rules.

In people's responses to COVID-19 social distancing measures, we can clearly see these two broad forces at play. In our study, we examined two motivations: (1) extrinsic motivations that shape people's behavior through positive and negative incentives, like punishments and the costs of compliance; and (2) intrinsic motivations that drive people's behavior through their own values, morals, and sense of duty. Extrinsic and intrinsic motivations also interact. If governments fail to punish individuals for rule breaking, they may be normalizing such rule breaking and creating a negative social norm. Yet if law enforcement becomes unfair and unjust, the punishments can backfire, undermine legitimacy, and erode people's sense of duty to obey the law.

Compliance with COVID-19 measures very much depended on the situation people were in. There are two types of situations here. One is the capacity people have to follow legal rules. In the case of COVID-19 compliance, this includes whether people know and understand the rules. The other sort of situation is when there is an opportunity to violate rules. For COVID-19, this meant whether people could still go to work or still meet with people outside their household.

Overall, whenever we want to address any type of unwanted or damaging conduct through law, we should use the behavioral code to diagnose what the root causes of the problem are, what motivations people have for engaging in the behavior, and what aspects of the situation matter. Then we must address each in the most effective and least intrusive manner. The insights about the behavioral code give us the knowledge required to conduct such an analysis through the following six steps:

*Step 1: What variation is there in the unwanted behavior?*
Before we do any analysis of causes, we must know what we are dealing with. For a series of homicides, are they passion killings or paid assassinations? For speeding, are we looking at people just driving 10 percent over the speed limit or 50 percent over? For industrial pollution, are we dealing with small companies with limited resources or large companies that have the expertise and capital to curb pollution? It is vital to know what variation there is in the behavior we want to address so that we can analyze and address each core type separately. Here we must also determine our unit of analysis: is the conduct just individual or are we dealing with community, organizational, or broader societal behavior? The remainder of the questions should be applied specifically to each type of the unwanted behavior.

*Step 2: How does the behavior work?*
In creating an effective approach to prevent unwanted behavior, it is vital to examine the situation before the motivation. This forces us to think of *how* they do it instead of *why*. By finding out how the wrongdoing operates, we may be able to eliminate a vital element in this process and make the behavior more difficult or even impossible. In this way, we might not even need to try to steer motivations. We saw earlier that terrorists planned to use carry-on liquids to bomb planes, so we focused on regulating the amount of liquids people could bring onto planes. This is cheap, easy, and highly effective. In the coronavirus crisis, we saw governments around the world force organizations to develop protocols that kept people

physically distanced from one another. Of course, making unwanted behavior harder may come at the cost of freedom.

*Step 3: What do people need in order to refrain from the behavior?*
This capacity approach is the flipside of the opportunity approach. The first step is to look at whether people know the rules. If they do not, we have to figure out if it is because the rules are too numerous, too technical, or just poorly disseminated. Next, we should identify whether people and organizations have sufficient technical, educational, and other skills necessary to follow the rules. Finally, we must examine whether people need help overcoming personal problems or individual concerns, such as low self-control, substance dependencies, or access to sufficient education, housing, employment, income, and opportunities. Unless people can do what the law asks of them, their motivation is irrelevant. You cannot do what you cannot do, no matter how much you wish you could.

*Step 4: Do people think the rules, rule makers, and rule enforcers are legitimate?*
It is much easier to improve behavior through law if people feel a general obligation to obey the law. People who see the system as unfair, biased, or unjust will feel less obligated to obey, and, if that is the case, we would need to address the way the law is made, implemented, and enforced in order to ensure that the public perceives it to be fair, unbiased, and just. When they do, they will follow the law even if they do not agree with it, even when others break it, even if there are no punishment threats, and even if it comes at considerable costs. They will just do it because it is the right thing to do.

*Step 5: What role do morals and social norms play?*
This step turns to other intrinsic motivations. For any successful intervention, we must know to what extent the unwanted behavior is rooted in existing morals and social norms. If the misbehavior is

largely rooted in the prevailing morals or social norms, then it is vital to avoid inadvertently focusing attention on them during interventions, campaigns, or messaging. But if the misbehavior is not grounded in existing morals and norms, then interventions should purposefully tap into these positive morals and norms to build behavioral change. In organizations or groups, we have to diagnose and address cultural norms that sustain wrongdoing, ideally long before a toxic culture has set in.

*Step 6: How do incentives and extrinsic motivations factor in?*
Finally, we must examine how the law's incentives play out in practice. For punishment and tort liability, for example, we clearly know that there is limited evidence that they create deterrence. We must assess not only what the certainty and severity of the existing sanction and liabilities are but also how people perceive them. We must ensure that their perceived certainty is sufficiently high. Moreover, we must check that sanctions and liabilities do not have unintended negative effects that undermine people's intrinsic motivations or capacity to comply with the law. For rewards and other positive incentives, similarly, we must assess how they are perceived, whether they play a positive role in improving behavior, or whether they crowd out the intrinsic motivations that are already at play.

There it is: the full behavioral code one needs to design and operate laws that can prevent and reduce wrongdoing. These specific questions enable us to generate a comprehensive accounting of law and human behavior. But knowledge alone is not enough. The scientific knowledge contained in this book has long existed, yet it has not been central in how we have designed and operated our legal system. Our legal system has much to learn from medicine, which over a century ago went through the same transformation our legal institutions require today.

In the early nineteenth century, Western medical practice was a cruel business. With little to no knowledge of the root causes of illness, doctors simply followed age-old practices. The logic behind these practices was first developed by Hippocrates in the fifth century BC and later expanded by Galen of Pergamon in the second century AD. The idea was that disease originated from an imbalance in the body, thus curing disease required restoring balance.[8] Doctors' preferred methods for rebalancing the body was to force patients to sweat, urinate, defecate, vomit, or bleed. Western physicians well into the nineteenth century prescribed laxatives, applied mustard plasters that caused blisters, and regularly bled people in attempts to cure. In fact, the name of the leading scientific medical journal today, *The Lancet*, refers directly to the instrument doctors would use to bleed their patients. Yet as the nineteenth century progressed, these age-old practices started to come under pressure. Oliver Wendell Holmes, the father of the famous US Supreme Court justice, summed it up nicely: "I firmly believe that if the whole *materia medica*, as now used, could be sunk to the bottom of the sea, it would all be better for mankind—and worse for the fishes."[9]

The world made major scientific advances in the fields of physics, chemistry, biology, and astronomy, and the emergence of the scientific method unlocked a new way of looking at disease, stimulating controlled experimentation and rigorous methods to test hypotheses. Such experimentation led James Lind in 1753 to discover that sailors could prevent scurvy by eating limes, which we would later find out was really just preventing a vitamin C deficiency. And Edward Jenner used rigorous methods in 1798 to show how people could get smallpox immunity through a vaccination with cowpox, a related virus that did not cause serious illness in humans.

Thus, views of medical practice started to change. Universities opened hospitals where they combined medical practice with science. Doctors began receiving training in scientific methods and came to view their profession as steeply rooted in scientific evidence. The combination of scientific and empirical methods led to major breakthroughs in curing and preventing disease. And today it seems impossible to separate medicine from science, just as it is unthinkable that a doctor would bleed a patient to lower a fever.

How different from medicine the field of law is in the twenty-first century! Legal training still follows an age-old logic, teaching students how they should interpret legal rules and cases and apply them to legal disputes. Scientific methods and scientific thinking are not central in the training of lawyers. Neither are empirical data nor statistical analysis. Instead, the lawyer is either trained as an advocate (as is the case in the US) who seeks to benefit their client, or as a judge (as is the case for instance in the Netherlands) who adjudicates disputes between parties based on case facts and law.

Yet law is not that different from medicine. Like medicine, law clearly serves to mitigate harm to humans. Although this is not its only function, the legal system plays a vital role to ensure that people do not suffer from violent crime, that they can breathe clean air, that they can drive safely, that they can trust that their pensions are not squandered, that they are not abused at work, and that they are not discriminated against. And just like medicine, law could also draw directly on scientific insights that have developed over the last fifty years. Yet somehow law has remained stuck in time, it seems, as it fails to make the science more central.

Of course, law and science have not remained entirely separate in all areas. There has been much empirical research in fields such as the sociology and anthropology of law, law and economics, and legal psychology. There is great work on eyewitness testimony, lineups, and judicial decision-making. Also, there has been extensive scholarship on the legal profession, the link between legal arrangements and economic growth, and what perceptions citizens have about the role law plays in their daily lives.

Yet much of the field of law, especially mainstream legal education and training, has so far remained isolated from vital social and behavioral science insights about how law shapes human behavior. Law professors teach in law schools while the criminologists, psychologists, sociologists, organizational scholars, and other social scientists teach in separate schools. There are important exceptions. Some law professors, some of whom have PhDs in social and behavioral sciences, have contributed to some of the core behavioral insights we have noted in this book, like Tom Tyler at Yale Law School, Franklin Zimring at Berkeley Law, Cass Sunstein at Harvard Law School, and Michele Alexander, who taught at Stanford Law School and the College of Law at Ohio State University.

But most law professors and the bulk of their courses are centered in law and legal analysis. Legal education and practice are all about learning how to apply legal rules to disputes and dispute resolution, to past behavior. In doing so, they pay little attention to understanding the behaviors that create the harms that cause such disputes, to understanding how the law shapes future behavior. When questions of law's impact on behavior are addressed in class, they are often deemed to be "policy questions," good for some lively debate but definitely not an important topic on exams. Just like doctors learned to look beyond bloodletting as a way to lower a fever and shifted to addressing the disease causing the fever, law practitioners must learn to address root causes and prevent misbehavior.

For a long time, the legal profession never needed to focus on the law's effect on shaping behavior and preventing harm. Lawyers and law professors were able to just focus on dispute resolution and legal analysis because that is what practice looked like, and practice was good business. Also, the internal logic of the legal field meant that empirical questions about whether law shapes behavior were hardly ever central in practice, and judges have not been very good at interpreting the science in the few instances we have seen behavioral arguments presented in court.[10] The US Supreme Court in the *Ewing* case (about the man facing a twenty-five-year sentence for stealing golf clubs) completely sidestepped all the scientific research that questioned whether the three strikes policies have a deterrent effect. In another case, Supreme Court Chief Justice John Roberts referred to social science data as "gobbledygook."[11]

But there is more at play. Our laws, the people that make them, and those who apply and enforce them are part of the larger fabric of our society and political system. There are strong moral, societal, and political forces stacked against successfully incorporating empirical insights to improve the functioning of our laws against misconduct.

In the public debate about crime and wrongdoing, people tend to focus on what the criminal or wrongdoer deserves for their acts. We saw this in Elizabeth Warren's calls for tougher punishment for corporate offenders. They deserved it, and isn't it fair that they get punished for what they did, just like street crime offenders do? Of course, we also see this in every call for getting tough on crime whenever another heinous act occurs. There is a focus on retributive justice, because people want to get even.

Certainly justice matters. If we focus singularly on ensuring that law changes behavior without addressing what's morally right and wrong, we can promote tyranny or injustice. But once our political process has figured out what the right rules are, we must ensure that they work, lest we make seemingly just laws that are in reality impotent. The problem here is that thinking exclusively about what serves justice prevents us from thinking about how to effectively prevent future injustice.

Science also faces objections from people who like certain interventions and dislike others. This is particularly true when it comes to our punishment reflex. In fact, research demonstrates that the urge to punish is hardwired in our brains. Humans not only derive neurological pleasure when we punish others, but many people have an inherent preference for punishment and a dislike for alternatives.[12] We may disagree about who needs to be punished more harshly, with progressives wanting stricter punishment for corporate offenses and conservatives wanting tougher sentences for street crimes.[13] Yet altogether, this punishment reflex will cause people to object to any science that shows it does not work the way they intuitively believe.

An important part of the problem is that people tend to equate their own preferences and their own sense of right and wrong with what they think will be effective. If you dislike capital punishment, you are not only more likely to think it does not deter crime, but you will more easily accept studies that show its failures. But if you are morally fine with the death penalty, you will likely reject those exact same scientific studies.

Science must also overcome deeply entrenched racism. Anti-Black racism is deeply ingrained in America following centuries of slavery, decades of Jim Crow apartheid, and continuing racial segregation, inequality, and abuses. Policing in the United States is rooted in slave patrols.[14] Politicians and media pundits frequently stoke fear of crime by people of color as a way to send coded, racist signals through both dog-whistles and bullhorns.[15] Such racism distorts how the science about crime and the ways to address it are discussed, received, and accepted. While some view creating better access to education, housing, and employment to be obvious, objective ways to create opportunity and reduce crime, others view them, through a racist lens, to be unfairly and unjustifiably preferential to racial minorities.

And there is also direct opposition to science. During protests against the pandemic lockdown and social distancing measures to mitigate against COVID-19, some protesters carried signs stating "Defund Science." Doubt in science has a long history. In 1615, Galileo Galilei was tried and found guilty by the Roman Inquisition for his astronomical discovery that Earth revolved around the Sun and not the other way around. There is widespread doubt in science in the cases of hot-button issues such as biological evolution and climate change, in which personal beliefs and core identities drive people to distrust and even outright attack the science, despite overwhelming empirical evidence contrary to those beliefs. Ill-informed populist politics and the barrage of attacks on science in popular media have not helped to promote trust in science and scientists.

And science itself sometimes betrays popular trust. There have been several instances where scientists fabricated data and engaged in anti-science. There have been many hyped studies that simply do not replicate or apply outside the social science laboratories. And sometimes scientists summarize their findings without sufficient nuance or make broad, sweeping claims that their data do not back up. This can undermine their neutrality, which becomes particularly problematic now that scholars are increasingly engaged in public debate and policymaking.

In light of all this, presenting the science alone is not enough to persuade. Yuval Noah Harari, the author of *Sapiens: A Brief History of Humankind*, has argued that humankind operates through two powers: the power of facts and the power of fiction. Facts matter; if one builds a house and gets the physical facts wrong, it may cave in and crush everyone inside. But fiction, or storytelling, is what binds people and allows them to form larger groups and collective identities. As such, to create convincing science, we need to tell the stories, tell the tales of the science itself and the anecdotes that provide context for these scientific discoveries.

Law is the most important system that we have to maintain our complex societies. Our laws protect our property, our safety, our health, our economy, and our natural environment. But law only works if it successfully shapes human and organizational behavior. In this book we have shown the invisible behavioral code that law must take into account in order to create effective and sustainable behavioral change. We have distilled the knowledge down to six clear steps that any legal coder must follow to address harmful and unwanted conduct. But outlining these steps and the science behind them is not enough. Our legal systems, our human intuitions, and our politics are stacked against the science.

We continue to face massive behavioral challenges. Just think of the ongoing opioid epidemic, continuing cases of sexual harassment that have emerged since the #MeToo movement, racist and brutal policing, massive financial fraud, and environmental pollution that is causing climate change. The problems humanity faces are too important to ignore the science that can help our legal system to address them more effectively. We suggest three reforms to ensure that our legal code incorporates the behavioral code.

REFORM 1: LEGAL TRAINING AND PRACTICE    Our legal system must embrace a *behavioral jurisprudence* that assesses and corrects flawed assumptions about behavior in the law. Through this, law must combine its traditional doctrinal and normative questions, questions of what the law is and should be, with empirical questions of how the law affects behavior. Instead of focusing on applying the law to singular cases, lawyers must learn to embrace policy questions and focus on how legal rules shape behavior across numerous cases.

Because of their professional placement, law professors and the lawyers they train have far more influence on what laws are adopted and how they operate than do the social and behavioral scientists who have been trained to understand how laws affect human behavior. Law schools must bring more social scientists into the fold and blend them into the core curricula, giving them the space to train lawyers to be able to combine legal and empirical analysis. Questions of whether people know the law, why they comply with laws, and why they break the law should be seen as critical legal questions, not merely social science questions. Such questions must become part and parcel of legal training, research, and practice. Rather than just open more clinics where law students get trained on how to advocate for clients and handle disputes, law schools should also open laboratories where they experiment with different types of rules and interventions. If law schools do so, and if legal practice makes behavioral change part of its business, they stand to gain enormously. And here we do not just mean intellectually and socially. According to a recent study, the market for compliance work globally was valued at $31.27 billion in 2019, and it is estimated to grow to $88 billion by 2027.[16] And if that is not enough to change law schools, future law students should demand to get behavioral training, since they will need to use it in practice.

REFORM 2: THE SCIENCE   Scientists also have a key role to play. Decades of scientific work have failed to impact our laws and make them better at changing behavior. Scientists must transform how they do law and behavioral science research and how they communicate about their findings.

They must ensure that studies about how people respond to the law connect with the real-life problems our societies face. It is not enough for scientists to test theoretical ideas and participate in lofty debates with other scholars. It is not enough to focus research on one potential cause for misconduct without integrating findings across disciplinary and theoretical silos. It is not enough for scientists to conduct lab experiments that have little to no relation to actual behavior in the real world. It is not enough to show that an intervention or program works in one study, without replicating and expanding these findings in the same and other contexts. And it is not enough to focus studies only on simple interventions that do not address the truly complex behaviors that produce the biggest harms to our society.

Social and behavioral scientists must focus on understanding the role law can play in influencing the most important behavioral problems, regardless of whether such studies have the right theoretical contribution or the surest chance of showing an immediate, publishable result. This means that scientists should look more at societal problems as their starting point for research and, if possible, also collaborate more with people who deal with such problems in their everyday lives to co-design and co-conduct impactful studies.

Scientists must also communicate better about their work to ensure that it leaves the academic community and has a fighting chance at shaping legal practice. To have a successful career in academia, scientists are incentivized to publish their work almost exclusively in peer-reviewed journals. But that means that their articles are replete with the theoretical and statistical jargon that they, uniquely, were trained in. Practitioners, by and large, simply do not have the expertise or time to read such articles, or even access to them behind journals' paywalls. This means that scientists must become bilingual; they must relearn to communicate in clear, plain language and translate their main findings to a broader audience that doesn't speak statistical "gobbledygook." They should write shorter pieces—for instance, commentary in newspapers or blog posts—that summarize what they did, what they found, why we should care, and what the limitations are in such a way that practitioners can get a taste for their work and get in touch to begin real-world applications and replications. Scientists have to take the extra step to find a way to package their science in a story that compels people to read, learn, and connect.

Scientists should also become more proactive. They must leave the ivory tower and engage in public debate to correct the flawed assumptions about law and behavior that are frequently touted. Scientists keep too much of what they do to themselves while the major policy decisions that affect law and the way it addresses behavior are discussed by politicians and media pundits with hardly any knowledge of the science, often on the basis of flawed intuition. Scientists have a duty to correct the public discourse.

In all of this, scientists must be honest. When studies fail to find an effect or a well-designed and promising intervention yields small effects, journal editors and reviewers must be willing to acknowledge that such null effects can be meaningful. They have a duty to open space in their prestigious journals to publicize such findings, if not to reward the risks researchers are taking by conducting impactful work, then at the very least to save other researchers their time and limited funding. Simultaneously, nothing hurts science more than cases of fraud, unethical conduct, or plagiarism. But dishonesty also lies in presenting solid findings in a way that does not do them justice and that in the heat of the fifteen minutes of media fame get presented too far out of context or without sufficiently portraying their complexity. For scientists to be heard, they need to be able to speak a simple language that maintains the nuance of the original research.

REFORM 3: OURSELVES    In the end, law and behavior is about all of us. We all have a stake in ensuring that our laws work better to keep us safe. We are all subject to these laws, all burdened by laws that limit freedom or induce costs without delivering a safer society. We all have a role to play in ensuring that law is always getting better at improving human conduct. But to do so, we must also look at ourselves and not just wait for legal practitioners, policymakers, and scientists to make these reforms for us.

As members of our shared community that is bound together by the fabric of law, we have to recognize that we have an immense collective influence on our laws. Living in democracies, we can use our vote and our contact with our elected politicians to shape the policies that determine the content and functioning of our laws. By learning about the behavioral code, we can come to distinguish ideas that might be effective in tackling big social behavioral problems from those that would clearly be ineffective. We have to demand policies that work, not just ones that sound good and feed our intuitions.

This advice, of course, is remarkably difficult to follow. As we saw, just learning the science is but a first step. We filter the science through our own intuitions, preferences, and biases. Try and think back to all the core insights we have learned in this book. Which did you find easy to accept? And which did you resist? Did you resist because you did not find the information convincing, because the study's methods or its data did not seem solid? Or did you just doubt some of the findings without being able to express why? For instance, did you have trouble accepting that there is no evidence that capital punishment and the death penalty deter crime? What about the finding that rehabilitation programs can work? Or that fairer policing can help to reduce crime? Think back in earnest and reread passages you had doubt about. In instances where you cannot attribute your doubt to the study's methodology or the quality of the data, consider whether you would actually be willing to accept such findings even if they were true. Only through such reflection can we truly come to terms with the fact that we—every single one of us— filter scientific insights. Once we recognize this and confront ourselves, maybe we can also come to accept findings that we do not like when we first read them.

The next step is to observe ourselves in our daily lives and daily discussions. Where do we continue to support ways to shape behavior that lack scientific evidence? Once we set aside this book, we will too easily forget what it means come election time or even when watch or read the daily news. But we should apply these insights to every single instance where someone notes a behavioral problem and proposes a solution to it. With every debate about police violence, every proposal about sexual harassment, every news article about illegal doping in sports, and every major tort case against a big company we hear about, we should be vigilant and ask the core behavioral questions: What situations and motivations promoted the behavior? How will the proposed policy influence them? Once we train ourselves to do so, both for the big policies in our countries but also for the smaller issues we may face at work or at home, we can truly come to separate the wheat from the chaff, the effective approaches from the useless ones.

Armed with the scientific knowledge, we can all serve as ambassadors of the behavioral code, initiating critical discussions about laws, rules, and human behavior. We can all act as fact-checkers, correcting statements that we now know are blatantly false or lack empirical evidence. We can all become our own critical observers, improving the ways we try to change misbehavior in our own lives. And we can all act as informed citizens, supporting policies grounded in science—not just intuition—that will actually keep us safe.

# Acknowledgments

We are thankful for Andrew Stuart, our agent, who understood what we hoped to do, and to our editor, Joanna Green, whose sharp and questioning eye helped us find our voice. Also, a great thanks to the whole production and marketing team at Beacon, who have been phenomenal. We will be forever grateful as well to Katherine Flynn and Laura Chasen for their initial guiding touches.

We would also like to thank the scholars who reviewed earlier drafts: Robert Cialdini, Tom Tyler, Dan Nagin, Greg Pogarsky, Yuval Feldman, Cortney Simons, Erich Kirchler, Alex Piquero, Francis Cullen, Hui Chen, Cary Coglianese, Travis Pratt, Lance Hannon, and David Harding.

Benjamin's research for this book was in part made possible through a generous grant from the European Research Council (ERC 2018-COG HomoJuridicus-817680).

Benjamin wishes to thank Adam for the fabulous collaboration and inspiration, and for sharing all the ups and downs of this project as a colleague and friend. I also thank all my colleagues and students at the University of Amsterdam and the University of California, Irvine, who over the years have provided invaluable input in the development of this project. Here especially, I wish to thank Mario Barnes, Bryant Garth, Kaaryn Gustafson, Alex Camacho, Sameer Ashar, Shauhin Talesh, Katie Porter, Jonathan Glater, Chris Reinders Folmer, and Rob Schwitters, who have patiently given feedback and answered the many questions I kept asking them. I also want to thank all colleagues at the Centre for Law and Behavior for providing feedback and joining me on this quest to correct behavioral assumptions in the law. Also, a special thanks to Beth Cauffman for guiding me into psychology and teaching me to think in process, and of course for introducing Adam to me. I also want to thank all my friends who have had to listen to endless new great ideas for the book; a special thanks to Eric, Victor, Mitran, Anouk, and Annemieke. I also want to thank my parents, Rene and Giny, for how they brought me up always to be curious and travel the world. I also want to thank Max and Mare for being the perfect living testimonies that I have not mastered the behavioral code but enjoy this every day. And last but not least, I want to thank Janine, for sharing this journey with me.

Adam wishes to begin by thanking Benjamin van Rooij, whose thirst for knowledge and bottomless energy continue to amaze me. I am also thankful for his patience with my affinity for both spirited debates and the "Delete" key. I would not be an academic without Beth Cauffman, my forever mentor whose wise counsel and quick wit have shaped my career immeasurably. At the root of it all are Deborah Phillips, Beth Meloy, Chandan Vaidya, Sarah Vidal, and Jennifer Woolard of Georgetown University, who opened every possible door for a young research assistant. I want to thank Tom Tyler, Ellen Cohn, Tracey Meares, Ben Bradford, Jonathan Jackson, and Rick Trinkner for their inspirational research, and Laurence Steinberg, Paul Frick, and Alex Piquero for their patient guidance through the years. I am lucky to teach at Arizona State University, where my colleagues have built a welcoming and vibrant community that continues to raise the bar for scholarship and impact. I may lead the Youth Justice Laboratory, but my students and collaborators teach me more every day. Finally, words cannot express my gratitude for my family. I am immensely grateful for a lifetime of support. Reaghan and the girls may never know just how much their perspective on what truly matters grounds me.

# Notes

CHAPTER 1: A TALE OF TWO CODES
1. For all examples cited above, as well as for the full text of the California Vehicle Code, see California Legislative Information 2020.
2. Levine and Reinarman 2004; Rorabaugh 1996; Whitebread 2000.
3. Ryan 1998.
4. Humphreys 2018.
5. Violation Tracker 2020.
6. OSHA 2020.
7. With 13 deaths per day, the total number of work-related deaths is 4,745 each year. See OSHA 2020. Iraq casualties have been 4,497 (3,529 in combat). See Griffiths 2020.
8. Baldwin and Houry 2015.
9. Williams and Wells 2004. See also Glassbrenner, Carra, and Nichols 2004; Solomon, Compton, and Preusser 2004.
10. Kidd, McCartt, and Oesch 2014.
11. Kidd, McCartt, and Oesch 2014.
12. NHTSA 2020.
13. Economics: see, for example, Kahneman and Tversky 1979; Tversky and Kahneman 1974; Thaler 2015. Ethics: Bazerman and Tenbrunsel 2012.

CHAPTER 2: THE PUNISHMENT DELUSION
1. "The Young Family," *Supernanny USA*, season 2, episode 13. Full episode on YouTube: https://www.youtube.com/watch?v=6VJIBKEczzk.
2. Warren 2016a.
3. Warren 2016c.
4. Carter 2016.
5. Warren 2016b.
6. Yates 2015.
7. Smith 2015.
8. Nixon 1973.

9. Reagan 1984.
10. Bush 1989.
11. Clinton 1993
12. Johnson 2014.
13. NOS Nieuws 2019; Kasper 2019.
14. Barry and Selsoe Sorensen 2018; Bendixen 2018.
15. Beccaria 2016: 9.
16. Beccaria 2016: 11.
17. Beccaria 2016: 33.
18. Fahmy et al. 2020.
19. APA n.d.
20. This section draws most directly in its analysis and sources from Nagin, Cullen, and Jonson 2009; Cullen, Jonson, and Nagin 2011.
21. Langan and Levin 2002.
22. Nieuwbeerta, Nagin, and Blokland 2009.
23. Cullen and Minchin 2000.
24. Gendreau et al. 2000.
25. Jonson 2010.
26. Cullen, Jonson, and Nagin 2011.
27. Taibbi 2013.
28. Hannaford 2016.
29. Beccaria 2016: 33.
30. Nagin 2013.
31. Travis, Western, and Redburn 2014: 149.
32. Zimring, Hawkins, and Kamin 2001.
33. Zimring and Kamin 2001: 607.
34. Males and Macallair 1999: 67.
35. Worrall 2004.
36. Kovandzic, Sloan III, and Vieraitis 2004.
37. Marvell and Moody 2001: 106.
38. Fisman 2008.
39. Shepherd 2002: 190.
40. Helland and Tabarrok 2007: 330.
41. Ehrlich 1975.
42. *Furman v. Georgia*, 408 U.S. 238 (1972).
43. Gregg v. Georgia, Proffitt v. Florida, Jurek v. Texas, Woodson v. North Carolina, and Roberts v. Louisiana, 428 U.S. 153 (1976).
44. Fagan 2014.
45. Fagan 2006.
46. Fagan 2006: 258.
47. The study: Mocan and Gittings 2003. Fagan 2006, 258n18 showed that it was cited in Gene Koretz, "Equality? Not on Death Row," *Business Week*, June 30, 2003, 28; Jeff Jacoby, "Execution Saves Innocents," *Boston Globe*, Sept. 28, 2003; Kieran Nicholson, "Study: Race, Gender of Governors Affect

Death-Row Decisions," *Denver Post*, Dec. 19, 2002; Richard Morin, "Lame Ducks and the Death Penalty," *Washington Post*, Jan. 20, 2002; Richard Morin, "Murderous Pardons?," *Washington Post*, Dec. 15, 2002.

48. Fagan 2006.
49. Fagan 2006. Shepherd's study: Shepherd 2004.
50. Fagan 2006.
51. For an overview, see Fagan 2006. Donohue and Wolfers reanalyzed much of the data published in new deterrence studies and published their findings in a *Stanford Law Review* paper not so subtly titled "The Uses and Abuses of Empirical Evidence in the Death Penalty Debate." They wrote, "We find that the existing evidence for deterrence is surprisingly fragile, and even small changes in specifications yield dramatically different results." Their study found numerous coding errors in the oft-cited studies, not to mention inappropriate study designs. Donohue and Wolfers conclude, "At the end of the day, the fact that all these analyses over such a long period of time using plausible data and models generate so little evidence of deterrence suggests that any effect is likely to be small, and that one should be highly dubious about 'new' claims that strong evidence of deterrence exists." Donohue and Wolfer 2006: 2. Tomislav Kovandzic and his colleagues also reviewed the new deterrence literature and came to a similar conclusion: "Our results provide no empirical support for the argument that the existence or application of the death penalty deters prospective offenders from committing homicide." They stressed that "policymakers should refrain from justifying its use by claiming that it is a deterrent to homicide and should consider less costly, more effective ways of addressing crime." Kovandzic, Vieraitis, and Boots 2009: 803.
52. Fagan 2006.
53. Donohue and Wolfers 2006.
54. Cochran and Chamlin 2000; Thomson 1999; Cochran, Chamlin, and Seth 1994.
55. Cochran and Chamlin 2000.
56. Shepherd 2005.
57. Nagin 2013.
58. Elvik 2016.
59. Schell-Busey et al. 2016; Simpson et al. 2014.
60. Beccaria 2016: 11.
61. Nagin 2013.
62. Brown 1978; Chamlin 1991.
63. Chamlin 1991.
64. Nagin 2013: 201.
65. Nagin 2013.
66. Helland and Tabarrok 2007; Nagin 2013.
67. Sherman, Gartin, and Buerger 1989.
68. Weisburd and Green 1995; Weisburd et al. 2004; Sherman and Weisburd 1995; Weisburd and Mazerolle 2000; Braga et al. 1999; Braga and Weisburd 2010;

Brantingham and Brantingham 1999; Eck, Gersh, and Taylor 2000; Weisburd et al. 2004.

69. Weisburd and Green 1995; Sherman and Weisburd 1995; Braga and Weisburd 2010; Braga et al. 1999; Weisburd et al. 2004; Weisburd and Mazerolle 2000.

70. Nagin 2013: 240.

71. Goldstein 2013.

72. NYCLU 2020. See also Mason 2016.

73. The whole analysis of the Uber Greyball system here is based on Isaac 2019.

74. Henriques 2011.

75. Ruiz et al. 2016.

76. Gray 2006; Gray and Silbey 2012; Gray and Silbey 2014: 117–19.

77. Plambeck and Taylor 2016.

78. *Guardian* 2019.

79. Ross and Pritikin 2010.

80. Based on communication with Henk Elffers, a Dutch tax compliance expert, who studied this in the 1990s.

81. Thornton, Gunningham, and Kagan 2005.

82. Thornton, Gunningham, and Kagan 2005: 272.

83. Kleck et al. 2005.

84. Apel 2013: 78.

85. Pogarsky and Piquero 2003.

86. Apel 2013: 78.

87. Engel, Tillyer, and Corsaro 2013.

88. Braga, Weisburd, and Turchan 2018. Some newer studies do find relatively strong effects of the intervention on crime reductions. See, for instance, Clark-Moorman, Rydberg, and McGarrell 2019.

89. Seabrook 2009.

90. De Quervain et al. 2004: 1254; Singer et al. 2006.

91. See Das Gupta 2007: 15, Plato 1975 (section 722): 181–82. See Aristotle 1976 (section 1180a15): 337; Deut. 13 and 21; Quran, 2:66; Xunzi 2003; Feizi 2003: 29.

92. Clark, Chen, and Ditto 2015.

93. US Senate Select Committee on Intelligence 2014.

94. Cullen, Jonson, and Nagin 2011.

CHAPTER 3: OF STICKS, CARROTS, AND ELEPHANTS

1. This description is based on Mendoza 1995.

2. The story here is based on Holiday 2018 and an interview with Holiday in the *Atlantic* (Thompson 2018).

3. Thompson 2018.

4. Thompson 2018.

5. Thompson 2018.

6. Landes 1982; McEwin 1989; Devlin 1992; McEwin 1989; Cummins, Phillips, and Weiss 2001; Cohen and Dehejia 2004; Cummins, Phillips, and Weiss 2001; Sloan, Reilly, and Schenzler 1994.

7. Kochanowski and Young 1985; Zador and Lund 1986; Kochanowski and Young 1985; Heaton and Helland 2009; Loughran 2001; Derrig et al. 2002; Heaton and Helland 2008.

8. Anderson, Heaton, and Carroll 2010: 82; Engstrom 2011: 333.

9. Kachalia and Mello 2011; Mello and Kachalia 2010; Agarwal, Gupta, and Gupta 2019: 6.

10. Dewees and Trebilcock 1992.

11. "Restating the earnings of the company": Cao and Narayanamoorthy 2011; DuCharme, Malatesta, and Sefcik 2004; Kim 2015; Gillan and Panasian 2015; Boyer and Hanon 2009. "Overpaying for corporations it acquires": Lin, Officer, and Zou 2011. "Taking the companies public when they are not ready to do so": Chalmers, Dann, and Harford 2002: 609.

12. Schwartz 2014.

13. Rappaport 2017.

14. This story is based on reporting in the *New York Times* and *Guardian*. See Sharma Rani 2017 and Motlag 2016.

15. Sharma Rani 2017

16. Motlag 2016.

17. Sharma Rani 2017.

18. Sharma Rani 2017.

19. Sharma Rani 2017.

20. Cameron and Pierce 1994; Nisan 1992.

21. Intrinsic motivation: Anderson, Manoogian, and Reznick 1976: 915; autonomy and independence: Kotaman 2017; self-regulation: Deci, Koestner, and Ryan 1999.

22. Baumrind 1996.

23. Dell'Antonia 2016.

24. Cooperation: see, for example, Andreoni, Harbaugh, and Vesterlund 2003; Balliet, Mulder, and Van Lange 2011; Bénabou and Tirole 2006; voting: John, MacDonald, and Sanders 2015; Koelle et al. 2017; pro-environmental conduct: Maki et al. 2016.

25. The literature reviewed here is based on Alm 2019.

26. Alm 2019. See also, for example, Brockmann, Genschel, and Seelkopf 2016.

27. Brockmann, Genschel, and Seelkopf 2016.

28. Koessler et al. 2019.

29. Fabbri, Barbieri, and Bigoni 2019.

30. Blackman 2000; Blackman and Bannister 1997; Blackman and Bannister 1998; Blackman et al. 2006.

31. Thornton, Kagan, and Gunningham 2008.

32. Here we draw on a review of the literature. See Reinders Folmer 2021.

33. Reinders Folmer 2021.

34. This is based on the description by Shu's coauthor Dan Ariely; see Ariely 2012.

35. Shu et al. 2012.

36. Kahneman 2011.

37. The terms "System 1" and "System 2" originally came from Stanovich and West 2000.

38. Drawn from SharpBrains 2006.

39. Haidt 2012.

40. When you take a step back, you may sense that the elephant is not the most apt symbol for System 1. Elephants aren't necessarily known for being fast. Maybe the image works best if you think about elephants stomping down everything in their path, as System 1 might do if left entirely unchecked by a healthy System 2.

41. This section draws on a recent review of the relevant literature. See Pogarsky 2021.

42. Tversky and Kahneman 1974.

43. Slovic, Fischhoff, and Lichtenstein 1979.

44. See, for example, Pogarsky, Roche, and Pickett 2017; Loughran 2019; Pickett and Bushway 2015; Pickett, Loughran, and Bushway 2015; Pickett, Loughran, and Bushaway 2016; Pogarsky and Herman 2019; Pogarsky, Roche, and Pickett 2018.

45. Kahneman 2011.

46. Van Gelder 2012.

47. Van Gelder and de Vries 2013.

48. Pogarsky, Roche, and Pickett 2017.

49. These examples are drawn directly from Kahneman 2011, chapters 25 and 26.

50. Kahneman and Tversky 1979.

51. Elffers and Hessing 1997.

52. Robben et al. 1990; Chang, Nichols, and Schultz 1987; Webley et al. 1991; Cox and Plumley 1988; Schepanski and Shearer 1995; Engström et al. 2015; Kirchler and Maciejovsky 2001.

53. Chang, Nichols, and Schultz 1987.

54. Robben et al. 1990.

55. Engström et al. 2015.

56. Ernest-Jones, Nettle, and Bateson 2011.

57. Gino, Norton, and Ariely 2010.

58. Van Gelder, Hershfield, and Nordgren 2013. For a study with a similar prime and effect, see van Gelder et al. 2015.

59. Novi Mores 2012.

60. Johnson et al. 2012.

61. Kristal et al. 2020.

62. Doyen et al. 2012.

CHAPTER 4: THE MORAL DIMENSION

1. Belgium 2014.

2. Henley 2018.

3. Chen 2019.

4. Urban Dictionary 2015.

5. NHTSA 2019a.
6. NHTSA 2019b.
7. Doyle 2021.
8. Botzas 2019.
9. AT&T 2013a.
10. AT&T 2013b.
11. The discussion of Tyler's original work is based on Tyler 1990.
12. Kagan and Skolnick 1993.
13. Kohlberg 1963: 19.
14. Kohlberg 1971.
15. Based on Kohlberg 1971.
16. Haidt, Koller, and Dias 1993: 617.
17. Haidt, Koller, and Dias 1993.
18. Haidt and Hersh 2001.
19. Haidt 2001: 17.
20. Haidt, Bjorklund, and Murphy 2000.
21. Haidt 2007: 998.
22. Greene et al. 2004.
23. Rooth 2009.
24. There is a large body of research about implicit bias. See Greenwald and
    Krieger 2006. While a review from 2009 found that the IAT indeed predicts
    real discrimination, a review from 2013 shows doubt about this. See Green-
    wald et al. 2009; Oswald et al. 2013.
25. Bazerman and Tenbrunsel 2012: 5.
26. Feldman 2018.
27. Bereby-Meyer et al. 2020.
28. Barnes, Gunia, and Wagner 2015.
29. Ruffle and Tobol 2014.
30. Shalvi, Eldar, and Bereby-Meyer 2012; Gunia et al. 2012; Kern and Chugh
    2009.
31. Tenbrunsel and Messick 2004.
32. Shu and Gino 2012.
33. Tenbrunsel and Messick 2004: 226.
34. Gino and Bazerman 2009.
35. Sykes and Matza 1957: 667. "Social controls that serve to check or inhibit devi-
    ant motivational patterns are rendered inoperative, and the individual is freed
    to engage in delinquency without serious damage to his self-image. In this
    sense, the delinquent both has his cake and eats it too, for he remains commit-
    ted to the dominant normative system and yet so qualifies its imperatives that
    violations are 'acceptable' if not 'right.'"
36. For a very elaborate model of many more neutralization techniques, see
    Kaptein and Van Helvoort 2019.
37. Sykes and Matza 1957: 667.
38. Maruna and Copes 2005: 233.

39. Klockars 1974.
40. Blanken, van de Ven, and Zeelenberg 2015.
41. Bandura 1999; Bandura et al. 1996.
42. Maruna and Copes 2005: 260; Maruna and Copes 2005: 259; Hollinger 1991; Stewart and Byrne 2000.
43. Helmond et al. 2015.
44. Cardwell and Copes 2021.
45. Cardwell, Mazerolle, and Piquero 2019.
46. Bouffard, Cooper, and Bergseth 2017; Jonas-van Dijk et al. 2020.
47. BBC News 2019.
48. Breslow 2015.
49. Feuer 2019.
50. Henriques 2011.
51. BBC News 2018.
52. Carreyrou 2018.
53. Farrow 2019.
54. Aristotle 1976 (section 1180a15): 337.
55. Kohlberg 1971.
56. Lardén et al. 2006.
57. Palmer 2003: 168. The review includes a review of a meta-analysis from 1990 that analyzes the effects from fifteen studies and finds that moral reasoning is less mature in offender populations. See Nelson, Smith, and Dodd 1990.
58. Nelson, Smith, and Dodd 1990.
59. Valliant et al. 2000.
60. Van Gelder and de Vries 2016: 705.
61. Sexual assault: Lee, Gizzarone, and Ashton 2003. Workplace delinquency: Lee, Ashton, and de Vries 2005; Lee, Ashton, and Shin 2005. Occupational crime: Van Gelder and de Vries 2016. Common misdemeanors: Van Gelder and de Vries 2013.
62. Paulhus and Williams 2002.
63. Corry et al. 2008.
64. Hare et al. 1990; Lilienfeld and Andrews 1996.
65. Jones and Paulhus 2009.
66. Paulhus and Williams 2002: 557.
67. Bullying: Baughman et al. 2012. Deception: Azizli et al. 2016. Deviant sexual behavior: Williams et al. 2009. Revenge: DeLongis, Nathanson, and Paulhus 2011, cited in Furnham, Richards, and Paulhus 2013. White-collar crime: Flexon et al. 2016. Academic dishonesty: Brunell et al. 2011. Violent crime: Wright et al. 2017.
68. APA 2013.
69. Yu, Geddes, and Fazel 2012.
70. Yu, Geddes, and Fazel 2012: 785.
71. Reising et al. 2019.
72. Stromberg 2013.

73. DeMatteo et al. 2020.
74. Kjøbli, Zachrisson, and Bjørnebekk 2018.
75. Muratori et al. 2017.
76. Waschbusch et al. 2019.
77. Feldman 2018.

CHAPTER 5: CIVIL OBEDIENCE
1. For details on Gandhi's salt water march, see Dalton 2012.
2. Fine and Van Rooij 2017; Fine et al. 2016.
3. Fine et al. 2020a.
4. Tyler 1990.
5. Brockner et al. 1997; Tyler 2000.
6. Tyler 1997.
7. Walters and Bolger 2019.
8. Tyler, Callahan, and Frost 2007.
9. Winter and May 2001.
10. Welfare fraud: Murphy, Tyler, and Curtis 2009. Tax evasion: Murphy 2003; Worsham 1996; Murphy 2005; Doyle et al. 2009; Hartner et al. 2008; Kogler et al. 2013; Kirchler 2007; Kirchler, Hoelzl, and Wahl 2008; Kirchler et al. 2010. For the original idea of how trust theoretically plays a role in tax compliance and how it relates to law enforcement, see the slippery slope framework developed by Erich Kirchler and colleagues: Kirchler, Hoelzl, and Wahl 2008. Nursing homes: Makkai and Braithwaite 1996.
11. MacCoun 2005.
12. Nagin and Telep 2017.
13. Doyle et al. 2009.
14. Simerman 2019; Reutter 2019.
15. Rappleye 2016.
16. Cases thrown out: Rappleye 2016. Cases that could be affected: Vaughn 2019.
17. Edwards, Lee, and Esposito 2019.
18. Fine et al. 2020b.
19. Fine et al 2020b.
20. Fine et al. 2020c.
21. Ramji-Nogales, Schoenholtz, and Schrag 2007.
22. Mashaw 1978.
23. Ho 2017.
24. 481 US 279 (1987).
25. Barnes and Chemerinsky 2017; Gronhovd 1986.
26. Lewis 1987.
27. President's Task Force on 21st Century Policing 2015.
28. McLean et al. 2019.
29. McLean et al. 2019.
30. McLean et al. 2019.
31. Rice and Lee 2015.

32. Beck and Rice 2016.
33. Rice and Lee 2015.
34. Beck and Rice 2016.
35. Leap 2020.
36. Rice and Lee 2015; Los Angeles Mayor's Office 2017.
37. Chang 2020.
38. Robin et al. 2020; Leap 2020.
39. Owens et al. 2018.
40. Mazerolle et al. 2013.
41. Chang 2020.
42. Ho 2017.
43. Kish-Gephart, Harrison, and Treviño 2010; Treviño and Youngblood 1990.
44. Wilson 2001.
45. Truth and Reconciliation Commission 2020.
46. Van der Merwe and Chapman 2008; Gibson 2005; Gibson 2004; Mamdani 2002.
47. O'Brien, Meares, and Tyler 2020.
48. Wang and Philips 2018.
49. Garcia 2019.
50. Fazlollah, McCoy, and Shaw 2018.
51. Bouboushian 2015.

CHAPTER 6: FOLLOWING THE HERD

1. Gneezy and Rustichini 2000.
2. Cialdini 2007.
3. Cialdini 2007.
4. Based on Schultz et al. 2007.
5. Perkins et al. 2010.
6. Perkins et al. 2010.
7. Perkins et al. 2010.
8. Bruce 2002.
9. Perceptions of dating violence: DeGue et al. 2014. Actual dating violence: Foshee et al. 2004.
10. Perkins, Perkins, and Craig 2019.
11. Wenzel 2005: 873.
12. Tang and Hall 1995; Lepper, Greene, and Nisbett 1973.
13. Nolan and Wallen 2021.
14. Nolan and Wallen 2021.
15. Smith and Louis 2008: 648.
16. For an overview of studies that show this, see Smith and Louis 2008: 649.
17. For an overview, see Smith and Louis 2008.
18. National Park Service 2018.
19. Cialdini et al. 2006: 12.

20. Twiley 2015.
21. Weiser 2019.
22. This paragraph draws directly from Twiley 2015.
23. See Cialdini 2003, Cialdini 2007; Cialdini et al. 2006; Cialdini and Goldstein 2004.
24. Honor and respect: Anderson 2000. Religious beliefs: Grijns and Horii 2018.
25. Maslin Nir 2017.
26. Keizer, Lindenberg, and Steg 2011.
27. Here we can think of cultural norms in communities; some make people always seek to enhance and breed their respect, and at times these can stimulate illegal and even violent behavior. See Anderson 2000. Or we can think of religious norms—for example, those that may sustain legally banned forms of underage marriage. See Grijns and Horii 2018.

CHAPTER 7: EMPOWERING CHANGE

1. For full video, see Public Apology Central 2017.
2. Dambrova et al. 2016.
3. USADA 2016.
4. Edited from Adams 2012.
5. Kim 1999.
6. Kim 1999.
7. Pleasence, Balmer, and Denvir 2017.
8. Sarat 1975.
9. Albrecht and Green 1977.
10. Darley, Sanderson, and LaMantia 1996. See also Darley, Carlsmith, and Robinson 2001.
11. Cavanagh and Cauffman 2017.
12. Pleasence and Balmer 2012: 322.
13. See reviews by Littleton 2008 (reviewing twenty-eight studies) and Eberwein III 2008 (reviewing seventy-seven studies). Examples of individual studies include Bowal 1998; Militello, Schimmel, and Eberwein 2009; Schimmel and Militello 2007.
14. Shuman and Weiner 1981; Givelber, Bowers, and Blitch 1984; Van McCrary et al. 1992; Saltstone, Saltstone, and Rowe 1997; Van McCrary and Swanson 1999; Chate 2008; White et al. 2012; White et al. 2014.
15. Van McCrary and Swanson 1999: 20.
16. See Edelman and Talesh 2011; Talesh 2015; Talesh 2009; Talesh and Pélisse 2019; Gray and Pelisse 2019; Abbott, Levi-Faur, and Snidal 2017.
17. Darley, Carlsmith, and Robinson 2001: 184.
18. Pleasence and Balmer 2012: 325.
19. Ellickson 1991: 115.
20. Beccaria 2016: 107.
21. Marlborough 2016.

22. Marlborough 2016.

23. Segall 2018.

24. *Psychology Today* 2019.

25. Gottfredson and Hirschi 1990.

26. The discussion here is strongly influenced by Pratt and Lloyd 2021.

27. Gottfredson and Hirschi 1990: 10, 16, 12.

28. Gottfredson and Hirschi 1990.

29. Gottfredson and Hirschi 1990: 90.

30. Hirschi and Gottfredson 1993.

31. Vazsonyi, Mikuška, and Kelley 2017.

32. De Ridder et al. 2012. Pratt and Cullen 2000: 952–53.

33. Akers and Sellers 2004, as cited in Vazsonyi, Mikuška, and Kelley 2017.

34. Akers 1991.

35. Gottfredson and Hirschi 1990: 90.

36. Hirschi 2004.

37. Piquero, Jennings, and Farrington 2010; Piquero et al. 2016.

38. Augimeri et al. 2018.

39. Augimeri et al. 2018: 44.

40. Burke and Loeber 2015.

41. Augimeri et al. 2018.

42. Steinberg and Scott 2003.

43. Stanley-Becker and Horton 2018.

44. Chason 2019.

45. Cooke and Farrington 2016.

46. Currie 2008, cited in Cooke and Farrington 2016.

47. Button 2007, cited in Cooke and Farrington 2016.

48. Cooke and Farrington 2016: 856. Of course, more research is necessary because there have only been a dozen or so studies. Duindam et al. 2020.

49. Craig, Gannon, and Dixon 2013: 8.

50. Joy Tong and Farrington 2006: 5.

51. Robinson and Porporino 2003.

52. Joy Tong and Farrington 2006: 5.

53. Joy Tong and Farrington 2006.

54. Weekes et al. 2013: 248.

55. Pelissier et al. 2001.

56. Porporino et al. 2002. For a more recent meta-analysis of a broader body of research, see Holloway, Bennett, and Farrington 2008.

57. Lipsey and Cullen 2007.

58. Martinson 1974.

59. Alexander 2012.

60. Alexander 2012: 149.

61. Visher, Winterfield, and Coggeshall 2005: 295–96; Sampson and Laub 1997: 17.

62. Alexander 2012: 148.

63. Visher, Winterfield, and Coggeshall 2005: 295–96.
64. Freeman 1991: 13.
65. Augustin 2016.
66. Lantigua-Williams 2016.
67. Pratt and Cullen 2005.
68. Pare and Felson 2014. See also Kang 2016 with further evidence of the link between poverty and crime, finding that neighborhoods with higher levels of poverty concentration will have more crime.
69. Lochner and Moretti 2004.
70. Lochner and Moretti 2004: 176.
71. Deming 2011.
72. Aizer and Doyle 2015.
73. Foley 2001; Macomber et al. 2010.
74. McCarthy and Hagan 1991.
75. Lens 2014. For a broader overview of the literature, see Lens 2013.
76. Woo and Joh 2015.
77. Pratt, Turner, and Piquero 2004.
78. Agnew 2006.
79. Botchkovar, Tittle, and Antonaccio 2009.
80. Botchkovar, Tittle, and Antonaccio 2009.
81. Here we draw on Kagan and Scholz 1984.

CHAPTER 8: SPEED BUMPS FOR TERRORISTS

 1. Van Natta Jr., Sciolino, and Grey 2006.
 2. Van Natta Jr., Sciolino, and Grey 2006.
 3. Casciani 2009.
 4. Van Natta Jr., Sciolino, and Grey 2006.
 5. This and the next paragraph are based on Calder 2016.
 6. Cohen and Felson 1979.
 7. Cohen and Felson 1979: 598.
 8. Cohen and Felson 1979: 599, 596.
 9. Cohen and Felson 1979: 596.
10. Sex crimes: Tewksbury and Mustaine 2001; Belknap 1987. Robbery: Groff 2007. Medical fraud: Benson, Madensen, and Eck 2009. Carbon emissions trading fraud: Gibbs, Cassidy, and Rivers III 2013.
11. McNeeley 2015.
12. Spano and Freilich 2009: 308.
13. Pratt, Holtfreter, and Reisig 2010: 281.
14. Holt and Bossler 2008.
15. Bossler and Holt 2009.
16. For all these points, see Mayhew, Clarke, and Elliott 1989: 2–3.
17. Mayhew, Clarke, Elliott 1989.
18. Clarke 1980.

19. Clarke 1980.
20. Farrington and Welsh 2007.
21. Maarse 2016.
22. Pope 2016.
23. Newman 1972.
24. Newman 1972 as summarized in Cullen, Agnew, and Wilcox 2014: 460.
25. Clarke 2005.
26. Bostwick 2010.
27. AFP (Agence France-Presse) 2019.
28. Associated Press 2016.
29. Robies 2018.
30. Robies 2018.
31. Robies 2018.
32. Ekblom 1988.
33. Clarke 2005.
34. Clarke 1980.
35. Guerette and Bowers 2009.
36. Scherdin 1986.
37. Pease 1991.
38. For all aspects of this case, see Castle 2019.
39. Travis, Western, and Redburn 2014.
40. Travis, Western, and Redburn 2014: 141–42.
41. Sentencing Project 2020.
42. Graves 2016.
43. See Howell 2009.
44. Glueck and Glueck 1937; Laub and Sampson 2003; Piquero 2008.
45. Sweeten, Piquero, and Steinberg 2013.
46. Schubert et al. 2004.
47. Mulvey et al. 2010.
48. Steinberg and Scott 2003.
49. Cohen and Casey 2014.
50. Travis, Western, and Redburn 2014.
51. Travis, Western, and Redburn 2014: 143.
52. Johnson and Raphael 2012: 302.
53. Miles and Ludwig 2007: 291.
54. Marvell and Moody 1994: 117.
55. Cup 2019.
56. Woodyatt 2019.
57. Welch 2019.
58. Richtel 2016.
59. Richtel 2016.
60. Kidd, McCartt, and Oesch 2014.
61. Kidd, McCartt, and Oesch 2014.
62. Fehling 2018.

63. Kivisto, Ray, and Phalen 2017.
64. Kellermann et al. 1993. A recent study also found a strong significant relationship between gun ownership and homicide rates. With each 1 percent more ownership there was an 0.9 percent increase in homicide. See Siegel, Ross, and King 2013.

CHAPTER 9: EATING SYSTEMS FOR BREAKFAST
1. Gow 2008. See also Dietz and Gillespie 2012.
2. Israel: Schubert and Miller 2008. Argentina: US Attorney's Office 2015; Schubert and Miller 2008.
3. Spiegel International 2007.
4. Schubert and Miller 2008.
5. Dietz and Gillespie 2012.
6. Dierks 2006.
7. Schubert and Miller 2008.
8. Spiegel International 2008.
9. Lopez 2011. "Death sentence with a two-year reprieve" means that the sentence will be commuted to life within two years in the case of good conduct.
10. US Department of Justice and District of Columbia 2008.
11. Gino, Ayal, and Ariely 2009; Kish-Gephart, Harrison, and Treviño 2010; Scholten and Ellemers 2016; Treviño and Youngblood 1990.
12. Simpson et al. 2014.
13. Federal Sentencing Guidelines §8B2.5, section F; see https://www.ussc.gov/guidelines/2018-guidelines-manual/annotated-2018-chapter-8.
14. Federal Sentencing Guidelines §8B2.1; see https://www.ussc.gov/guidelines/2018-guidelines-manual/annotated-2018-chapter-8.
15. Coglianese and Nash 2021.
16. Sarbanes-Oxley Act of 2002 (Public Company Accounting Reform and Investor Protection Act), Pub. L. No. 107–204, 116 Stat. 745 (codified as amended in scattered sections of U.S.C. titles 11, 15, 18, 28, and 29).
17. Coglianese and Nash 2021. Dodd-Frank Wall Street Reform and Consumer Protection Act, Pub. L. No. 111- 203, 124 Stat. 1367 (codified as amended in scattered sections of U.S.C. titles 7, 12, 15, and 31).
18. Coglianese and Nash 2021.
19. Our discussion here is based in part on Coglianese and Nash 2021.
20. Prakash and Potoski 2006.
21. Ge, Koester, and McVay 2017.
22. Kish-Gephart, Harrison, and Treviño 2010; Schell-Busey 2009.
23. Parker and Nielsen 2009
24. Parker and Nielsen 2009: 24.
25. Parker and Nielsen 2009: 28.
26. Weaver 2014; Treviño 1999; Goebel and Weißenberger 2017; Hofeditz et al. 2017.
27. Hofeditz et al. 2017.

28. Warren, Gaspar, and Laufer 2014.
29. McKendall, DeMarr, and Jones-Rikkers 2002.
30. "Does not impact": Laufer 1999; Laufer and Robertson 1997; McCabe, Treviño, and Butterfield 1996; Stansbury and Barry 2007. "Temporary": Richards 1999.
31. Kaptein and Schwartz 2008.
32. McKendall, DeMarr, and Jones-Rikkers 2002: 380.
33. Treviño and Weaver 2001.
34. Treviño et al. 1999: 132.
35. McKendall, DeMarr, and Jones-Rikkers 2002: 379; Parker and Nielsen 2009.
36. Krawiec 2003: 487.
37. Weaver, Treviño, and Cochran 1999.
38. Laufer 1999.
39. Krawiec 2003.
40. Krawiec 2003: 491–92.
41. Edelman 1992.
42. Chen and Soltes 2018.
43. Independent oversight: Coglianese and Lazer 2003: 725. Corporate leadership commitment and organizational climate: Kish-Gephart, Harrison, and Treviño 2010; Coglianese and Nash 2021; Parker and Nielsen 2009.
44. Discussion of this story is based on Hensley 2009 and Berkrot 2009.
45. Hensley 2009.
46. Hensley 2009.
47. Berkrot 2009.
48. Based on Waxman 2019.
49. False Claims Act (FCA), 31 U.S.C. § 3730(d). See also US Department of Justice 2011.
50. Pontell, Calavita, and Tillman 1994.
51. Demotion: Sawyer, Johnson, and Holub 2010: 4. Firing: Alford 2007: 223; Dyck, Morse, and Zingales: 2010; Sawyer, Johnson, and Holub 2010. Quitting under duress: Dyck, Morse, and Zingales 2010: 2216.
52. Alford 2007: 230.
53. Liyanarachchi and Newdick 2009: 41.
54. Liyanarachchi and Newdick 2009: 40; Dyck, Morse, and Zingales 2010.
55. Earle and Madek 2007; Carson, Verdu, and Wokutch 2008.
56. Sawyer, Johnson, and Holub 2010.
57. Alford 2007; Rapp 2012.
58. Dyck, Morse, and Zingales 2010.
59. Liyanarachchi and Newdick 2009, Curtis 2006, Taylor and Curtis 2010, Dasgupta and Kesharwani 2010.
60. US Department of Justice 2004.
61. Morgenson 2016.
62. Moberly 2012.
63. Moberly 2012: 37.

64. Near and Miceli 1996; Miceli, Near, and Dworkin 2008. Dasgupta and Kesharwani, in their survey of the relevant literature, only write a little about the effects of whistle-blowing on reducing corporate wrongdoing. Mostly they repeat the observations from Miceli and colleagues. They conclude with a statement about the complexity entailed in predictions: "A number of factors determine the outcome but these factors and the outcome itself vary from organization to organization and from individual to individual." Dasgupta and Kesharwani 2010: 63.

65. McKendall, DeMarr, and Jones-Rikkers 2002: 379, Parker and Nielsen 2009: 28, Gunningham and Sinclair 2014; Coglianese and Nash 2021; Steinberg 2011: 33; Ely and Meyerson 2010; Kish-Gephart, Harrison, and Treviño 2010; Near and Miceli 1996; Miceli, Near, and Dworkin 2008; Dasgupta and Kesharwani 2010: 63.

66. Gunningham and Sinclair 2014.

67. Volkov 2020.

68. DeJesus 2019

69. Sharma 2017.

70. Geertz 2000.

71. Geertz 2000.

72. Geertz 2000: 27.

73. For an elaborate explanation of all this, see Geertz 1973.

74. Schein 2010.

75. This section draws (sometimes directly) from Van Rooij and Fine 2018.

76. Overall discussion of BP here is based on Baker et al. 2007; Balmer, Powell, and Greyser 2011; Bozeman 2011; Domenec 2012; Frey 2002; Goldenberg 2010; Hoffman and Devereaux Jennings 2011; Kollewe 2010; Lustgarten 2010; Lustgarten 2012; Lustgarten and Knutson 2010; Lyall 2010; Mattera 2016; Pardosi 1997; PBS 2010; Smithson and Venette 2013; Steffy 2010; Sylves and Comfort 2012; US Chemical Safety and Hazard Investigation Board 2007.

77. Goldenberg 2010.

78. Overall discussion of VW draws on Chossière et al. 2017; Ewing 2017; Glinton 2016; Manske and Quoos 2018; Nelson 2016; Reuters 2016.

79. Discussion of Wells Fargo draws on Arnold 2016a; Associated Press 2017; Colvin 2017; Corkery 2016; Cowley 2017; Cowley and Kingson 2017; Egan 2017; Frost 2017; Glazer 2017; Independent Directors of the Board of Wells Fargo 2017; Kellaway 2015; Lakatos, Davidson, and Sanney n.d.; Lubin 2017; Puzzanghera 2017; Reckard 2013; Roberts 2017.

80. Independent Directors of the Board of Wells Fargo 2017.

81. Reckard 2013.

82. Lustgarten and Knutson 2010.

83. Arnold 2016b.

84. Reckard 2013.

85. Colvin 2017.

86. Morgenson 2017.

87. Ewing 2017: 216.
88. Woodward 2019.
89. Volkswagen 2017.
90. Alvesson and Sveningsson 2015; Bass and Avolio 1993; Cameron and Quinn 2006; Harrison and Stokes 1992; Hatch 1993; Hofstede et al. 1990; Jones, Jimmieson, and Griffiths 2005; Scalzi et al. 2006; Scott et al. 2003; Warren, Gaspar, and Laufer 2014; Schein 2010.
91. Schein 2010.
92. Ogbonna and Wilkinson 2003.

## CHAPTER 10: BEHAVIORAL JURISPRUDENCE

1. Shear, Crowley, and Glanz 2020.
2. Soper 1919.
3. De Bruijn et al. 2020; Kooistra et al. 2020; Kuiper et al. 2020; Van Rooij et al. 2020.
4. Bacon and Ortiz 2020. For a similar appeal from Michigan governor Gretchen Whitmer, see Fox 2 Detroit 2020.
5. Rijksoverheid 2020.
6. Johnson 2020.
7. Rijksoverheid 2020.
8. The opening paragraphs on the historical development of scientific medicine and medical practice are based on Barry 2005.
9. Barry 2005: 31.
10. For some studies on how judges in the US have misapplied empirical evidence, see Finkel 1995; Monahan and Walker 2011; Fradella 2003; Rustad and Koenig 1993: 91.
11. Flaherty 2017.
12. De Quervain et al. 2004 1254; Singer et al. 2006; Unnever and Cullen 2009.
13. Unnever and Cullen 2009.
14. Balko 2013.
15. Haney-López 2015.
16. Grand View Research 2020.

# Bibliography

Abbott, Kenneth W., David Levi-Faur, and Duncan Snidal. 2017. "Theorizing Regulatory Intermediaries: The RIT Model." *Annals of the American Academy of Political and Social Science* 670 (1): 14–35.

Abdullah, Halimah. 2016. "HUD Seeks to End Housing Discrimination Against Ex-Offenders." NBC News, April 4. https://www.nbcnews.com/news/us-news/hud-seeks-end-housing-discrimination-against-ex-offenders-n550471.

Adams, Orny. 2012. "Third Amendment and Commandments." YouTube, October 30. https://www.youtube.com/watch?v=zKXLhOnDdNw.

AFP (Agence France-Presse). 2019. "Death of the 500 Euro Note, Bill Favoured by Criminals . . . and Germans." *South China Morning Post,* January 27. https://www.scmp.com/news/world/europe/article/2183801/death-500-euro-note-bill-favoured-criminals-and-germans.

Agarwal, Rajender, Ashutosh Gupta, and Shweta Gupta. 2019. "The Impact of Tort Reform on Defensive Medicine, Quality of Care, and Physician Supply: A Systematic Review." *Health Services Research* 54 (4): 851–59.

Agnew, Robert. 2006. *Pressured into Crime: An Overview of General Strain Theory.* Oxford: Oxford University Press.

Aizer, Anna, and Joseph J. Doyle Jr. 2015. "Juvenile Incarceration, Human Capital, and Future Crime: Evidence from Randomly Assigned Judges." *Quarterly Journal of Economics* 130 (2): 759–803.

Akers, Ronald L. 1991. "Self-Control as a General Theory of Crime." *Journal of Quantitative Criminology* 7 (2): 201–11.

Akers, Ronald L., and Christine Sharon Sellers. 2004. *Criminological Theories: Introduction, Evaluations, and Application.* 4th ed. Los Angeles: Roxbury.

Albrecht, Stan L., and Miles Green. 1977. "Cognitive Barriers to Equal Justice Before the Law." *Journal of Research in Crime and Delinquency* 14 (2): 206–21.

Alexander, Michelle. 2012. *The New Jim Crow: Mass Incarceration in the Age of Colorblindness.* New York: New Press.

Alford, C. Fred. 2007. "Whistle-Blower Narratives: The Experience of Choiceless Choice." *Social Research* 74 (10): 223–48.

Alm, James. 2019. "What Motivates Tax Compliance?" *Journal of Economic Surveys* 33 (2): 353–88.

Alvesson, Mats, and Stefan Sveningsson. 2015. *Changing Organizational Culture: Cultural Change Work in Progress.* New York: Routledge.

Anderson, Elijah. 2000. *Code of the Street: Decency, Violence, and the Moral Life of the Inner City.* New York: W. W. Norton.

Anderson, J. M., Paul Heaton, and Stephen Carroll. 2010. *The US Experience with No-Fault Automobile Insurance: A Retrospective.* Santa Monica, CA: RAND Corporation.

Anderson, Rosemarie, Sam T. Manoogian, and J. Steven Reznick. 1976. "The Undermining and Enhancing of Intrinsic Motivation in Preschool Children." *Journal of Personality and Social Psychology* 34 (5): 915–22.

Andreoni, James, William Harbaugh, and Lise Vesterlund. 2003. "The Carrot or the Stick: Rewards, Punishments, and Cooperation." *American Economic Review* 93 (3): 893–902.

APA (American Psychological Association). 2013. "Personality Disorders." *DSM-V.* https://www.psychiatry.org/File%20Library/Psychiatrists/Practice/DSM/APA_DSM-5-Personality-Disorder.pdf.

———. 2016. "Solitary Confinement of Juvenile Offenders." https://www.apa.org/advocacy/criminal-justice/solitary.pdf.

Apel, Robert. 2013. "Sanctions, Perceptions, and Crime: Implications for Criminal Deterrence." *Journal of Quantitative Criminology* 29 (1): 67–101.

Ariely, Dan. 2012. *The (Honest) Truth About Dishonesty: How We Lie to Everyone—Especially Ourselves.* London: HarperCollins.

Aristotle. 1976. *Ethics.* London: Penguin Books.

Arnold, Chris. 2016a. "Former Wells Fargo Employees Describe Toxic Sales Culture, Even at HQ." NPR, October 4. https://www.npr.org/2016/10/04/496508361/former-wells-fargo-employees-describe-toxic-sales-culture-even-at-hq.

Arnold, Chris. 2016b. "Workers Say Wells Fargo Unfairly Scarred Their Careers." NPR, October 21. https://www.npr.org/2016/10/21/498804659/former-wells-fargo-employees-join-class-action-lawsuit?t=1593764772819.

Associated Press. 2016. "European Central Bank to Discontinue 500-Euro Note." CBC News, May 5. https://www.cbc.ca/news/business/500-euro-ended-1.3568182.

———. 2017. "Wells Fargo Fired a Worker for Refusing to Scam Customers, Lawsuit Says." *Los Angeles Times*, April 17. http://www.latimes.com/business/la-fi-wells-fargo-lawsuit-20170417-story.html.

AT&T. 2013a. "An Instant Can Change Your Life." YouTube. https://www.youtube.com/watch?v=cQS_hMq2Lqo&feature=youtu.be.

———. 2013b. "Texting While Driving: Chandler." YouTube. https://www.youtube.com/watch?v=PN1eljqxs44&feature=youtu.be.

Augimeri, Leena K., et al. 2018. "SNAP (Stop Now and Plan): Helping Children Improve Their Self-Control and Externalizing Behavior Problems." *Journal of Criminal Justice* 56: 43–49.

Augustin, Stanley. 2016. "Lawyers' Committee Opens Nationwide Inquiry into Housing Providers That Impose 'Blanket Bans' upon Applicants Who Have Had Contact with the Criminal Justice System." April 4. https://lawyers

committee.org/lawyers-committee-opens-nationwide-inquiry-housing
-providers-impose-blanket-bans-upon-applicants-contact-criminal-justice-system.

Azizli, Nicole, et al. 2016. "Lies and Crimes: Dark Triad, Misconduct, and High-Stakes Deception." *Personality and Individual Differences* 89: 34–39.

Bacon, John, and Jorge L. Ortiz. 2020. "Coronavirus Live Updates: Californians Ordered to Stay Home; Italy Surpasses China's Death Toll; US Death Toll Tops 200." *USA Today*, March 19. https://eu.usatoday.com/story/news/health /2020/03/19/coronavirus-updates-us-china-nyc-cases-testing-unemployment -cdc/2866751001.

Baker, James, et al. 2007. *The Report of the BP US Refineries Independent Safety Review Panel.* US Chemical Safety and Hazard Investigation Board. https://www .csb.gov/assets/1/20/baker_panel_report1.pdf?13842.

Baldwin, Grant T., and Debra Houry. 2015. "Getting Everyone to Buckle Up on Every Trip: What More Can Be Done?" *Annals of Internal Medicine* 163 (3): 234–35.

Balko, Radley. 2013. *Rise of the Warrior Cop: The Militarization of America's Police Forces.* New York: PublicAffairs.

Balliet, Daniel, Laetitia B. Mulder, and Paul A. M. Van Lange. 2011. "Reward, Punishment, and Cooperation: A Meta-Analysis." *Psychological Bulletin* 137 (4): 594–615.

Balmer, John M. T., Shaun M. Powell, and Stephen A. Greyser. 2011. "Explicating Ethical Corporate Marketing: Insights from the BP Deepwater Horizon Catastrophe: The Ethical Brand That Exploded and Then Imploded." *Journal of Business Ethics* 102 (1): 1.

Bandura, Albert. 1999. "Moral Disengagement in the Perpetration of Inhumanities." *Personality and Social Psychology Review* 3 (3): 193–209.

Bandura, Albert, et al. 1996. "Mechanisms of Moral Disengagement in the Exercise of Moral Agency." *Journal of Personality and Social Psychology* 71 (2): 364–74.

Barnes, Christopher M., Brian C. Gunia, and David T. Wagner. 2015. "Sleep and Moral Awareness." *Journal of Sleep Research* 24 (2): 181–88.

Barnes, Mario L., and Erwin Chemerinsky. 2017. "What Can Brown Do for You: Addressing *McCleskey v. Kemp* as a Flawed Standard for Measuring the Constitutionally Significant Risk of Race Bias." *Northwestern University Law Review* 112: 1293–1336.

Barry, Ellen, and Martin Selsoe Sorensen. 2018. "In Denmark, Harsh New Laws for Immigrant 'Ghettos.'" *New York Times*, July 1. https://www.nytimes.com /2018/07/01/world/europe/denmark-immigrant-ghettos.html.

Barry, John M. 2005. *The Great Influenza: The Epic Story of the Deadliest Plague in History.* New York: Penguin.

Bass, Bernard M., and Bruce J. Avolio. 1993. "Transformational Leadership and Organizational Culture." *Public Administration Quarterly*: 112–21.

Baughman, Holly M., et al. 2012. "Relationships Between Bullying Behaviours and the Dark Triad: A Study with Adults." *Personality and Individual Differences* 52 (5): 571–75.

Baumrind, Diana. 1996. "The Discipline Controversy Revisited." *Family Relations* 45 (4): 405–14.

Bazerman, Max H., and Ann E. Tenbrunsel. 2012. *Blind Spots: Why We Fail to Do What's Right and What to Do About It*. Princeton, NJ: Princeton University Press.

BBC News. 2018. "Larry Nassar: Disgraced US Olympics Doctor Jailed for 175 Years." BBC. January 25. https://www.bbc.com/news/world-us-canada -42811304.

————. 2019. "El Chapo Trial: Mexican Drug Lord Joaquín Guzmán Gets Life in Prison." BBC. July 17. https://www.bbc.com/news/world-us-canada -49022208.

Beccaria, Cesare. 2016. *On Crimes and Punishments*. Transaction Publishers.

Beck, Charlie, and Connie Rice. 2016. "How Community Policing Can Work." *New York Times*. August 12. https://www.nytimes.com/2016/08/12/opinion /how-community-policing-can-work.html.

Belknap, Joanne. 1987. "Routine Activity Theory and the Risk of Rape: Analyzing Ten Years of National Crime Survey Data." *Criminal Justice Policy Review* 2 (4): 337–56.

Bénabou, Roland, and Jean Tirole. 2006. "Incentives and Prosocial Behavior." *American Economic Review* 96 (5): 1652–78.

Bendixen, Machala. 2018. "Denmark's 'Anti-Ghetto' Laws Are a Betrayal of Our Tolerant Values." *Guardian*, July. https://www.theguardian.com/commentis free/2018/jul/10/denmark-ghetto-laws-niqab-circumcision-islamophobic.

Benson, Michael L., Tamara D. Madensen, and John E. Eck. 2009. "White-Collar Crime from an Opportunity Perspective." In *The Criminology of White Collar Crime*. Edited by Sally Simpson and David Weisburd, 175–95. New York: Springer.

Bereby-Meyer, Yoella, et al. 2020. "Honesty Speaks a Second Language." *Topics in Cognitive Science* 12: 632–43.

Berkrot, Bill. 2009. "Pfizer Whistleblower's Ordeal Reaps Big Rewards." Reuters. September 3. https://www.reuters.com/article/us-pfizer-whistleblower -idUSN021592920090903.

Blackman, Allen, and Geoffrey J. Bannister. 1997. "Pollution Control in the Informal Sector: The Ciudad Juárez Brickmakers' Project." *Natural Resources Journal* 37 (Fall): 829–56.

————. "Pollution Control in the Informal Sector: The Ciudad Juárez Brickmakers' Project." *Resources for the Future Discussion Paper* (February): 98–15.

Blackman, Allen. 2000. "Informal Sector Pollution Control: What Policy Options Do We Have?" *World Development* 28 (12): 2067–82.

Blackman, Allen, et al. 2006. "The Benefits and Costs of Informal Sector Pollution Control: Mexican Brick Kilns." *Environment and Development Economics* 11 (5): 603–27.

Blanken, Irene, Niels van de Ven, and Marcel Zeelenberg. 2015. "A Meta-Analytic Review of Moral Licensing." *Personality and Social Psychology Bulletin* 41 (4): 540–58.

Bossler, Adam M., and Thomas J. Holt. 2009. "On-Line Activities, Guardianship, and Malware Infection: An Examination of Routine Activities Theory." *International Journal of Cyber Criminology* 3 (1): 400–420.

Bostwick, William. 2010. "Safer Suds: U.K.'s Design Bridge Invents a More Bar Fight–Friendly Pint Glass." *Fast Company.* https://www.fastcompany.com /1543276/safer-suds-uks-design-bridge-invents-more-bar-fight-friendly -pint-glass.

Botchkovar, Ekaterina V., Charles R. Tittle, and Olena Antonaccio. 2009. "General Strain Theory: Additional Evidence Using Cross-Cultural Data." *Criminology* 47 (1): 131–76.

Botzas, Senay. 2019. "Bicycle Lovers in the Netherlands to Be Hit with Fine for Using Mobile Phones While Cycling." *Telegraph*, June 28. https://www .telegraph.co.uk/news/2019/06/28/bicycle-lovers-netherlands-hit-fine-using -mobile-phones-cycling.

Bouboushian, Rose. 2015. "$4.75M Kids for Cash Settlement Approved." Courthouse News Service, August 13. https://www.courthousenews.com/4-75m -kids-for-cash-settlement-approved.

Bouffard, Jeff, Maisha Cooper, and Kathleen Bergseth. 2017. "The Effectiveness of Various Restorative Justice Interventions on Recidivism Outcomes Among Juvenile Offenders." *Youth Violence and Juvenile Justice* 15 (4): 465–80.

Bowal, Peter. 1998. "A Study of Lay Knowledge of Law in Canada." *Indiana International & Comparative Law Review* 9 (1): 121–41.

Boyer, M. Martin, and Hanon Amandine. 2012. "Protecting Directors and Officers from Liability Arising from Aggressive Earnings Management." *Insurance and Risk Management* 77 (1): 33–58.

Bozeman, Barry. 2011. "The 2010 BP Gulf of Mexico Oil Spill: Implications for Theory of Organizational Disaster." *Technology in Society* 33 (3–4): 244–52.

Braga, Anthony Allan, and David Weisburd. 2010. *Policing Problem Places: Crime Hot Spots and Effective Prevention.* New York: Oxford University Press.

Braga, Anthony A., David Weisburd, and Brandon Turchan. 2018. "Focused Deterrence Strategies and Crime Control: An Updated Systematic Review and Meta-Analysis of the Empirical Evidence." *Criminology and Public Policy* 17 (1): 205–50.

Braga, Anthony A., et al. 1999. "Problem-Oriented Policing in Violent Crime Places: A Randomized Controlled Experiment." *Criminology* 37 (3): 541–80.

Brantingham, Patricia L., and Paul J. Brantingham. 1999. "A Theoretical Model of Crime Hot Spot Generation." *Studies on Crime and Crime Prevention* 8 (1): 7–26.

Breslow, Jason M. 2015. "The Staggering Death Toll of Mexico's Drug War." *Frontline.* PBS. July 27. https://www.pbs.org/wgbh/frontline/article/the -staggering-death-toll-of-mexicos-drug-war.

Brockmann, Hilke, Philipp Genschel, and Laura Seelkopf. 2016. "Happy Taxation: Increasing Tax Compliance Through Positive Rewards?" *Journal of Public Policy* 36 (3): 381–406.

Brockner, Joel, et al. 1997. "When Trust Matters: The Moderating Effect of Outcome Favorability." *Administrative Science Quarterly* 42 (3): 558–83.

Brown, Don W. 1978. "Arrest Rates and Crime Rates: When Does a Tipping Effect Occur?" *Social Forces* 57 (2): 671–82.

Bruce, S. 2002. "The 'A Man' Campaign: Marketing Social Norms to Men to Prevent Sexual Assault." In *Report on Social Norms.* Working Paper 5. Little Falls, NJ: PaperClip Communications.

Brunell, Amy B., et al. 2011. "Narcissism and Academic Dishonesty: The Exhibitionism Dimension and the Lack of Guilt." *Personality and Individual Differences* 50 (3): 323–28.

Burke, Jeffrey D., and Rolf Loeber. 2015. "The Effectiveness of the Stop Now and Plan (SNAP) Program for Boys at Risk for Violence and Delinquency." *Prevention Science* 16 (2): 242–53.

Bush, George H. W. 1989. "Address to the Nation on the National Drug Control Strategy." American Presidency Project. https://www.presidency.ucsb.edu /documents/address-the-nation-the-national-drug-control-strategy.

Button, A. 2007. "Gendered Mechanisms of Control, Power, and Resistance in Prison Dog Training Programs." Doctoral dissertation. Kansas State University, Manhattan.

Calder, Simon. 2016. "It's the 10th Anniversary of the Liquids Ban on Flights— but Is It Still Necessary?" *Independent*, August 9. https://www.independent .co.uk/travel/news-and-advice/liquids-ban-on-flights-10th-anniversary-do -we-still-need-it-a7181216.html.

California Legislative Information. 2020. "Vehicle Code." https://leginfo.legislature .ca.gov/faces/codesTOCSelected.xhtml.

Cameron, Judy, and W. David Pierce. 1994. "Reinforcement, Reward, and Intrinsic Motivation: A Meta-Analysis." *Review of Educational Research* 64 (3): 363–423.

Cameron, K. S., and R. E. Quinn. 2006. *Diagnosing and Changing Organizational Culture: Based on the Competing Values Framework.* Jossey-Bass.

Cao, Zhiyan, and Ganapathi S. Narayanamoorthy. 2011. "The Effect of Litigation Risk on Management Earnings Forecasts." *Contemporary Accounting Research* 28 (1): 125–73.

Cardwell, Stephanie, and Heith Copes. 2021 (forthcoming). "Neutralization." In *The Cambridge Handbook on Compliance.* Edited by Benjamin Van Rooij and D. Daniel Sokol. Cambridge, UK: Cambridge University Press.

Cardwell, Stephanie M., Lorraine Mazerolle, and Alex R. Piquero. 2019. "Parental Attachment and Truant Rationalizations of Antisocial Behavior: Findings from a Randomized Controlled Trial." *Journal of Crime and Justice* 43 (3): 1–19.

Carreyrou, John. 2018. *Bad Blood: Secrets and Lies in a Silicon Valley Startup.* New York: Knopf.

Carson, Thomas L., Mary Ellen Verdu, and Richard E. Wokutch. 2008. "Whistle-Blowing for Profit: An Ethical Analysis of the Federal False Claims Act." *Journal of Business Ethics* 77 (3): 361–76.

Carter, Zachary D. 2016. "Elizabeth Warren: American Justice Is 'Rigged' in Favor of the Rich." *Huffington Post*, February 3. http://www.huffingtonpost .com/entry/elizabeth-warren-american-justice-rigged-for-rich_us_56b205 a2e4b04f9b57d7e5fe.

Casciani, Dominic. 2009. "Liquid Bomb Plot: What Happened." BBC News, September 7. http://news.bbc.co.uk/2/hi/uk_news/8242479.stm.

Castle, Stephen. 2019. "London Attack Spurs Heroism and Questions About a Prisoner's Release." *New York Times*, November 30. https://www.nytimes .com/2019/11/30/world/europe/london-bridge-attack.html.

Cavanagh, Caitlin, and Elizabeth Cauffman. 2017. "What They Don't Know Can Hurt Them: Mothers' Legal Knowledge and Youth Re-Offending." *Psychology, Public Policy, and Law* 23 (2): 141–53.

Center for Research on Health Care Data Center. 2017. "Pathways to Desistance: A Study of Serious Adolescent Offenders as They Transition to Adulthood and out of Crime." http://www.pathwaysstudy.pitt.edu/index.html.

Chalmers, John M. R., Larry Y. Dann, and Jarrad Harford. 2002. "Managerial Opportunism? Evidence from Directors' and Officers' Insurance Purchases." *Journal of Finance* 57 (2): 609–36.

Chamlin, Mitchell B. 1991. "A Longitudinal Analysis of the Arrest-Crime Relationship: A Further Examination of the Tipping Effect." *Justice Quarterly* 8 (2): 187–99.

Chang, Cindy. 2020. "LAPD Community Policing Has Prevented Crime and Made Residents Feel Safer, Study Finds." *Los Angeles Times*, May 13. https://www.latimes.com/california/story/2020–05–13/lapd-community-policing-program-prevented-crime-made-residents-feel-safer-study-finds.

Chang, Otto H., Donald R. Nichols, and Joseph J. Schultz. 1987. "Taxpayer Attitudes Toward Tax Audit Risk." *Journal of Economic Psychology* 8 (3): 299–309.

Chason, Rachel. 2019. "His First Job Was Training Service Dogs in Prison. The Dogs Go on to Transform Veterans' Lives." *Washington Post*, October 27. https://www.washingtonpost.com/local/his-first-job-was-training-service-dogs-in-prison-the-dogs-go-on-to-transform-veterans-lives/2019/10/26/9ee3e828-f5c7-11e9-ad8b-85e2aa00b5ce_story.html.

Chate, R. A. C. 2008. "An Audit of the Level of Knowledge and Understanding of Informed Consent Amongst Consultant Orthodontists in England, Wales and Northern Ireland." *British Dental Journal* 205 (12): 665–73.

Chen, Brian X. 2019. "Texting While Walking Is Dangerous. Here Is How to Stop." *New York Times*, November 13. https://www.nytimes.com/2019/11/13/technology/personaltech/distracted-walking-twalking.html.

Chen, Hui, and Eugene Soltes. 2018. "Why Compliance Programs Fail and How to Fix Them." *Harvard Business Review* 96 (2): 115–25.

Chossière, Guillaume P., et al. 2017. "Public Health Impacts of Excess NOx Emissions from Volkswagen Diesel Passenger Vehicles in Germany." *Environmental Research Letters* 12: 1–14. https://iopscience.iop.org/article/10.1088/1748-9326/aa5987/pdf.

Cialdini, Robert B. 2003. "Crafting Normative Messages to Protect the Environment." *Current Directions in Psychological Science* 12 (4): 105–9.

———. 2007. "Descriptive Social Norms as Underappreciated Sources of Social Control." *Psychometrika* 72 (2): 263–68.

Cialdini, Robert B., and Noah J. Goldstein. 2004. "Social Influence: Compliance and Conformity." *Annual Review of Psychology* 55: 591–621.

Cialdini, Robert B., et al. 2006. "Managing Social Norms for Persuasive Impact." *Social Influence* 1 (1): 3–15.

Clark, Cory J., Eric Evan Chen, and Peter H. Ditto. 2015. "Moral Coherence Processes: Constructing Culpability and Consequences." *Current Opinion in Psychology* 6: 123–28.

Clarke, Ronald V. 1980. "'Situational' Crime Prevention: Theory and Practice." *British Journal of Criminology* 20 (2): 136–47.

————. 2005. "Seven Misconceptions of Situational Crime Prevention." In *Handbook of Crime Prevention and Community Safety*. Edited by Nick Tilley, 39–70. New York: Routledge.

Clark-Moorman, Kyleigh, Jason Rydberg, and Edmund F. McGarrell. 2019. "Impact Evaluation of a Parolee-Based Focused Deterrence Program on Community-Level Violence." *Criminal Justice Policy Review* 30 (9): 1408–30.

Clinton, William J. 1993. "Remarks Announcing the Anticrime Initiative and an Exchange With Reporters." Washington, DC: US Government Publishing Office. https://www.govinfo.gov/content/pkg/PPP-1993-book2/html/PPP -1993-book2-doc-pg1360-4.htm.

Cochran, John K., and Mitchell B. Chamlin. 2000. "Deterrence and Brutalization: The Dual Effects of Executions." *Justice Quarterly* 17 (4): 685–706.

Cochran, John K., Mitchell B. Chamlin, and Mark Seth. 1994. "Deterrence or Brutalization—An Impact Assessment of Oklahoma's Return to Capital Punishment." *Criminology* 32: 107–34.

Coglianese, Cary, and David Lazer. 2003. "Management-Based Regulation: Prescribing Private Management to Achieve Public Goals." *Law and Society Review* 37 (4): 691–730.

Coglianese, Cary, and Jennifer Nash. 2021 (forthcoming). "Compliance Management Systems: Do They Make A Difference?" In *The Cambridge Handbook of Compliance*. Edited by Benjamin Van Rooij and D. Daniel Sokol. Cambridge, UK: Cambridge University Press.

Cohen, Alexandra O., and Betty J. Casey. 2014. "Rewiring Juvenile Justice: The Intersection of Developmental Neuroscience and Legal Policy." *Trends in Cognitive Sciences* 18 (2): 63–65.

Cohen, Alma, and Rajeev Dehejia. 2004. "The Effect of Automobile Insurance and Accident Liability Laws on Traffic Fatalities." *Journal of Law and Economics* 47 (2): 357–93.

Cohen, Lawrence E., and Marcus Felson. 1979. "Social Change and Crime Rate Trends: A Routine Activity Approach." *American Sociological Review* 44 (4): 588–608.

Colvin, Geoff. 2017. "Inside Wells Fargo's Plan to Fix Its Culture Post-Scandal." *Fortune*, June 11. http://fortune.com/2017/06/11/wells-fargo-scandal-culture.

Cooke, Barbara J., and David P. Farrington. 2016. "The Effectiveness of Dog-Training Programs in Prison: A Systematic Review and Meta-Analysis of the Literature." *Prison Journal* 96 (6): 854–76.

Corkery, Michael. 2016. "Elizabeth Warren Accuses Wells Fargo Chief of 'Gutless Leadership.'" *New York Times*, September 20. https://www.nytimes.com/2016 /09/21/business/dealbook/wells-fargo-ceo-john-stumpf-senate-testimony.html.

Corry, Nida, et al. 2008. "The Factor Structure of the Narcissistic Personality Inventory." *Journal of Personality Assessment* 90 (6): 593–600.

Cowley, Stacy. 2017. "Wells Fargo Review Finds 1.4 Million More Suspect Accounts." *New York Times*, August 31. https://www.nytimes.com/2017/08/31 /business/dealbook/wells-fargo-accounts.html.

Cowley, Stacy, and Jennifer A. Kingson. 2017. "Wells Fargo to Claw Back $75 Million from 2 Former Executives." *New York Times*, April 10. https://www .nytimes.com/2017/04/10/business/wells-fargo-pay-executives-accounts -scandal.html.

Cox, Dennis, and Alan Plumley. 1988. "Analyses of Voluntary Compliance Rates for Different Income Source Classes." Unpublished manuscript, Research Division, Internal Revenue Service, Washington, DC.

Craig, Leam A., Theresa A. Gannon, and Louise Dixon. 2013. *What Works in Offender Rehabilitation: An Evidence-Based Approach to Assessment and Treatment.* Chichester: John Wiley & Sons.

Cullen, Christopher, and Martin Minchin. 2000. *The Prison Population in 1999: A Statistical Review.* Home Office Research Findings 118. London: Home Office.

Cullen, Francis T., Robert Agnew, and Pamela Wilcox. 2014. *Criminological Theory: Past to Present.* Oxford, UK: Oxford University Press.

Cullen, Francis T., Cheryl Lero Jonson, and Daniel S. Nagin. 2011. "Prisons Do Not Reduce Recidivism: The High Cost of Ignoring Science." *Prison Journal* 91 (3 suppl.): 48S–65S.

Cummins, J. David, Richard D. Phillips, and Mary A. Weiss. 2001. "The Incentive Effects of No-Fault Automobile Insurance." *Journal of Law and Economics* 44 (2): 427–64.

Cup, Ine. 2019. "739 bekeuringen bij Touringcar-controle op smartphonegebruik (739 Fines Through Coach-Bus Inspections)." *AD*, September 19. https:// www.ad.nl/binnenland/739-bekeuringen-bij-touringcar-controle-op-smart phonegebruik~a01c04a95.

Currie, Nikki. 2008. "A Case Study of Incarcerated Males Participating in a Canine Training Program." Doctoral dissertation. Kansas State University, Manhattan.

Curtis, Mary B. 2006. "Are Audit-Related Ethical Decisions Dependent upon Mood?" *Journal of Business Ethics* 68 (2): 191–209.

Dalton, Dennis. 2012. *Mahatma Gandhi: Nonviolent Power in Action*: New York: Columbia University Press.

Dambrova, Maija, et al. 2016. "Pharmacological Effects of Meldonium: Biochemical Mechanisms and Biomarkers of Cardiometabolic Activity." *Pharmacological Research* 113: 771–80.

Darley, John M., Kevin M. Carlsmith, and Paul H. Robinson. 2001. "The Ex Ante Function of the Criminal Law." *Law and Society Review* 35 (1): 165–90.

Darley, John M., Catherine A. Sanderson, and Peter S. LaMantia. 1996. "Community Standards for Defining Attempt Inconsistencies with the Model Penal Code." *American Behavioral Scientist* 39 (4): 405–20.

Das Gupta, Ram Prasad. 2007. *Crime and Punishment in Ancient India.* Delhi: BKP.

Dasgupta, Siddhartha, and Ankit Kesharwani. 2010. "Whistleblowing: A Survey of Literature." *IUP Journal of Corporate Governance* 9 (4): 57–70.

De Bruijn, Anne Leonore, et al. 2020. "Why Did Israelis Comply with COVID-19 Mitigation Measures During the Initial First Wave Lockdown?" Available at SSRN: https://papers.ssrn.com/sol3/papers.cfm?abstract_id=3681964.

Deci, Edward L, Richard Koestner, and Richard M. Ryan. 1999. "A Meta-Analytic Review of Experiments Examining the Effects of Extrinsic Rewards on Intrinsic Motivation." *Psychological Bulletin* 125 (6): 627–68.

DeGue, Sarah, et al. 2014. "A Systematic Review of Primary Prevention Strategies for Sexual Violence Perpetration." *Aggression and Violent Behavior* 19 (4): 346–62.

DeJesus, Ivey. 2019. "Jerry Sandusky Scandal at Penn State: The Culture of Silence." *PennLive*, January 5. https://www.pennlive.com/midstate/2012/07/jerry_sandusky_scandal_at_penn.html.

Dell'Antonia, K. J. 2016. "The Right Way to Bribe Your Kids to Read." *New York Times*, July 23. http://www.nytimes.com/2016/07/24/opinion/sunday/the-right-way-to-bribe-your-kids-to-read.html.

DeLongis, A., C. Nathanson, and D. L. Paulhus. 2011. "Revenge: Who, When, and Why." Unpublished manuscript, University of British Columbia, Vancouver.

DeMatteo, David, et al. 2020. "Statement of Concerned Experts on the Use of the Hare Psychopathy Checklist—Revised in Capital Sentencing to Assess Risk for Institutional Violence." *Psychology, Public Policy, and Law* 26 (2): 133–44.

Deming, David J. 2011. "Better Schools, Less Crime?" *Quarterly Journal of Economics* 126 (4): 2063–115.

De Quervain, Dominique J. F., et al. 2004. "The Neural Basis of Altruistic Punishment." *Science* 305 (5688): 1254–58.

De Ridder, Denise T. D., et al. 2012. "Taking Stock of Self-Control: A Meta-Analysis of How Trait Self-Control Relates to a Wide Range of Behaviors." *Personality and Social Psychology Review* 16 (1): 76–99.

Derrig, Richard A., et al. 2002. "The Effect of Population Safety Belt Usage Rates on Motor Vehicle-Related Fatalities." *Accident Analysis and Prevention* 34 (1): 101–10.

Devlin, Rose Anne. 1992. "Liability Versus No-Fault Automobile Insurance Regimes: An Analysis of the Experience in Quebec." In *Contributions to Insurance Economics*. Edited by George Dionne, 499–520. New York: Springer.

Dewees, Don, and Michael Trebilcock. 1992. "The Efficacy of the Tort System and Its Alternatives: A Review of Empirical Evidence." *Osgoode Hall Law Journal* 30 (1): 57-138.

Dierks, Benjamin. 2006. "Corruption Probe Reaches Ever Higher at Siemens." *Guardian*. December 13. https://www.theguardian.com/business/2006/dec/13/internationalnews.

Dietz, Graham, and Nicole Gillespie. 2012. "Rebuilding Trust: How Siemens Atoned for Its Sins." *Guardian*. March 26. https://www.theguardian.com/sustainable-business/recovering-business-trust-siemens.

Domenec, Fanny. 2012. "The 'Greening' of the Annual Letters Published by Exxon, Chevron and BP Between 2003 and 2009." *Journal of Communication Management* 16 (3): 296–311.

Donohue, John J., and Justin Wolfers. 2006. "Estimating the Impact of the Death Penalty on Murder." *American Law and Economics Review* 11 (2): 249–309.

Doyen, Stéphane, et al. 2012. "Behavioral Priming: It's All in the Mind, but Whose Mind?" *PLOS One* 7 (1): e29081 1-7, https://journals.plos.org/plosone/article?id=10.1371/journal.pone.0029081.

Doyle, Elaine, et al. 2009. "Procedural Justice Principles and Tax Compliance in Ireland: A Preliminary Exploration in the Context of Reminder Letters." *Journal of Finance and Management in Public Services* 8 (1): 49–62.

Doyle, Krista. 2021. "Texting While Driving Penalties by State." Aceable, https://www.aceable.com/blog/texting-and-driving-fines-by-state.

DuCharme, Larry L., Paul H. Malatesta, and Stephan E. Sefcik. 2004. "Earnings Management, Stock Issues, and Shareholder Lawsuits." *Journal of Financial Economics* 71 (1): 27–49.

Duindam, Hanne M., Jessica J. Asscher, Machteld Hoeve, Geert Jan J. M. Stams, and Hanneke E. Creemers. 2020. "Are We Barking up the Right Tree? A Meta-Analysis on the Effectiveness of Prison-Based Dog Programs." *Criminal Justice and Behavior* 47: 749–67.

Dyck, Alexander, Adair Morse, and Luigi Zingales. 2010. "Who Blows the Whistle on Corporate Fraud?" *Journal of Finance* 65 (6): 2213–53.

Earle, Beverley H., and Gerald A. Madek. 2007. "The Mirage of Whistleblower Protection Under Sarbanes-Oxley: A Proposal for Change." *American Business Law Journal* 44 (1): 1–54.

Eberwein, Howard Jacob, III. 2008. "Raising Legal Literacy in Public Schools, a Call for Principal Leadership: A National Study of Secondary School Principals' Knowledge of Public School Law." Doctoral dissertation. University of Massachusetts, Amherst.

Eck, John E., Jeffrey S. Gersh, and Charlene Taylor. 2000. "Finding Crime Hot Spots Through Repeat Address Mapping." In *Analyzing Crime Patterns: Frontiers of Practice*. Edited by Victor Goldsmith, Philip G. McGuire, John B. Mollenkopf, Timothy A. Ross, 49–64. New York: Sage.

Edelman, Lauren B. 1992. "Legal Ambiguity and Symbolic Structures: Organizational Mediation of Civil Rights Law." *American Journal of Sociology* 97 (6): 1531–76.

Edelman, Lauren B., and Shauhin A. Talesh. 2011. "To Comply or Not to Comply—That Isn't the Question: How Organizations Construct the Meaning of Compliance." In *Explaining Compliance: Business Responses to Regulation*. Edited by Christine Parker and Vibeke Lehmann Nielsen, 103–22. Cheltenham, UK: Edward Elgar.

Edwards, Frank, Hedwig Lee, and Michael Esposito. 2019. "Risk of Being Killed by Police Use of Force in the United States by Age, Race–Ethnicity, and Sex." *Proceedings of the National Academy of Sciences* 116 (34): 16793–98.

Egan, Matt. 2017. "More Wells Fargo Workers Allege Retaliation for Whistleblowing." CNN, November 7. http://money.cnn.com/2017/11/06/investing/wells-fargo-retaliation-whistleblower/index.html.

Ehrlich, Isaac. 1975. "The Deterrent Effect of Capital Punishment: A Question of Life and Death." *American Economic Review* 65 (3): 397–417.

Ekblom, Paul. 1988. "Preventing Post Office Robberies in London: Effects and Side Effects." *Journal of Security Administration* 11 (2): 36–43.

Elffers, Henk, and Dick J. Hessing. 1997. "Influencing the Prospects of Tax Evasion." *Journal of Economic Psychology* 18 (2): 289–304.

Ellickson, Robert C. 1991. *Order Without Law*. Cambridge, MA: Harvard University Press.

Elvik, Rune. 2016. "Association Between Increase in Fixed Penalties and Road Safety Outcomes: A Meta-Analysis." *Accident Analysis and Prevention* 92: 202–10.

Ely, Robin J., and Debra E. Meyerson. 2010. "An Organizational Approach to Undoing Gender: The Unlikely Case of Offshore Oil Platforms." *Research in Organizational Behavior* 30: 3–34.

Engel, Robin S., Marie Skubak Tillyer, and Nicholas Corsaro. 2013. "Reducing Gang Violence Using Focused Deterrence: Evaluating the Cincinnati Initiative to Reduce Violence (CIRV)." *Justice Quarterly* 30 (3): 403–39.

Engstrom, Nora Freeman. 2011. "An Alternative Explanation for No-Fault's Demise." *DePaul Law Review* 61: 303–82.

Engström, Per, et al. 2015. "Tax Compliance and Loss Aversion." *American Economic Journal: Economic Policy* 7 (4): 132–64.

Ernest-Jones, Max, Daniel Nettle, and Melissa Bateson. 2011. "Effects of Eye Images on Everyday Cooperative Behavior: A Field Experiment." *Evolution and Human Behavior* 32 (3): 172–78.

Ewing, Jack. 2017. *Faster, Higher, Farther: The Volkswagen Scandal*. New York: W. W. Norton.

Fabbri, Marco, Paolo Nicola Barbieri, and Maria Bigoni. 2006. "Death and Deterrence Redux: Science, Law and Causal Reasoning on Capital Punishment." *Ohio State Journal of Criminal Law* 4: 255.

———. 2019. "Ride Your Luck! A Field Experiment on Lottery-Based Incentives for Compliance." *Management Science* 65 (9): 4336–48.

Fagan, Jeffrey. 2014. "Capital Punishment: Deterrent Effects and Capital Costs." Columbia Law School. https://colburnjusticeleague.files.wordpress.com/2014/10/capital-punishment_-deterrent-effects-capital-costs-_-columbia-law-school.pdf.

Fahmy, Chantal, et al. 2020. "Head Injury in Prison: Gang Membership and the Role of Prison Violence." *Journal of Criminal Justice* 67 (March–April), article 101658: 1–11.

Farrington, David P., and Brandon C. Welsh. 2007. *Improved Street Lighting and Crime Prevention: A Systematic Review*. Stockholm: National Council for Crime Prevention.

Farrow, Ronan. 2019. *Catch and Kill: Lies, Spies and a Conspiracy to Protect Predators*. New York: Fleet.

Fazlollah, Mark, Craig R. McCoy, and Julie Shaw. 2018. "Under Court Order, District Attorney Krasner Releases List of Tainted Police." *Philadelphia Inquirer*, March 6. https://www.inquirer.com/philly/news/larry-krasner-philadelphia-police-tainted-misconduct-secret-list-20180306.html.

Fehling, Donald E., Jr. 2018. "School Shooting: Don't Blame Guns for Human Failings." *News Tribune* (Tacoma). February 21. https://www.thenewstribune.com/opinion/letters-to-the-editor/article201414504.html.

Feizi, Ha. 2003. *Basic Writings*. Translated by Burton Watson. New York: Columbia University Press.

Feldman, Yuval. 2018. *The Law of Good People: Challenging States' Ability to Regulate Human Behavior*. New York: Cambridge University Press.

Feuer, Alan. 2019. "'El Chapo' Guzmán Sentenced to Life in Prison, Ending No-torious Criminal Career." *New York Times*, July 17. https://www.nytimes.com/2019/07/17/nyregion/el-chapo-sentencing.html.

Fine, Adam, and Benjamin Van Rooij. 2017. "For Whom Does Deterrence Affect Behavior? Identifying Key Individual Differences." *Law and Human Behavior* 41 (4): 356–60.

Fine, Adam, et al. 2020a. "Age-Graded Differences and Parental Influences on Ad-olescents' Obligation to Obey the Law." *Journal of Developmental and Life-Course Criminology* 6 (1): 26–42.

Fine, A., et al. 2020b. "Youth Perceptions of Law Enforcement and Worry About Crime from 1976–2016." *Criminal Justice & Behavior* 47 (5): 564–81.

Fine, A., et al. 2020c. "Police Legitimacy: Identifying Developmental Trends and Whether Youths' Perceptions Can Be Changed." *Journal of Experimental Crimi-nology* (early view online). https://doi.org/10.1007/s11292-020-09438-7.

Fine, Adam, et al. 2016. "Rule Orientation and Behavior: Development and Validation of a Scale Measuring Individual Acceptance of Rule Violation." *Psychology, Public Policy, and Law* 22 (3): 314–29.

Finkel, Norman J. 1995. "Prestidigitation, Statistical Magic, and Supreme Court Numerology in Juvenile Death Penalty Cases." *Psychology, Public Policy, and Law* 1 (3): 612–42.

Fisman, Ray. 2008. "Going Down Swinging." *Slate*, March 20. http://www.slate.com/articles/business/the_dismal_science/2008/03/going_down_swinging.html.

Flaherty, Colleen. 2017. "Sociology's 'Mic Drop' Moment." *Inside Higher Ed*, Oc-tober 12. https://www.insidehighered.com/news/2017/10/12/chief-justice-john-roberts-calls-data-gerrymandering-sociological-gobbledygook.

Flexon, Jamie L., et al. 2016. "Low Self-Control and the Dark Triad: Disentan-gling the Predictive Power of Personality Traits on Young Adult Substance Use, Offending and Victimization." *Journal of Criminal Justice* 46: 159–69.

Foley, Regina M. 2001. "Academic Characteristics of Incarcerated Youth and Correctional Educational Programs: A Literature Review." *Journal of Emotional and Behavioral Disorders* 9 (4): 248–59.

Foshee, Vangie A., et al. 2004. "Assessing the Long-Term Effects of the Safe Dates Program and a Booster in Preventing and Reducing Adolescent Dating Vio-lence Victimization and Perpetration." *American Journal of Public Health* 94 (4): 619–24.

Fox 2 Detroit. 2020. "Gov. Gretchen Whitmer Urges Michigan Residents to Stay the Course on Social Distancing as Protesters Loom." April 15. https://www.fox2detroit.com/news/gov-gretchen-whitmer-urges-michigan-residents-to-stay-the-course-on-social-distancing-as-protesters-loom.

Fradella, Henry F. 2003. "A Content Analysis of Federal Judicial Views of the Social Science Researcher's Black Arts." *Rutgers Law Journal* 35: 103–70.

Freeman, Richard B. 1991. *Crime and the Employment of Disadvantaged Youths*. Cam-bridge, MA: National Bureau of Economic Research.

Frey, Darcy. 2002. "How Green Is BP?" *New York Times*, December 8. https://www.nytimes.com/2002/12/08/magazine/how-green-is-bp.html.

Frost, William. 2017. "Wells Fargo Report Gives Inside Look at the Culture That Crushed the Bank's Reputation." *CNBC*, April 10. https://www.cnbc.com /2017/04/10/wells-fargo-report-shows-culture-that-crushed-banks -reputation.html.

Furnham, Adrian, Steven C. Richards, and Delroy L. Paulhus. 2013. "The Dark Triad of Personality: A 10 Year Review." *Social and Personality Psychology Compass* 7 (3): 199–216.

Garcia, Uriel J. 2019. "Phoenix Police Union Backs Off No-Confidence Vote Against Chief Jeri Williams." *AZCentral*, November 11. https://www.azcentral.com/story /news/local/phoenix/2019/11/01/phoenix-police-union-officers-avoid-no -confidence-vote-against-chief/4129121002.

Ge, Weili, Allison Koester, and Sarah McVay. 2017. "Benefits and Costs of Sarbanes-Oxley Section 404 (B) Exemption: Evidence from Small Firms' Internal Control Disclosures." *Journal of Accounting and Economics* 63 (2–3): 358–84.

Geertz, Clifford. 1973. "Thick Description: Toward and Interpretive Theory of Culture." In *The Interpretation of Cultures: Selected Essays*, 3–30. New York: Basic Books.

———. 2000. "Deep Play: Notes on the Balinese Cockfight." In *Culture and Politics: A Reader.* Edited by Lane Crothers and Charles Lockhart, 175–201. New York: St. Martin's Press.

Gendreau, Paul, et al. 2000. "The Effects of Community Sanctions and Incarceration on Recidivism." *Forum on Corrections Research* 12 (2): 10–13.

Gibbs, Carole, Michael B. Cassidy, and Louie Rivers III. 2013. "A Routine Activities Analysis of White-Collar Crime in Carbon Markets." *Law and Policy* 35 (4): 341–74.

Gibson, James L. 2004. "Does Truth Lead to Reconciliation? Testing the Causal Assumptions of the South African Truth and Reconciliation Process." *American Journal of Political Science* 48 (2): 201–17.

———. 2005. "The Truth About Truth and Reconciliation in South Africa." *International Political Science Review* 26 (4): 341–61.

Gillan, Stuart L., and Christine A. Panasian. 2015. "On Lawsuits, Corporate Governance, and Directors' and Officers' Liability Insurance." *Journal of Risk and Insurance* 82 (4): 793–822.

Gino, Francesca, Shahar Ayal, and Dan Ariely. 2009. "Contagion and Differentiation in Unethical Behavior: The Effect of One Bad Apple on the Barrel." *Psychological Science* 20 (3): 393–98.

Gino, Francesca, and Max H. Bazerman. 2009. "When Misconduct Goes Unnoticed: The Acceptability of Gradual Erosion in Others' Unethical Behavior." *Journal of Experimental Social Psychology* 45 (4): 708–19.

Gino, Francesca, Michael I. Norton, and Dan Ariely. 2010. "The Counterfeit Self: The Deceptive Costs of Faking It." *Psychological Science* 21 (5): 712–20.

Givelber, Daniel J., William J. Bowers, and Carolyn L. Blitch. 1984. "Tarasoff, Myth and Reality: An Empirical Study of Private Law in Action." *Wisconsin Law Review* 1984 (2): 443–98.

Glassbrenner, Donna, Joseph S. Carra, and James Nichols. 2004. "Recent Estimates of Safety Belt Use." *Journal of Safety Research* 35 (2): 237–44.

Glazer, Emily. 2017. "Wells Fargo Digs Deeper into Its Culture Issues." *Wall Street Journal*, March 21. https://www.wsj.com/articles/wells-fargo-digs-deeper-into -its-culture-issues-1490124295.

Glinton, Sonari. 2016. "'We Didn't Lie,' Volkswagen CEO Says of Emissions Scandal." National Public Radio, January 11. https://www.npr.org/sections /thetwo-way/2016/01/11/462682378/we-didnt-lie-volkswagen-ceo-says-of -emissions-scandal.

Glueck, Sheldon, and Eleanor Glueck. 1937. *Later Criminal Careers*. New York: Commonwealth Fund.

Gneezy, Uri, and Aldo Rustichini. 2000. "A Fine Is a Price." *Journal of Legal Studies* 29: 1-17.

Goebel, Sebastian, and Barbara E. Weißenberger. 2017. "The Relationship Between Informal Controls, Ethical Work Climates, and Organizational Performance." *Journal of Business Ethics* 141 (3): 505–28.

Goldenberg, Suzanne. 2010. "US Oil Spill Inquiry Chief Slams BP's 'Culture of Complacency.'" *Guardian*, November 9. https://www.theguardian.com /environment/2010/nov/09/oil-spill-inquiry-culture-complacency-bp.

Goldstein, Joseph. 2013. "Judge Rejects New York's Stop-and-Frisk Policy." *New York Times*, April 12. https://www.nytimes.com/2013/08/13/nyregion/stop -and-frisk-practice-violated-rights-judge-rules.html.

Gottfredson, Michael R., and Travis Hirschi. 1990. *A General Theory of Crime*. Stanford, CA: Stanford University Press.

Gow, David. 2008. "Siemens Boss Admits Setting Up Slush Funds." *Guardian*. May 27. https://www.theguardian.com/business/2008/may/27/technology.europe.

Grand View Research. 2020. *Enterprise Governance, Risk and Compliance Market Size, Share and Trends Analysis Report by Component, by Software, by Service, by Enterprise Type, by Vertical, and Segment Forecasts, 2020–2027*. San Francisco: Grand View Research.

Graves, Allison. 2016. "Did Hillary Clinton Call African-American Youth 'Superpredators?'" PolitiFact, August 28. http://www.politifact.com/truth-o-meter /statements/2016/aug/28/reince-priebus/did-hillary-clinton-call-african -american-youth-su.

Gray, Garry C. 2006. "The Regulation of Corporate Violations Punishment, Compliance, and the Blurring of Responsibility." *British Journal of Criminology* 46 (5): 875–92.

Gray, Garry C., and Susan S. Silbey. 2012. "The Other Side of the Compliance Relationship." In *Explaining Compliance: Business Responses to Regulation*. Edited by Christine Parker and Vibeke Lehmann Nielsen, 123–38. Cheltenham: Edgar Elden.

———. 2014. "Governing Inside the Organization: Interpreting Regulation and Compliance." *American Journal of Sociology* 120 (1): 96–145.

Gray, Garry, and Jérôme Pélisse. 2019. "Frontline Workers and the Role of Legal and Regulatory Intermediaries." HAL. https://hal.archives-ouvertes.fr/hal -02316029/document.

Greene, Joshua D., et al. 2004. "The Neural Bases of Cognitive Conflict and Control in Moral Judgment." *Neuron* 44 (2): 389–400.

Greenwald, Anthony G., and Linda Hamilton Krieger. 2006. "Implicit Bias: Scientific Foundations." *California Law Review* 94 (4): 945–67.

Greenwald, Anthony G., et al. 2009. "Understanding and Using the Implicit Association Test: III. Meta-Analysis of Predictive Validity." *Journal of Personality and Social Psychology* 97 (1): 17–41.

Griffiths, Margaret, ed. 2020. "Casualties in Iraq: The Human Cost of Occupation." Antiwar.com. https://antiwar.com/casualties.

Grijns, Mies, and Hoko Horii. 2018. "Child Marriage in a Village in West Java (Indonesia): Compromises Between Legal Obligations and Religious Concerns." *Asian Journal of Law and Society* 5 (2): 453–66.

Groff, Elizabeth R. 2007. "Simulation for Theory Testing and Experimentation: An Example Using Routine Activity Theory and Street Robbery." *Journal of Quantitative Criminology* 23 (2): 75–103.

Gronhovd, Sheri L. 1986. "Social Science Statistics in the Courtroom: The Debate Resurfaces in McCleskey v. Kemp." *Notre Dame Law Review* 62: 688–712.

*Guardian*. 2019. "New Zealand: Just 11% of Sexual Violence Reports Lead to Conviction." November 1. https://www.theguardian.com/world/2019/nov/01/new-zealand-just-11-of-sexual-violence-reports-lead-to-conviction.

Guerette, Rob T., and Kate J. Bowers. 2009. "Assessing the Extent of Crime Displacement and Diffusion of Benefits: A Review of Situational Crime Prevention Evaluations." *Criminology* 47 (4): 1331–68.

Gunia, Brian C., et al. 2012. "Contemplation and Conversation: Subtle Influences on Moral Decision Making." *Academy of Management Journal* 55 (1): 13–33.

Gunningham, Neil, and Darren Sinclair. 2014. "The Impact of Safety Culture on Systemic Risk Management." *European Journal of Risk Regulation* 5: 505–16.

Haidt, Jonathan. 2001. "The Emotional Dog and Its Rational Tail: A Social Intuitionist Approach to Moral Judgment." *Psychological Review* 108 (4): 814–34.

———. 2007. "The New Synthesis in Moral Psychology." *Science* 316 (5827): 998–1002.

———. 2012. *The Righteous Mind: Why Good People Are Divided by Politics and Religion*. New York: Vintage.

Haidt, Jonathan, Fredrik Bjorklund, and Scott Murphy. 2000. "Moral Dumbfounding: When Intuition Finds No Reason." Unpublished manuscript, University of Virginia.

Haidt, Jonathan, and Matthew A. Hersh. 2001. "Sexual Morality: The Cultures and Emotions of Conservatives and Liberals." *Journal of Applied Social Psychology* 31 (1): 191–221.

Haidt, Jonathan, Silvia Helena Koller, and Maria G. Dias. 1993. "Affect, Culture, and Morality, or Is It Wrong to Eat Your Dog?" *Journal of Personality and Social Psychology* 65 (4): 613–28.

Haney-López, Ian. 2015. *Dog Whistle Politics: How Coded Racial Appeals Have Reinvented Racism and Wrecked the Middle Class*: New York: Oxford University Press.

Hannaford, Alex. 2016. "No Exit." *Texas Observer*, October 3. https://www.texasobserver.org/three-strikes-law-no-exit.

Hare, Robert D., et al. 1990. "The Revised Psychopathy Checklist: Reliability and Factor Structure." *Psychological Assessment: A Journal of Consulting and Clinical Psychology* 2 (3): 338–41.

Harrison, Roger, and Herb Stokes. 1992. *Diagnosing Organizational Culture.* San Francisco: Pfeiffer.

Hartner, Martina, et al. 2008. "Procedural Fairness and Tax Compliance." *Economic Analysis and Policy* 38 (1): 137–52.

Hatch, Mary Jo. 1993. "The Dynamics of Organizational Culture." *Academy of Management Review* 18 (4): 657–93.

Heaton, Paul, and Eric Helland. 2008. "No-Fault Insurance and Automobile Accidents." Working Paper WR-551-1-ICJ. RAND.

Helland, Eric, and Alexander Tabarrok. 2007. "Does Three Strikes Deter? A Nonparametric Estimation." *Journal of Human Resources* 42 (2): 309–30.

Helmond, Petra, et al. 2015. "A Meta-Analysis on Cognitive Distortions and Externalizing Problem Behavior: Associations, Moderators, and Treatment Effectiveness." *Criminal Justice and Behavior* 42 (3): 245–62.

Henley, Jon. 2018. "Dutch Cyclists Face Mobile Phone Ban." *Guardian.* September 27. https://www.theguardian.com/world/2018/sep/27/dutch-cyclists-face -mobile-phone-ban.

Henriques, Diana B. 2011. *The Wizard of Lies: Bernie Madoff and the Death of Trust.* New York: Macmillan.

Hensley, Scott. 2009. "Pfizer Whistleblower Tells His Bextra Story." NPR, September 3. https://www.npr.org/sections/health-shots/2009/09/pfizer _whistleblower_tells_his.html.

Hirschi, Travis. 2004. "Self-Control and Crime." In *Handbook of Self-Regulation: Regulation, Theory, and Applications.* Edited by Roy F. Baumeister and Kathleen D. Vohs, 537–52. New York: Guilford Press.

Hirschi, Travis, and Michael Gottfredson. 1993. "Commentary: Testing the General Theory of Crime." *Journal of Research in Crime and Delinquency* 30 (1): 47–54.

Ho, Daniel E. 2017. "Does Peer Review Work: An Experiment of Experimentalism." *Stanford Law Review* 69: 1–120.

Hofeditz, Marcel, et al. 2017. "'Want To' Versus 'Have To': Intrinsic and Extrinsic Motivators as Predictors of Compliance Behavior Intention." *Human Resource Management* 56 (1): 25–49.

Hoffman, Andrew J., and P. Devereaux Jennings. 2011. "The BP Oil Spill as a Cultural Anomaly? Institutional Context, Conflict, and Change." *Journal of Management Inquiry* 20 (2): 100–112.

Hofstede, G., et al. 1990. "Measuring Organizational Cultures: A Qualitative and Quantitative Study Across Twenty Cases." *Administrative Science Quarterly* 35 (2): 286–316.

Holiday, Ryan. 2018. *Conspiracy: Peter Thiel, Hulk Hogan, Gawker, and the Anatomy of Intrigue.* New York: Portfolio.

Hollinger, Richard C. 1991. "Neutralizing in the Workplace: An Empirical Analysis of Property Theft and Production Deviance." *Deviant Behavior* 12 (2): 169–202.

Holloway, Katy R., Trevor Bennett, and David P. Farrington. 2008. *Effectiveness of Treatment in Reducing Drug-Related Crime: Report Prepared for the National Council for Crime Prevention, Sweden.* Swedish National Council for Crime Prevention (BRÅ).

Holt, Thomas J., and Adam M. Bossler. 2008. "Examining the Applicability of Lifestyle-Routine Activities Theory for Cybercrime Victimization." *Deviant Behavior* 30 (1): 1–25.

Howell, James C. 2009. "Superpredators and Other Myths About Juvenile Delinquency." In *Preventing and Reducing Juvenile Delinquency: A Comprehensive Framework*, 2nd ed., 3–16. Los Angeles: SAGE.

Humphreys, Keith. 2018. "Opioid Epidemic Is Deadlier Than the Vietnam War in '68, Study Says." *Washington Post*, June 7. https://www.washingtonpost.com /news/wonk/wp/2018/06/07/the-opioid-epidemic-is-deadlier-than-the -vietnam-war-study-says.

Independent Directors of the Board of Wells Fargo. 2017. *Sales Practice Investigation Report*. April 10. https://www08.wellsfargomedia.com/assets/pdf/about /investor-relations/presentations/2017/board-report.pdf.

Isaac, Mike. 2019. *Super Pumped: The Battle for Uber*. New York: W. W. Norton.

Johnson, Boris. 2020. "This country has made a huge effort, a huge sacrifice, and done absolutely brilliantly well in delaying the spread of the virus." Twitter. April 4. https://twitter.com/borisjohnson/status/1246349201711288320.

Johnson, Carrie. 2014. "20 Years Later, Parts of Major Crime Bill Viewed as Terrible Mistake." NPR. September 12. https://www.npr.org/2014/09/12 /347736999/20-years-later-major-crime-bill-viewed-as-terrible-mistake?t =1608801496559.

Johnson, Eric J., et al. 2012. "Beyond Nudges: Tools of a Choice Architecture." *Marketing Letters* 23 (2): 487–504.

Johnson, Rucker, and Steven Raphael. 2012. "How Much Crime Reduction Does the Marginal Prisoner Buy?" *Journal of Law and Economics* 55 (2): 275–310.

Jonas-van Dijk, Jiska, et al. 2020. "Victim–Offender Mediation and Reduced Reoffending: Gauging the Self-Selection Bias." *Crime and Delinquency* 66 (6–7): 949–72.

Jones, Daniel N., and Delroy L. Paulhus. 2009. "Machiavellianism." In *Handbook of Individual Differences in Social Behavior*. Edited by Mark R. Leary and Rick H. Hoyle, 93–108. New York: Guilford Press.

Jones, Renae A., Nerina L. Jimmieson, and Andrew Griffiths. 2005. "The Impact of Organizational Culture and Reshaping Capabilities on Change Implementation Success: The Mediating Role of Readiness for Change." *Journal of Management Studies* 42 (2): 361–86.

Jonson, Cheryl L. 2010. "The Impact of Imprisonment on Reoffending: A Meta-Analysis." Doctoral dissertation. University of Cincinnati.

Joy Tong, L. S., and David P. Farrington. 2006. "How Effective Is the 'Reasoning and Rehabilitation' Programme in Reducing Reoffending? A Meta-Analysis of Evaluations in Four Countries." *Psychology, Crime and Law* 12 (1): 3–24.

Kachalia, Allen, and Michelle M. Mello. 2011. "New Directions in Medical Liability Reform." *New England Journal of Medicine* 364 (16): 1564–72.

Kagan, Robert A., and John T. Scholz. 1984. "The 'Criminology of the Corporation' and Regulatory Enforcement Strategies." In *Regulatory Enforcement*. Edited by Keith Hawkins and John M. Thomas, 67–95. Boston: Kluwer-Nijhoff.

Kagan, Robert A., and Jerome H. Skolnick. 1993. "Banning Smoking: Compliance Without Enforcement." In *Smoking Policy: Law, Politics, and Culture*.

Edited by Robert L. Rabin and Stephen D. Sugarman, 69–94. New York: Oxford University Press.

Kahneman, Daniel. 2011. *Thinking, Fast and Slow.* New York: Macmillan.

Kahneman, Daniel, and Amos Tversky. 1979. "Prospect Theory: An Analysis of Decision Under Risk." *Econometrica: Journal of the Econometric Society* 47 (2): 263–91.

Kang, Songman. 2016. "Inequality and Crime Revisited: Effects of Local Inequality and Economic Segregation on Crime." *Journal of Population Economics* 29 (2): 593–626.

Kaptein, Muel, and Mark S. Schwartz. 2008. "The Effectiveness of Business Codes: A Critical Examination of Existing Studies and the Development of an Integrated Research Model." *Journal of Business Ethics* 77 (2): 111–27.

Kaptein, Muel, and Martien Van Helvoort. 2019. "A Model of Neutralization Techniques." *Deviant Behavior* 40 (10): 1260–85.

Kasper, van Laarhoven. 2019. "Kabinet wil gegarandeerde celstraffen voor belagers hulpverleners (Government wants mandatory prison for harassment of safety and enforcement personnel)." *NRC Handelsblad*, October 14. https://www.nrc .nl/nieuws/2019/10/14/kabinet-wil-gegarandeerde-celstraffen-voor-belagen -hulpverleners-a3976643.

Keizer, Kees, Siegwart Lindenberg, and Linda Steg. 2011. "The Reversal Effect of Prohibition Signs." *Group Processes and Intergroup Relations* 14 (5): 681–88.

Kellaway, Lucy. 2015. "Wells Fargo's Happy:Grumpy Ratio Is No Way to Audit Staff." *Financial Times*, February 8. https://www.ft.com/content/31967ba6 -aacb-11e4-81bc-00144feab7de.

Kellermann, Arthur L., et al. 1993. "Gun Ownership as a Risk Factor for Homicide in the Home." *New England Journal of Medicine* 329 (15): 1084–91.

Kern, Mary C., and Dolly Chugh. 2009. "Bounded Ethicality: The Perils of Loss Framing." *Psychological Science* 20 (3): 378–84.

Kidd, David G., Anne T. McCartt, and Nathan J. Oesch. 2014. "Attitudes Toward Seat Belt Use and In-Vehicle Technologies for Encouraging Belt Use." *Traffic Injury Prevention* 15 (1): 10–17.

Kim, Irene. 2015. "Directors' and Officers' Insurance and Opportunism in Accounting Choice." *Accounting and Taxation* 7 (1): 51–65.

Kim, Pauline T. 1999. "Norms, Learning and Law: Exploring the Influences of Workers' Legal Knowledge." *University of Illinois Legal Review* 1999 (2): 447–516.

Kirchler, Erich. 2007. *The Economic Psychology of Tax Behaviour.* New York: Cambridge University Press.

Kirchler, Erich, Erik Hoelzl, and Ingrid Wahl. 2008. "Enforced Versus Voluntary Tax Compliance: The 'Slippery Slope' Framework." *Journal of Economic Psychology* 29 (2): 210–25.

Kirchler, Erich, and Boris Maciejovsky. 2001. "Tax Compliance Within the Context of Gain and Loss Situations, Expected and Current Asset Position, and Profession." *Journal of Economic Psychology* 22 (2): 173–94.

Kirchler, Erich, et al. 2010. "Why Pay Taxes? A Review of Tax Compliance Decisions." In *Developing Alternative Frameworks for Explaining Tax Compliance.* Edited James Alm, Jorge Martinez-Vazquez, and Benno Torgler, 59. New York: Routledge.

Kish-Gephart, Jennifer J., David A. Harrison, and Linda Klebe Treviño. 2010. "Bad
    Apples, Bad Cases, and Bad Barrels: Meta-Analytic Evidence About Sources of
    Unethical Decisions at Work." *Journal of Applied Psychology* 95 (1): 1-31.
Kivisto, Aaron J., Bradley Ray, and Peter L. Phalen. 2017. "Firearm Legislation
    and Fatal Police Shootings in the United States." *American Journal of Public
    Health* 107 (7): 1068-75.
Kjøbli, John, Henrik Daae Zachrisson, and Gunnar Bjørnebekk. 2018. "Three
    Randomized Effectiveness Trials—One Question: Can Callous-Unemotional
    Traits in Children Be Altered?" *Journal of Clinical Child and Adolescent Psychol-
    ogy* 47 (3): 436-43.
Kleck, Gary, et al. 2005. "The Missing Link in General Deterrence Research."
    *Criminology* 43: 623-60.
Klockars, Carl B. 1974. *The Professional Fence.* New York: Free Press.
Kochanowski, Paul S., and Madelyn V. Young. 1985. "Deterrent Aspects of
    No-Fault Automobile Insurance: Some Empirical Findings." *Journal of Risk
    and Insurance* 52 (2): 269-88.
Koelle, Felix, et al. 2017. "Nudging the Electorate: What Works and Why?"
    CeDEx Discussion Paper 2017-16. https://www.nottingham.ac.uk/cedex
    /documents/papers/cedex-discussion-paper-2017-16.pdf.
Koessler, Ann-Kathrin, et al. 2019. "Commitment to Pay Taxes: Results from
    Field and Laboratory Experiments." *European Economic Review* 115: 78-98.
Kogler, Christoph, et al. 2013. "Trust and Power as Determinants of Tax Com-
    pliance: Testing the Assumptions of the Slippery Slope Framework in Austria,
    Hungary, Romania and Russia." *Journal of Economic Psychology* 34: 169-80.
Kohlberg, Lawrence. 1963. "The Development of Children's Orientations Toward
    a Moral Order: I. Sequence in the Development of Moral Thought." *Vita
    Humana* 6 (1): 11-33.
———. 1971. "Stages of Moral Development." *Moral Education* 1 (51): 23-92.
Kollewe, Julia. 2010. "BP Chief Executive Tony Hayward in His Own Words."
    *Guardian.* May 14. https://www.theguardian.com/environment/2010/may/14
    /tony-hayward-bp.
Kooistra, Emmeke, et al. 2020. "Mitigating COVID-19 in a Nationally Represen-
    tative UK Sample: Personal Abilities and Obligation to Obey the Law Shape
    Compliance with Mitigation Measures." Working paper. https://psyarxiv.com
    /zuc23.
Kotaman, Hüseyin. 2017. "Impact of Rewarding and Parenting Styles on Young
    Children's Cheating Behavior." *European Journal of Developmental Psychology* 14
    (2): 127-40.
Kovandzic, Tomislav V., John J. Sloan III, and Lynne M. Vieraitis. 2004. "'Strik-
    ing Out' as Crime Reduction Policy: The Impact of 'Three Strikes' Laws on
    Crime Rates in US Cities." *Justice Quarterly* 21 (2): 207-39.
Kovandzic, Tomislav V., Lynne M. Vieraitis, and Denise Paquette Boots. 2009.
    "Does the Death Penalty Save Lives?" *Criminology and Public Policy* 8 (4):
    803-43.
Krawiec, Kimberly D. 2003. "Cosmetic Compliance and the Failure of Negotiated
    Governance." *Washington University Law Quarterly* 81: 487-544.

Kristal, Ariella S., et al. 2020. "Signing at the Beginning Versus at the End Does Not Decrease Dishonesty." *Proceedings of the National Academy of Sciences* 117 (13): 7103–7.

Kuiper, Malouke Esra, et al. 2020. "The Intelligent Lockdown: Compliance with COVID-19 Mitigation Measures in the Netherlands." Working paper. https://psyarxiv.com/5wdb3.

Lakatos, Joseph, Bethany Davidson, and Kenneth Sanney. 2017. "Calling Wells Fargo's CEO: Drive Widespread Cultural Change via Implementation of the Dynamic Organizational Model and Permeation of Servant Leadership Throughout the Financial Institution." *Journal of International Management Studies* 12 (1): 1–8.

Landes, Elisabeth M. 1982. "Insurance, Liability, and Accidents: A Theoretical and Empirical Investigation of the Effect of No-Fault Accidents." *Journal of Law and Economics* 25 (1): 49–65.

Langan, Patrick A., and David J. Levin. 2002. "Recidivism of Prisoners Released in 1994." *Federal Sentencing Reporter* 15 (1): 58–65.

Lantigua-Williams, Juleyka. 2016. "Giving Students a Second Chance." *Atlantic.* June 10. https://www.theatlantic.com/politics/archive/2016/06/fair-chance-education-pledge/486518.

Lardén, Martin, et al. 2006. "Moral Judgement, Cognitive Distortions and Empathy in Incarcerated Delinquent and Community Control Adolescents." *Psychology, Crime and Law* 12 (5): 453–62.

Laub, John H., and Robert J. Sampson. 2003. *Shared Beginnings, Divergent Lives.* Cambridge, MA: Harvard University Press.

Laufer, William S. 1999. "Corporate Liability, Risk Shifting, and the Paradox of Compliance." *Vanderbilt Law Review* 52: 1341–420.

Laufer, William S., and Diana C. Robertson. 1997. "Corporate Ethics Initiatives as Social Control." *Journal of Business Ethics* 16 (10): 1029–47.

Leap, Jorja. 2020. *Evaluation of the LAPD Community Safety Partnership.* Los Angeles: UCLA Luskin. http://www.lapdpolicecom.lacity.org/051220/CSP%20Evaluation%20Report_2020_FINAL.pdf.

Lee, Kibeom, Michael C. Ashton, and Reinout E. de Vries. 2005. "Predicting Workplace Delinquency and Integrity with the HEXACO and Five-Factor Models of Personality Structure." *Human Performance* 18 (2): 179–97.

Lee, Kibeom, Michael C. Ashton, and Kang-Hyun Shin. 2005. "Personality Correlates of Workplace Anti-Social Behavior." *Applied Psychology* 54 (1): 81–98.

Lee, Kibeom, Marie Gizzarone, and Michael C. Ashton. 2003. "Personality and the Likelihood to Sexually Harass." *Sex Roles* 49 (1–2): 59–69.

Lens, Michael C. 2013. "Subsidized Housing and Crime: Theory, Mechanisms, and Evidence." *Journal of Planning Literature* 28 (4): 352–63.

———. 2014. "The Impact of Housing Vouchers on Crime in US Cities and Suburbs." *Urban Studies* 51 (6): 1274–89.

Lepper, Mark R., David Greene, and Richard E. Nisbett. 1973. "Undermining Children's Intrinsic Interest with Extrinsic Reward: A Test of the 'Overjustification' Hypothesis." *Journal of Personality and Social Psychology* 28 (1): 129–37.

Levine, Harry G., and Craig Reinarman. 2004. *Alcohol Prohibition and Drug Prohibition. Lessons from Alcohol Policy for Drug Policy.* Amsterdam: CEDRO.

Lewis, Anthony. 1987. "Abroad at Home: Bowing to Racism." *New York Times.* April 28. https://www.nytimes.com/1987/04/28/opinion/abroad-at-home -bowing-to-racism.html.

Lilienfeld, Scott O., and Brian P. Andrews. 1996. "Development and Preliminary Validation of a Self-Report Measure of Psychopathic Personality Traits in Noncriminal Population." *Journal of Personality Assessment* 66 (3): 488–524.

Lin, Chen, Micah S. Officer, and Hong Zou. 2011. "Directors' and Officers' Liability Insurance and Acquisition Outcomes." *Journal of Financial Economics* 102 (3): 507–25.

Lipsey, Mark W., and Francis T. Cullen. 2007. "The Effectiveness of Correctional Rehabilitation: A Review of Systematic Reviews." *Annual Review of Law and Social Science* 3: 297–320.

Littleton, Mark. 2008. "Teachers' Knowledge of Education Law." *Action in Teacher Education* 30 (2): 71–78.

Liyanarachchi, Gregory, and Chris Newdick. 2009. "The Impact of Moral Reasoning and Retaliation on Whistle-Blowing: New Zealand Evidence." *Journal of Business Ethics* 89 (1): 37–57.

Lochner, Lance, and Enrico Moretti. 2004. "The Effect of Education on Crime: Evidence from Prison Inmates, Arrests, and Self-Reports." *American Economic Review* 94 (1): 155–89.

Lopez, Linette. 2011. "China Mobile Executive Gets Death Penalty for Taking Bribes from Siemens." *Business Insider,* June 21. https://www.businessinsider. com/chinese-exec-gets-death-penalty-for-taking-bribes-from-siemens-2011–6.

Los Angeles Mayor's Office. 2017. "Mayor Garcetti Announces New Expansion of Community Safety Partnership." March 3. https://www.lamayor.org/mayor -garcetti-announces-new-expansion-community-safety-partnership.

Loughran, David S. 2001. *The Effect of No-Fault Automobile Insurance on Driver Behavior and Automobile Accidents in the United States.* Santa Monica: Rand Institute for Civil Justice.

Loughran, Thomas A. 2019. "Behavioral Criminology and Public Policy." *Criminology and Public Policy* 18 (4): 737–58.

Lubin, Joann S. 2017. "After Uber and Wells Fargo, Boards Wake Up to Culture." *Wall Street Journal,* October 5. https://www.wsj.com/articles/after-uber-boards -wake-up-to-company-culture-1507046401.

Lustgarten, Abrahm. 2010. "Furious Growth and Cost Cuts Led to BP Accidents Past and Present." ProPublica, October 26. https://www.propublica.org/article /bp-accidents-past-and-present.

Lustgarten, Abrahm. 2012. *Run to Failure: BP and the Making of the Deepwater Horizon Disaster.* New York: W. W. Norton.

Lustgarten, Abrahm, and Ryan Knutson. 2010. "Years of Internal BP Probes Warned That Neglect Could Lead to Accidents." ProPublica, June 7. https:// www.propublica.org/article/years-of-internal-bp-probes-warned-that-neglect -could-lead-to-accidents.

Lyall, Sarah. 2010. "In BP's Record, a History of Boldness and Costly Blunders." *New York Times,* July 12. https://www.nytimes.com/2010/07/13/business /energy-environment/13bprisk.html.

Maarse, Geert. 2016. "Het is heel moeilijk om wildplassers op heterdaad te betrappen" (It is very difficult to catch public urinators in the act). *Erasmus Magazine*, December 12. https://www.erasmusmagazine.nl/2016/12/22/het-is-heel -moeilijk-om-wildplassers-op-heterdaad-te-betrappen.

MacCoun, Robert J. 2005. "Voice, Control, and Belonging: The Double-Edged Sword of Procedural Fairness." *Annual Review of Law and Social Science* 1: 171–201.

MacDonald, John, et al. 2015. "Targeting Voter Registration with Incentives: A Randomized Controlled Trial of a Lottery in a London Borough." *Electoral Studies* 40: 170–75.

Macomber, Donna, et al. 2010. "Education in Juvenile Detention Facilities in the State of Connecticut: A Glance at the System." *Journal of Correctional Education* 61 (3): 223–61.

Maki, Alexander, et al. 2016. "Paying People to Protect the Environment: A Meta-Analysis of Financial Incentive Interventions to Promote Proenvironmental Behaviors." *Journal of Environmental Psychology* 47: 242–55.

Makkai, T., and John Braithwaite. 1996. "Procedural Justice and Regulatory Compliance." *Law and Human Behavior* 20 (1): 83–98.

Males, Mike, and Dan Macallair. 1999. "Striking Out: The Failure of California's Three Strikes and You're Out Law." *Stanford Law and Policy Review* 11: 65–74.

Mamdani, Mahmood. 2002. "Amnesty or Impunity? A Preliminary Critique of the Report of the Truth and Reconciliation Commission of South Africa (TRC)." *Diacritics* 32 (3–4): 33–59.

Manske, Michael, and Jana Quoos. 2018. "Secret Lab-Report on the Monkey Testing: Why Nobody Was Supposed to Learn About the Animal Testing." *Bild*, January 30. https://www.bild.de/geld/wirtschaft/volkswagen/the -secret-lab-report-54648270.bild.html.

Marlborough, Patrick. 2016. "My Life as a Kleptomaniac." *Vice*, April 29. https://www.vice.com/en_ca/article/bnpw88/what-its-like-to-live-with -kleptomania.

Martinson, Robert. 1974. "What Works? Questions and Answers About Prison Reform." *Public Interest* 35: 22–56.

Maruna, Shadd, and Heith Copes. 2005. "What Have We Learned from Five Decades of Neutralization Research?" *Crime and Justice* 32: 221–320.

Marvell, Thomas B., and Carlisle E. Moody. 1994. "Prison Population Growth and Crime Reduction." *Journal of Quantitative Criminology* 10 (2): 109–40.

———. 2001. "The Lethal Effects of Three-Strikes Laws." *Journal of Legal Studies* 30: 89–106.

Mashaw, Jerry L. 1978. *Social Security Hearings and Appeals: A Study of the Social Security Administration Hearing System*. Lexington, MA: Lexington Books.

Mason, Melanie. 2016. "Stop-and-Frisk's Effect on Crime Is Hotly Debated. Its Disproportionate Impact on Minorities Is Not." *Los Angeles Times*, September 26. http://www.latimes.com/politics/la-na-pol-crime-debate-factcheck -20160926-snap-story.html.

Mattera, Philip. 2016. "BP: Corporate Rap Sheet." Corporate Research Project. https://www.corp-research.org/BP.

Mayhew, Pat, Ronald V. Clarke, and David Elliott. 1989. "Motorcycle Theft, Helmet Legislation and Displacement." *Howard Journal of Criminal Justice* 28 (1): 1–8.

Mazerolle, Lorraine, et al. 2013. "Shaping Citizen Perceptions of Police Legitimacy: A Randomized Field Trial of Procedural Justice." *Criminology* 51 (1): 33–63.

McCabe, Donald L., Linda Klebe Trevino, and Kenneth D. Butterfield. 1996. "The Influence of Collegiate and Corporate Codes of Conduct on Ethics-Related Behavior in the Workplace." *Business Ethics Quarterly* 6 (4): 461–76.

McCarthy, Bill, and John Hagan. 1991. "Homelessness: A Criminogenic Situation?" *British Journal of Criminology* 31 (4): 393–410.

McEwin, R. Ian. 1989. "No-Fault and Road Accidents: Some Australasian Evidence." *International Review of Law and Economics* 9 (1): 13–24.

McKendall, Marie, Beverly DeMarr, and Catherine Jones-Rikkers. 2002. "Ethical Compliance Programs and Corporate Illegality: Testing the Assumptions of the Corporate Sentencing Guidelines." *Journal of Business Ethics* 37 (4): 367–83.

McLean, Kyle, et al. 2019. "Police Officers as Warriors or Guardians: Empirical Reality or Intriguing Rhetoric?" *Justice Quarterly:* 1–23.

McNeeley, Susan. 2015. "Lifestyle-Routine Activities and Crime Events." *Journal of Contemporary Criminal Justice* 31 (1): 30–52.

Mello, Michelle M., and Allen Kachalia. 2010. *Evaluation of Options for Medical Malpractice System Reform*. Washington, DC: MedPAC.

Mendoza, Martha. 1995. "Mexican Kilns Cast Pall on El Paso: Industry: Scientist at Los Alamos Lab Is Trying to Perfect a Clean-Burning, Economical Alternative to Brick Making in Which Old Tires Are Burned." *Los Angeles Times*, December 15. https://www.latimes.com/archives/la-xpm-1995-12-15-fi-14450 -story.html.

Miceli, Marcia P., Janet Pollex Near, and Terry M. Dworkin. 2008. *Whistle-Blowing in Organizations*. Rev. ed. New York: Routledge.

Miles, Thomas J., and Jens Ludwig. 2007. "The Silence of the Lambdas: Deterring Incapacitation Research." *Journal of Quantitative Criminology* 23 (4): 287–301.

Militello, Matthew, David Schimmel, and H. Jake Eberwein. 2009. "If They Knew, They Would Change: How Legal Knowledge Impacts Principals' Practice." *NASSP Bulletin* 93 (1): 27–52.

Moberly, Richard. 2012. "Sarbanes-Oxley's Whistleblower Provisions: Ten Years Later." *South Carolina Law Review* 64: 1–54.

Mocan, H. Naci, and R. Kaj Gittings. 2003. "Getting off Death Row: Commuted Sentences and the Deterrent Effect of Capital Punishment." *Journal of Law and Economics* 46: 453–78.

Monahan, John, and Laurens Walker. 2011. "Twenty-Five Years of Social Science in Law." *Law and Human Behavior* 35 (1): 72–82.

Morgenson, Gretchen. 2016. "Monsanto Whistle-Blower: $22 Million Richer, but Not Satisfied." *New York Times*, September 9. https://www.nytimes.com/2016 /09/11/business/for-monsanto-whistle-blower-a-22-million-award-that-fell -short.html.

———. 2017. "Wells Fargo's Testimony Left Some Feeling Shortchanged." *New York Times*, August 31. https://www.nytimes.com/2017/08/31/business /wells-fargo-testimony.html.

Motlag, Jason. 2016. "A Radical Approach to Gun Crime, Paying People Not to Kill Each Other." *Guardian*, June 9. https://www.theguardian.com/us-news/2016/jun/09/richmond-california-ons-gun-crime.

Mulvey, Edward P., et al. 2010. "Trajectories of Desistance and Continuity in Antisocial Behavior Following Court Adjudication Among Serious Adolescent Offenders." *Development and Psychopathology* 22 (2): 453–75.

Muratori, Pietro, et al. 2017. "Evaluation of Improvement in Externalizing Behaviors and Callous-Unemotional Traits in Children with Disruptive Behavior Disorder: A 1-Year Follow-Up Clinic-Based Study." *Administration and Policy in Mental Health and Mental Health Services Research* 44 (4): 452–62.

Murphy, Kristina. 2003. "Procedural Justice and Tax Compliance." *Australian Journal of Social Issues* 38 (3): 379–408.

———. 2005. "Regulating More Effectively: The Relationship Between Procedural Justice, Legitimacy, and Tax Non-Compliance." *Journal of Law and Society* 32 (4): 562–89.

Murphy, Kristina, Tom R. Tyler, and Amy Curtis. 2009. "Nurturing Regulatory Compliance: Is Procedural Justice Effective When People Question the Legitimacy of the Law?" *Regulation and Governance* 3 (1): 1–26.

Nagin, Daniel S. 2013. "Deterrence in the Twenty-First Century." *Crime and Justice* 42 (1): 199–263.

Nagin, Daniel S., Francis T. Cullen, and Cheryl Lero Jonson. 2009. "Imprisonment and Reoffending." *Crime and Justice* 38 (1): 115–200.

Nagin, Daniel S., and Cody W. Telep. 2017. "Procedural Justice and Legal Compliance." *Annual Review of Law and Social Science* 13: 5–28.

National Park Service. 2018. "Petrified Wood." https://www.nps.gov/pefo/learn/nature/petrified-wood.htm.

Near, Janet P., and Marcia P. Miceli. 1996. "Whistle-Blowing: Myth and Reality." *Journal of Management* 22 (3): 507–26.

Nelson, J. Ron, Deborah J. Smith, and John Dodd. 1990. "The Moral Reasoning of Juvenile Delinquents: A Meta-Analysis." *Journal of Abnormal Child Psychology* 18 (3): 231–39.

Nelson, J. S. 2016. "The Criminal Bug: Volkswagen's Middle Management." Unpublished paper. https://papers.ssrn.com/sol3/papers.cfm?abstract_id=2767255.

Newman, Oscar. 1972. *Defensible Space*. New York: Macmillan.

NHTSA. 2019a. "Distracted Driving." National Highway Traffic Safety Administration. https://www.nhtsa.gov/risky-driving/distracted-driving#resources.

———. 2019b. "Distracted Driving in Fatal Crashes 2017." National Highway Traffic Safety Administration. https://crashstats.nhtsa.dot.gov/Api/Public/ViewPublication/812700.

———. 2020. "Seat Belts." National Highway Traffic Safety Administration. https://www.nhtsa.gov/risky-driving/seat-belts.

Nieuwbeerta, Paul, Daniel S. Nagin, and Arjan Blokland. 2009. "The Relationship Between First Imprisonment and Criminal Career Development: A Matched Samples Comparison." *Journal of Quantitative Criminology* 25 (3): 227–57.

Nir, Sarah Maslin. 2017. "A Free-Riding Tortoise (and Other Violations) as Subway Delays Mount." *New York Times*, June 2. https://www.nytimes.com/2017/06/02/nyregion/subway-rules-of-conduct.html.

Nisan, Mordecai. 1992. "Beyond Intrinsic Motivation: Cultivating a Sense of the Desirable." In *Effective and Responsible Teaching: The New Synthesis.* Edited by Fritz Oser, Andreas Dick, and Jean-Luc Patry, 126–38. San Francisco: Jossey-Bass.

Nixon, Richard. 1973. "Radio Address About the State of the Union Message on Law Enforcement and Drug Abuse Prevention." https://www.presidency.ucsb.edu/documents/radio-address-about-the-state-the-union-message-law-enforcement-and-drug-abuse-prevention.

Nolan, Jessica M., and Kenneth E. Wallen. 2021 (forthcoming). "Social Norms and Persuasion." In *The Cambridge Handbook of Compliance.* Edited by Benjamin van Rooij and D. Daniel Sokol. Cambridge, UK: Cambridge University Press.

NOS Nieuws. 2019. "Beschonken bestuurders raken eerder hun rijbewijs kwijt (Drunk drivers to lose their license more swiftly)." *NOS,* November 7. https://nos.nl/artikel/2309386-beschonken-bestuurders-raken-eerder-hun-rijbewijs-kwijt.html#:~:text=Automobilisten%20onder%20invloed%20die%20achter,Grapperhaus%20van%20Justitie%20en%20Veiligheid.

Novi Mores. 2012. "Gedragsverandering in de stiltecoupé (Behavioral change in the silent compartment)." October 25. http://www.novimores.nl/2012/10/gedragsverandering-in-de-stiltecoupe.

NYCLU (New York Civil Liberties Union). 2020. "Annual Stop-and-Frisk Numbers." http://www.nyclu.org/content/stop-and-frisk-data.

O'Brien, Thomas C., Tracey L. Meares, and Tom R. Tyler. 2020. "Reconciling Police and Communities with Apologies, Acknowledgements, or Both: A Controlled Experiment." *Annals of the American Academy of Political and Social Science* 687 (1): 202–15.

Ogbonna, Emmanuel, and Barry Wilkinson. 2003. "The False Promise of Organizational Culture Change: A Case Study of Middle Managers in Grocery Retailing." *Journal of Management Studies* 40 (5): 1151–78.

OSHA. 2020. "Commonly Used Statistics." https://www.osha.gov/oshstats/commonstats.html.

Oswald, Frederick L., et al. 2013. "Predicting Ethnic and Racial Discrimination: A Meta-Analysis of IAT Criterion Studies." *Journal of Personality and Social Psychology* 105 (2): 171–92.

Owens, Emily, et al. 2018. "Can You Build a Better Cop? Experimental Evidence on Supervision, Training, and Policing in the Community." *Criminology and Public Policy* 17 (1): 41–87.

Painter, Kate, and David P. Farrington. 1997. "The Crime Reducing Effect of Improved Street Lighting: The Dudley Project." *Situational Crime Prevention: Successful Case Studies* 2: 209–26.

Palmer, Emma J. 2003. "An Overview of the Relationship Between Moral Reasoning and Offending." *Australian Psychologist* 38 (3): 165–74.

Pardosi, T. 1997. *Profil Migran Msuk di Enam Kota Besar: Medan, Bandung, Surabaya, Jakarta, Semarang, Ujung Pandang, Hasil Survei Urbanisasi 1995.* Jakarta: Biro Pusat Statistik (BPS) Indonesia.

Pare, Paul-Philippe, and Richard Felson. 2014. "Income Inequality, Poverty and Crime Across Nations." *British Journal of Sociology* 65 (3): 434–58.

Parker, Christine, and Vibeke Lehmann Nielsen. 2009. "Corporate Compliance Systems: Could They Make Any Difference?" *Administration and Society* 41 (1): 3–37.

Paulhus, Delroy L., and Kevin M. Williams. 2002. "The Dark Triad of Personality: Narcissism, Machiavellianism, and Psychopathy." *Journal of Research in Personality* 36 (6): 556–63.

PBS. 2010. "BP's Troubled Past." *Frontline*, October 26. http://www.pbs.org/wgbh /pages/frontline/the-spill/bp-troubled-past.

Pease, Ken. 1991. "The Kirkholt Project: Preventing Burglary on a British Public Housing Estate." *Security Journal* 2 (2): 73–77.

Pelissier, Bernadette, et al. 2001. "Federal Prison Residential Drug Treatment Reduces Substance Use and Arrests After Release." *American Journal of Drug and Alcohol Abuse* 27 (2): 315–37.

Perkins, H. Wesley, et al. 2010. "Effectiveness of Social Norms Media Marketing in Reducing Drinking and Driving: A Statewide Campaign." *Addictive Behaviors* 35 (10): 866–74.

Perkins, Jessica M., H. Wesley Perkins, and David W. Craig. 2019. "Misperceiving a Code of Silence: Peer Support for Telling Authorities About Weapons at School Among Middle School and High School Students in the United States." *Youth and Society* 51 (6): 814–39.

Pickett, Justin T., and Shawn D. Bushway. 2015. "Dispositional Sources of Sanction Perceptions: Emotionality, Cognitive Style, Intolerance of Ambiguity, and Self-Efficacy." *Law and Human Behavior* 39 (6): 624-40.

Pickett, Justin T., Thomas A. Loughran, and Shawn Bushway. 2015. "On the Measurement and Properties of Ambiguity in Probabilistic Expectations." *Sociological Methods and Research* 44 (4): 636–76.

———. 2016. "Consequences of Legal Risk Communication for Sanction Perception Updating and White-Collar Criminality." *Journal of Experimental Criminology* 12 (1): 75–104.

Piquero, Alex R. 2008. "Taking Stock of Developmental Trajectories of Criminal Activity over the Life Course." In *The Long View of Crime: A Synthesis of Longitudinal Research*. Edited by Akiva M. Liberman, 23–78. New York: Springer.

Piquero, Alex R., Wesley G. Jennings, and David P. Farrington. 2010. "On the Malleability of Self-Control: Theoretical and Policy Implications Regarding a General Theory of Crime." *Justice Quarterly* 27 (6): 803–34.

Piquero, Alex R., Wesley G. Jennings, David P. Farrington, Brie Diamond, and Jennifer M. Reingle Gonzalez. 2016. "A Meta-Analysis Update on the Effectiveness of Early Self-Control Improvement Programs to Improve Self-Control and Reduce Delinquency." *Journal of Experimental Criminology* 12 (2): 249–64.

Plambeck, Erica L., and Terry A. Taylor. 2016. "Supplier Evasion of a Buyer's Audit: Implications for Motivating Supplier Social and Environmental Responsibility." *Manufacturing and Service Operations Management* 18 (2): 184–97.

Plato. 1975. *The Laws*. London: Penguin.

Pleasence, Pascoe, and Nigel J. Balmer. 2012. "Ignorance in Bliss: Modeling Knowledge of Rights in Marriage and Cohabitation." *Law and Society Review* 46 (2): 297–333.

Pleasence, Pascoe, Nigel J. Balmer, and Catrina Denvir. 2017. "Wrong About Rights: Public Knowledge of Key Areas of Consumer, Housing and Employment Law in England and Wales." *Modern Law Review* 80 (5): 836–59.

Pogarsky, Greg. 2021 (forthcoming). "Heuristics and Biases in the Criminology of Compliance." In *Cambridge Handbook of Compliance*. Edited by Benjamin Van Rooij and D. Daniel Sokol. Cambridge, UK: Cambridge University Press.

Pogarsky, Greg, and Shaina Herman. 2019. "Nudging and the Choice Architecture of Offending Decisions." *Criminology and Public Policy* 18 (4): 823–39.

Pogarsky, Greg, and Alex R. Piquero. 2003. "Can Punishment Encourage Offending? Investigating the 'Resetting' Effect." *Journal of Research in Crime and Delinquency* 40 (1): 95–120.

Pogarsky, Greg, Sean Patrick Roche, and Justin T. Pickett. 2017. "Heuristics and Biases, Rational Choice, and Sanction Perceptions." *Criminology* 55 (1): 85–111.

———. 2018. "Offender Decision-Making in Criminology: Contributions from Behavioral Economics." *Annual Review of Criminology* 1: 379–400.

Pontell, Henry N., Kitty Calavita, and Robert Tillman. 1994. "Corporate Crime and Criminal Justice System Capacity: Government Response to Financial Institution Fraud." *Justice Quarterly* 11 (3): 383–410.

Pope, Shelby. 2016. "Can San Francisco Stop Public Urination with Paint That Pees Back?" *Narratively*, July 28. https://narratively.com/can-san-francisco -stop-public-urination-with-paint-that-pees-back.

Porporino, Frank J., et al. 2002. "An Outcome Evaluation of Prison-Based Treatment Programming for Substance Users." *Substance Use and Misuse* 37 (8–10): 1047–77.

Prakash, Aseem, and Matthew Potoski. 2006. *The Voluntary Environmentalists: Green Clubs, ISO 14001, and Voluntary Environmental Regulations*. Cambridge, UK: Cambridge University Press.

Pratt, Travis C., and Francis T. Cullen. 2000. "The Empirical Status of Gottfredson and Hirschi's General Theory of Crime: A Meta-Analysis." *Criminology* 38 (3): 931–64.

———. 2005. "Assessing Macro-Level Predictors and Theories of Crime: A Meta-Analysis." *Crime and Justice* 32: 373–450.

Pratt, Travis C., Kristy Holtfreter, and Michael D. Reisig. 2010. "Routine Online Activity and Internet Fraud Targeting: Extending the Generality of Routine Activity Theory." *Journal of Research in Crime and Delinquency* 47 (3): 267–96.

Pratt, Travis C., and Kristin Lloyd. 2021 (forthcoming). "Self-Control and Offending." In *The Cambridge Handbook on Compliance*. Edited by Benjamin Van Rooij and D. Daniel Sokol. Cambridge UK: Cambridge University Press.

Pratt, Travis C., Michael G. Turner, and Alex R. Piquero. 2004. "Parental Socialization and Community Context: A Longitudinal Analysis of the Structural Sources of Low Self-Control." *Journal of Research in Crime and Delinquency* 41 (3): 219–43.

President's Task Force on 21st Century Policing. 2015. *Final Report of the President's Task Force on 21st Century Policing*. Washington, DC: Office of Community Oriented Policing Services. https://cops.usdoj.gov/pdf/taskforce/TaskForce _FinalReport.pdf.

*Psychology Today.* 2019. "Kleptomania." https://www.psychologytoday.com/us /conditions/kleptomania.

Public Apology Central. 2017. "Maria Sharapova Explains Failed Drug Test in Press Conference." March 7, 2016, press conference. YouTube. https://www .youtube.com/watch?v=Nxd5X7wl9dE&feature=emb_logo.

Publicis Groupe Belgium. 2014. "Responsible Young Drivers: The Impossible Texting and Driving Test." YouTube. https://www.youtube.com/watch?v =n7pv4fyZhxc.

Puzzanghera, Jim. 2017. "What's Wrong with Bank Culture? A Top Fed Official Points to Wells Fargo Scandal." *Los Angeles Times*, March 21. http://www. latimes.com/business/la-fi-wells-fargo-fed-20170321-story.html.

Ramji-Nogales, Jaya, Andrew I. Schoenholtz, and Philip G. Schrag. 2007. "Refugee Roulette: Disparities in Asylum Adjudication." *Stanford Law Review* 60: 295-412.

Rapp, Geoffrey Christopher. 2012. "Mutiny by the Bounties? The Attempt to Reform Wall Street by the New Whistleblower Provisions of the Dodd-Frank Act." *Brigham Young University Law Review* 2012 (1): 73–152.

Rappaport, John. 2016. "How Private Insurers Regulate Public Police." *Harvard Law Review.* 130: 1539–614.

Rappleye, Hannah. 2016. "Shocking Trial, but Louisiana Sheriff Cleared of Civil Rights Abuses." NBC News, November 5. https://www.nbcnews.com/news /us-news/shocking-trial-louisiana-sheriff-cleared-civil-rights-abuses-n678031.

Reagan, Ronald. 1984. "Radio Address to the Nation on Proposed Crime Legislation." American Presidency Project. https://www.presidency.ucsb.edu /documents/radio-address-the-nation-proposed-crime-legislation.

Reckard, E. Scott. 2013. "Wells Fargo's Pressure-Cooker Sales Culture Comes at a Cost." *Los Angeles Times*, December 21. http://www.latimes.com/business/la -fi-wells-fargo-sale-pressure-20131222-story.html.

Reinders Folmer, Christopher P. 2021 (forthcoming). "Crowding-Out Effects of Laws, Policies and Incentives on Compliant Behavior." In *Cambridge Handbook of Compliance.* Edited by Benjamin Van Rooij and D. Daniel Sokol. Cambridge, UK: Cambridge University Press.

Reising, Kim, et al. 2019. "Childhood Risk Factors for Personality Disorder Symptoms Related to Violence." *Aggression and Violent Behavior* 49: 1–14.

Reuters. 2016. "VW Says Defeat Device in Conformity with European Law." Reuters, November 3. https://www.reuters.com/article/us-volkswagen -emissions-lawsuit/vw-says-defeat-device-in-conformity-with-european -law-idUSKBN12Y2VJ.

Reutter, David M. 2019. "Infamous Louisiana Sheriff on His Way Out." *Prison Legal News*, last modified October 4. https://www.prisonlegalnews.org/news /2019/oct/4/infamous-louisiana-sheriff-his-way-out.

Rice, Constance, and Susan K. Lee. 2015. *Relationship-Based Policing: Achieving Safety in Watts: A Report for the President's Task Force on 21st Century Policing.* Urban Peace Institute.

Richards, Clinton. 1999. "The Transient Effects of Limited Ethics Training." *Journal of Education for Business* 74 (6): 332–34.

Richtel, Matt. 2016. "Phone Makers Could Cut Off Drivers. So Why Don't They?" *New York Times*, September 24. https://www.nytimes.com/2016/09/25/technology /phone-makers-could-cut-off-drivers-so-why-dont-they.html.

Rijksoverheid. 2020. "Letterlijke tekst persconferentie minister-president Rutte, ministers Grapperhaus, De Jonge en Van Rijn over aangescherpte maatregelen coronavirus (verbatim text of press conference on stringent coronavirus measures)." March 23. https://www.rijksoverheid.nl/documenten/mediateksten /2020/03/23/persconferentie-minister-president-rutte-ministers-grapperhaus -de-jonge-en-van-rijn-over-aangescherpte-maatregelen-coronavirus.

Robben, Henry S. J., et al. 1990. "Decision Frame and Opportunity as Determinants of Tax Cheating: An International Experimental Study." *Journal of Economic Psychology* 11 (3): 341–64.

Roberts, Dean. 2017. "A Year After Scandal, Claims of Sales Pressure Linger at Wells Fargo." *Charlotte Observer*, September 2. http://www.charlotteobserver .com/news/business/banking/article170791647.html.

Robies, Frances. 2018. "Meth, the Forgotten Killer, Is Back. And It's Everywhere." *New York Times*, February 13. https://www.nytimes.com/2018/02 /13/us/meth-crystal-drug.html.

Robin, Lily, et al. 2020. *The Los Angeles Community Safety Partnership: 2019 Assessment.* Urban Institute. https://www.urban.org/sites/default/files/publication/101827 /the_los_angeles_community_safety_partnership_2019_assessment.pdf.

Robinson, David, and Frank J. Porporino. 2003. "Programming in Cognitive Skills: The Reasoning and Rehabilitation Programme." In *The Essential Handbook of Offender Assessment and Treatment.* Edited by Clive R. Hollin, 63–78. New York: John Wiley and Sons

Rooth, Dan-Olof. 2009. "Obesity, Attractiveness, and Differential Treatment in Hiring: A Field Experiment." *Journal of Human Resources* 44 (3): 710–35.

Rorabaugh, W. J. 1996. "Reexamining the Prohibition Amendment." *Yale Journal of Law and the Humanities* 8: 285–94.

Ross, Ezra, and Martin Pritikin. 2010. "Collection Gap: The Underenforcement of Corporate and White-Collar Fines and Penalties." *Yale Law and Policy Review* 29: 453–526.

Ruffle, Bradley J., and Yossef Tobol. 2014. "Honest on Mondays: Honesty and the Temporal Separation Between Decisions and Payoffs." *European Economic Review* 65: 126–35.

Ruiz, Rebecca R., et al. 2016. "Russian Doctor Explains How He Helped Beat Doping Tests at the Sochi Olympics." *New York Times*, May 13. https://www .nytimes.com/interactive/2016/05/13/sports/russia-doping-sochi-olympics -2014.html.

Rustad, Michael, and Thomas Koenig. 1993. "The Supreme Court and Junk Social Science: Selective Distortion in Amicus Briefs." *North Carolina Law Review* 72: 91–162.

Ryan, Kevin F. 1998. "Clinging to Failure: The Rise and Continued Life of US Drug Policy." *Law and Society Review* 32: 221–42.

Saltstone, Scot P., Robert Saltstone, and Brian H. Rowe. 1997. "Knowledge of Medical-Legal Issues. Survey of Ontario Family Medicine Residents." *Canadian Family Physician* 43: 669–73.

Sampson, Robert J, and John H. Laub. 1997. "A Life-Course Theory of Cumulative Disadvantage and the Stability of Delinquency." *Developmental Theories of Crime and Delinquency* 7: 133–61.

Sarat, Austin. 1975. "Support for the Legal System: An Analysis of Knowledge, Attitudes, and Behavior." *American Politics Quarterly* 3 (1): 3–24.

Sawyer, Kim R., Jackie Johnson, and Mark Holub. 2010. "The Necessary Illegitimacy of the Whistleblower." *Business and Professional Ethics Journal* 29 (1): 85–107.

Scalzi, Cynthia C., et al. 2006. "Barriers and Enablers to Changing Organizational Culture in Nursing Homes." *Nursing Administration Quarterly* 30 (4): 368–72.

Schein, E. H. 2010. *Organizational Culture and Leadership*. 4th ed. New York: Jossey-Bass.

Schell-Busey, Natalie Marie. 2009. "The Deterrent Effects of Ethics Codes for Corporate Crime: A Meta-Analysis." Unpublished PhD dissertation, University of Maryland, https://drum.lib.umd.edu/bitstream/handle/1903/9289 /SchellBusey_umd_0117E_10313.pdf.

Schell-Busey, Natalie, et al. 2016. "What Works? A Systematic Review of Corporate Crime Deterrence." *Criminology and Public Policy* 15 (2): 387–416.

Schepanski, Albert, and Teri Shearer. 1995. "A Prospect Theory Account of the Income Tax Withholding Phenomenon." *Organizational Behavior and Human Decision Processes* 63 (2): 174–86.

Scherdin, Mary Jane. 1986. "The Halo Effect: Psychological Deterrence of Electronic Security Systems." *Information Technology and Libraries* 5 (3): 232–35.

Schimmel, David, and Matthew Militello. 2007. "Legal Literacy for Teachers: A Neglected Responsibility." *Harvard Educational Review* 77 (3): 257–84.

Scholten, Wieke, and Naomi Ellemers. 2016. "Bad Apples or Corrupting Barrels? Preventing Traders' Misconduct." *Journal of Financial Regulation and Compliance* 24 (4): 366–82.

Schubert, Carol A., et al. 2004. "Operational Lessons from the Pathways to Desistance Project." *Youth Violence and Juvenile Justice* 2 (3): 237–55.

Schubert, Siri, and T. Christian Miller. 2008. "At Siemens, Bribery Was Just a Line Item." *New York Times*, December 20. http://www.nytimes.com/2008/12/21 /business/worldbusiness/21siemens.html.

Schultz, P. Wesley, et al. 2007. "The Constructive, Destructive, and Reconstructive Power of Social Norms." *Psychological Science* 18 (5): 429–34.

Schwartz, Joanna C. 2014. "Introspection Through Litigation." *Notre Dame Law Review* 90: 1055–104.

Scott, Tim, et al. 2003. "The Quantitative Measurement of Organizational Culture in Health Care: A Review of the Available Instruments." *Health Services Research* 38 (3): 923–45.

Seabrook, John. 2009. "Don't Shoot: A Radical Approach to the Problem of Gang Violence." *New Yorker*, June 15, 2009. https://www.newyorker.com/magazine /2009/06/22/dont-shoot-2.

Segall, Eleanor. 2018. "'Admitting It Was Shameful and Embarrassing'—What It's Really Like to Have Kleptomania." *Metro*, May 11. https://metro.co.uk/2018 /05/11/admitting-it-was-shameful-and-embarrassing-what-its-really-like-to -have-kleptomania-7510046.

Sentencing Project. 2020. "Trends in US Corrections." http://sentencingproject
.org/wp-content/uploads/2016/01/Trends-in-US-Corrections.pdf.

Shalvi, Shaul, Ori Eldar, and Yoella Bereby-Meyer. 2012. "Honesty Requires
Time (and Lack of Justifications)." *Psychological Science* 23 (10): 1264–70.

Sharma, Gaurav. 2017. "Insider Reveals 'Culture of Fear' That Drove Kobe Steel
Scandal." *International Business Times*, October 27. https://www.ibtimes.co.uk
/insider-reveals-culture-fear-that-drove-kobe-steel-scandal-1644749.

Sharma Rani, Rikha. 2017. "Building Trust Cuts Violence. Cash Also Helps."
*New York Times*, February 21. https://www.nytimes.com/2017/02/21/opinion
/building-trust-cuts-violence-cash-also-helps.html.

SharpBrains. 2006. "Brain Teaser: Can You Count the Fs in This Sentence?"
https://sharpbrains.com/blog/2006/09/10/brain-exercise-brain-teaser.

Shear, Michael D., Michael Crowley, and James Glanz. 2020. "Coronavirus May
Kill 100,000 to 240,000 in US Despite Actions, Officials Say." *New York Times*,
March 31. https://www.nytimes.com/2020/03/31/us/politics/coronavirus
-death-toll-united-states.html.

Shepherd, Joanna M. 2002. "Fear of the First Strike: The Full Deterrent Effect of California's Two- and Three-Strikes Legislation." *Journal of Legal Studies* 31 (1): 159–201.

———. 2004. "Murders of Passion, Execution Delays, and the Deterrence of Capital Punishment." *Journal of Legal Studies* 33 (2): 283–321.

———. 2005. "Deterrence Versus Brutalization: Capital Punishment's Differing
Impacts Among States." *Michigan Law Review* 104: 203–56.

Sherman, Lawrence W., Patrick R. Gartin, and Michael E. Buerger. 1989. "Hot
Spots of Predatory Crime: Routine Activities and the Criminology of Place."
*Criminology* 27 (1): 27–56.

———. 1995. "General Deterrent Effects of Police Patrol in Crime 'Hot Spots': A
Randomized, Controlled Trial." *Justice Quarterly* 12 (4): 625–48.

Shu, Lisa L., and Francesca Gino. 2012. "Sweeping Dishonesty Under the Rug:
How Unethical Actions Lead to Forgetting of Moral Rules." *Journal of Personality and Social Psychology* 102 (6): 1164–77.

Shu, Lisa L., et al. 2012. "Signing at the Beginning Makes Ethics Salient and
Decreases Dishonest Self-Reports in Comparison to Signing at the End." *Proceedings of the National Academy of Sciences* 109 (38): 15197–200.

Shuman, Daniel W., and Myron S. Weiner. 1981. "The Privilege Study: An Empirical Examination of the Psychotherapist-Patient Privilege." *North Carolina
Law Review* 60: 893–942.

Siegel, Michael, Craig S. Ross, and Charles King III. 2013. "The Relationship
Between Gun Ownership and Firearm Homicide Rates in the United States,
1981–2010." *American Journal of Public Health* 103 (11): 2098–105.

Simerman, John. 2019. "$3 Million in New Payouts as Iberia Parish Sheriff's Of-
fice Settles More Abuse Suits." Nola.com, March 2. https://www.nola.com
/news/courts/article_f17160ee-a7fe-50fd-a1f8-0b9b55ca5a26.html.

Simpson, Sally, et al. 2014. "Corporate Crime Deterrence: A Systematic Review."
*Campbell Systematic Reviews* 10 (4): 5–88.

Singer, Tania, et al. 2006. "Empathic Neural Responses Are Modulated by the
Perceived Fairness of Others." *Nature* 439 (7075): 466–69.

Sloan, Frank A., Bridget A. Reilly, and Christoph M. Schenzler. 1994. "Tort Liability Versus Other Approaches for Deterring Careless Driving." *International Review of Law and Economics* 14 (1): 53–71.

Slovic, Paul, Baruch Fischhoff, and Sarah Lichtenstein. 1979. "Rating the Risks." *Environment: Science and Policy for Sustainable Development* 21 (3): 14–39.

Smith, Joanne R., and Winnifred R. Louis. 2008. "Do as We Say and as We Do: The Interplay of Descriptive and Injunctive Group Norms in the Attitude–Behaviour Relationship." *British Journal of Social Psychology* 47 (4): 647–66.

Smith, Randall. 2015. "Two Former Traders Found Guilty in Libor Manipulation Case." *New York Times*, November 5. http://www.nytimes.com/2015/11/06/business/dealbook/two-former-traders-found-guilty-in-libor-manipulation-case.html.

Smithson, Joy, and Steven Venette. 2013. "Stonewalling as an Image-Defense Strategy: A Critical Examination of BP's Response to the Deepwater Horizon Explosion." *Communication Studies* 64 (4): 395–410.

Solomon, Mark G., Richard P. Compton, and David F. Preusser. 2004. "Taking the Click It or Ticket Model Nationwide." *Journal of Safety Research* 35 (2): 197–201.

Soper, George A. 1919. "The Lessons of the Pandemic." *Science* 49 (1274): 501–6.

Spano, Richard, and Joshua D. Freilich. 2009. "An Assessment of the Empirical Validity and Conceptualization of Individual Level Multivariate Studies of Lifestyle/Routine Activities Theory Published from 1995 to 2005." *Journal of Criminal Justice* 37 (3): 305–14.

Spiegel International. 2007. "Siemens Corruption Scandal Deepens: New Allegations of Bribes to Saddam." *Der Spiegel*, January 3. https://www.spiegel.de/international/siemens-corruption-scandal-deepens-new-allegations-of-bribes-to-saddam-a-457549.html.

———. 2008. "Siemens Verdict: Former Manager Convicted of Corruption." *Der Spiegel*, July 28. http://www.spiegel.de/international/business/siemens-verdict-former-manager-convicted-of-corruption-a-568504.html.

Stanley-Becker, Isaac, and Alex Horton. 2018. "Sully, Bush's Service Dog, Lies Before the President's Flag-Draped Casket in the Capitol Rotunda." *Washington Post*, December 4. https://www.washingtonpost.com/nation/2018/12/03/sully-bushs-service-dog-lies-before-his-casket-before-one-last-journey-with-former-president.

Stanovich, Keith E., and Richard F. West. 2000. "Advancing the Rationality Debate." *Behavioral and Brain Sciences* 23 (5): 701–17.

Stansbury, Jason, and Bruce Barry. 2007. "Ethics Programs and the Paradox of Control." *Business Ethics Quarterly* 17 (2): 239–61.

Steffy, Loren C. 2010. *Drowning in Oil: BP and the Reckless Pursuit of Profit.* New York: McGraw Hill Professional.

Steinberg, Laurence, and Elizabeth S. Scott. 2003. "Less Guilty by Reason of Adolescence: Developmental Immaturity, Diminished Responsibility, and the Juvenile Death Penalty." *American Psychologist* 58 (12): 1009–18.

Steinberg, Richard M. 2011. *Governance, Risk Management, and Compliance: It Can't Happen to Us—Avoiding Corporate Disaster While Driving Success.* Hoboken, NJ: John Wiley & Sons.

Stewart, Mary White, and Catherine Byrne. 2000. "Genocide, Political Violence, and the Neutralization of Evil." Paper presented at the American Sociological Association Annual Meeting, Washington, DC.

Stromberg, Joseph. 2013. "The Neuroscientist Who Discovered He Was a Psychopath." *Smithsonian Magazine*, November 22. https://www.smithsonianmag.com /science-nature/the-neuroscientist-who-discovered-he-was-a-psychopath -180947814.

Sweeten, Gary, Alex R. Piquero, and Laurence Steinberg. 2013. "Age and the Explanation of Crime, Revisited." *Journal of Youth and Adolescence* 42 (6): 921–38.

Sykes, Gresham M., and David Matza. 1957. "Techniques of Neutralization: A Theory of Delinquency." *American Sociological Review* 22 (6): 664–70.

Sylves, Richard T., and Louise K. Comfort. 2012. "The Exxon Valdez and BP Deepwater Horizon Oil Spills: Reducing Risk in Socio-Technical Systems." *American Behavioral Scientist* 56 (1): 76–103.

Taibbi, Matt. 2013. "Cruel and Unusual Punishment: The Shame of Three Strikes Laws." *Rolling Stone*, March 27. https://www.rollingstone.com/politics /politics-news/cruel-and-unusual-punishment-the-shame-of-three-strikes -laws-92042.

Talesh, Shauhin A. 2009. "The Privatization of Public Legal Rights: How Manufacturers Construct the Meaning of Consumer Law." *Law and Society Review* 43 (3): 527–62.

———. 2015. "Rule-Intermediaries in Action: How State and Business Stakeholders Influence the Meaning of Consumer Rights in Regulatory Governance Arrangements." *Law and Policy* 37 (1–2): 1–31.

Talesh, Shauhin, and Jérôme Pélisse. 2019. "How Legal Intermediaries Facilitate or Inhibit Social Change." *Studies in Law, Politics, and Society* 79: 111–45.

Tang, Shu-Hua, and Vernon C. Hall. 1995. "The Overjustification Effect: A Meta-Analysis." *Applied Cognitive Psychology* 9 (5): 365–404.

Taylor, Eileen Z., and Mary B. Curtis. 2010. "An Examination of the Layers of Workplace Influences in Ethical Judgments: Whistleblowing Likelihood and Perseverance in Public Accounting." *Journal of Business Ethics* 93 (1): 21–37.

Tenbrunsel, Ann E., and David M. Messick. 2004. "Ethical Fading: The Role of Self-Deception in Unethical Behavior." *Social Justice Research* 17 (2): 223–36.

Tewksbury, Richard, and Elizabeth Ehrhardt Mustaine. 2001. "Lifestyle Factors Associated with the Sexual Assault of Men: A Routine Activity Theory Analysis." *Journal of Men's Studies* 9 (2): 153–82.

Thaler, Richard H. 2015. *Misbehaving: The Making of Behavioral Economics*. New York: W. W. Norton.

Thompson, Derek. 2018. "The Most Expensive Comment in Internet History?" *Atlantic*, February 23. https://www.theatlantic.com/business/archive/2018 /02/hogan-thiel-gawker-trial/554132.

Thomson, Ernie. 1999. "Effects of an Execution on Homicides in California." *Homicide Studies* 3 (2): 129–50.

Thornton, Dorothy, Neil Gunningham, and Robert A. Kagan. 2005. "General Deterrence and Corporate Environmental Behavior." *Law and Policy* 27 (2): 262–88.

Thornton, Dorothy, Robert A. Kagan, and Neil Gunningham. 2008. "Compliance Costs, Regulation, and Environmental Performance: Controlling Truck Emissions in the US." *Regulation and Governance* 2 (3): 275–92.

Travis, Jeremy, Bruce Western, and Steve Redburn. 2014. *The Growth of Incarceration in the United States: Exploring Causes and Consequences.* Washington, DC: National Academies Press.

Treviño, Linda Klebe, and Gary R. Weaver. 2001. "Organizational Justice and Ethics Program Follow-Through: Influences on Employees' Harmful and Helpful Behavior." *Business Ethics Quarterly* 11 (4): 651–71.

Treviño, Linda Klebe, Gary R. Weaver, David G. Gibson, and Barbara Ley Toffler. 1999. "Managing Ethics and Legal Compliance: What Works and What Hurts." *California Management Review* 41 (2): 131–51.

Treviño, Linda K., and Stuart A. Youngblood. 1990. "Bad Apples in Bad Barrels: A Causal Analysis of Ethical Decision-Making Behavior." *Journal of Applied Psychology* 75 (4): 378–85.

Truth and Reconciliation Commission (South Africa). 2020. "Amnesty Hearings and Decisions." https://www.justice.gov.za/trc/amntrans/index.htm.

Tversky, Amos, and Daniel Kahneman. 1974. "Judgment Under Uncertainty: Heuristics and Biases." *Science* 185 (4157): 1124–31.

Twiley, Nicola. 2015. "Rocks, Paper, Sinners." *New Yorker,* January 23. http://www.newyorker.com/tech/elements/slide-show-bad-luck-petrified-forest.

Tyler, Tom R. 1990. *Why People Obey the Law.* Princeton, NJ: Princeton University Press.

———. 1997. "Procedural Fairness and Compliance with the Law." *Swiss Journal of Economics and Statistics* 133 (2): 219–40.

———. 2000. "Social Justice: Outcome and Procedure." *International Journal of Psychology* 35 (2): 117–25.

Tyler, Tom R., Patrick E. Callahan, and Jeffrey Frost. 2007. "Armed, and Dangerous (?): Motivating Rule Adherence Among Agents of Social Control." *Law and Society Review* 41 (2): 457–92.

Unnever, James D., and Francis T. Cullen. 2009. "Empathetic Identification and Punitiveness: A Middle-Range Theory of Individual Differences." *Theoretical Criminology* 13 (3): 283–312.

Urban Dictionary. 2015. "Twalking." https://www.urbandictionary.com/define.php?term=Twalking.

USADA (US Anti-Doping Agency). 2016. "Substance Profile: Meldonium." March 30. https://www.usada.org/spirit-of-sport/meldonium.

US Attorney's Office. 2015. "Former Siemens Chief Financial Officer Pleads Guilty in Manhattan Federal Court to $100 Million Foreign Bribery Scheme." FBI News. September 30. https://www.fbi.gov/contact-us/field-offices/newyork/news/press-releases/former-siemens-chief-financial-officer-pleads-guilty-in-manhattan-federal-court-to-100-million-foreign-bribery-scheme.

US Chemical Safety and Hazard Investigation Board. 2007. "Investigation Report: Refinery Explosion and Fire, Texas City, Texas, March 23, 2005." https://www.hsdl.org/?abstract&did=234995.

US Department of Justice. 2004. "Warner-Lambert to Pay $430 Million to Re-
    solve Criminal and Civil Health Care Liability Relating to Off-Label Promo-
    tion." Press release. May 13. https://www.justice.gov/archive/opa/pr/2004
    /May/04_civ_322.htm.
————. 2011. "The False Claims Act: A Primer." April 22. https://www.justice.gov
    /sites/default/files/civil/legacy/2011/04/22/C-FRAUDS_FCA_Primer.pdf.
US Department of Justice, and US Attorney for the District of Columbia. 2008.
    "Siemens Sentencing Memo." December 12. https://www.justice.gov/sites
    /default/files/opa/legacy/2008/12/19/siemens-sentencing-memo.pdf.
US Senate Select Committee on Intelligence. 2014. "Committee Study of the
    Central Intelligence Agency's Detention and Interrogation Program." https://
    www.intelligence.senate.gov/sites/default/files/documents/CRPT-113srpt
    288.pdf.
Valliant, Paul M., et al. 2000. "Moral Reasoning, Interpersonal Skills, and Cogni-
    tion of Rapists, Child Molesters, and Incest Offenders." *Psychological Reports* 86
    (1): 67–75.
Van der Merwe, Hugo, and Audrey R. Chapman. 2008. *Truth and Reconciliation
    in South Africa: Did the TRC Deliver?* Philadelphia: University of Pennsylva-
    nia Press.
Van Gelder, Jean-Louis. 2012. "Beyond Rational Choice: The Hot/Cool Perspec-
    tive of Criminal Decision Making." *Psychology, Crime and Law* 19 (9): 745–63.
Van Gelder, Jean-Louis, and Reinout E. de Vries. 2013. "Rational Misbehavior?
    Evaluating an Integrated Dual-Process Model of Criminal Decision Making."
    *Journal of Quantitative Criminology* 30: 1–27.
————. 2016. "Traits and States at Work: Lure, Risk and Personality as Predictors
    of Occupational Crime." *Psychology, Crime and Law* 22 (7): 701–20.
Van Gelder, Jean-Louis, Hal E. Hershfield, and Loran F. Nordgren. 2013. "Vividness
    of the Future Self Predicts Delinquency." *Psychological Science* 24 (6): 974–80.
Van Gelder, Jean-Louis, et al. 2015. "Friends with My Future Self: Longitudinal
    Vividness Intervention Reduces Delinquency." *Criminology* 53 (2): 158–79.
Van McCrary, S., and Jeffrey W. Swanson. 1999. "Physicians' Legal Defensiveness
    and Knowledge of Medical Law: Comparing Denmark and the USA." *Scandi-
    navian Journal of Public Health* 27 (1): 18–21.
Van McCrary, S., et al. 1992. "Treatment Decisions for Terminally Ill Patients:
    Physicians' Legal Defensiveness and Knowledge of Medical Law." *Law, Medi-
    cine and Health Care* 20 (4): 364–76.
Van Natta, Don, Jr., Elaine Sciolino, and Stephen Grey. 2006. "Details Emerge in
    British Terror Case." *New York Times*, August 28. https://www.nytimes.com
    /2006/08/28/world/europe/28plot.html.
Van Rooij, Benjamin, and Adam Fine. 2018. "Toxic Corporate Culture: Assessing
    Organizational Processes of Deviancy." *Administrative Sciences* 8 (3): 23–61.
Van Rooij, Benjamin, et al. 2020. "Compliance with COVID-19 Mitigation Mea-
    sures in the United States" Working paper. https://psyarxiv.com/qymu3.
Vaughn, Joshua. 2019. "In a Louisiana Parish, Hundreds of Cases May Be Tainted
    by Sherriff's Office Misconduct." *Appeal*, November 25. https://theappeal.org

/iberia-parish-brady-letters/?utm_source=the+Appeal&utm_campaign
=1ed105eb2c-.

Vazsonyi, Alexander T., Jakub Mikuška, and Erin L. Kelley. 2017. "It's Time: A
Meta-Analysis on the Self-Control-Deviance Link." *Journal of Criminal Justice*
48: 48–63.

Violation Tracker. 2020. "100 Most Penalized Parent Companies." https://
violationtracker.goodjobsfirst.org/top-100-parents.

Visher, Christy A., Laura Winterfield, and Mark B. Coggeshall. 2005. "Ex-Offender
Employment Programs and Recidivism: A Meta-Analysis." *Journal of Experimental
Criminology* 1 (3): 295–316.

Volkov, Michael. 2020. "The Boeing Scandal and the Demise of a Corporate Culture (Part I of III)." JD Supra. https://www.jdsupra.com/legalnews/the-boeing
-scandal-and-the-demise-of-a-71150.

Volkswagen. 2017. "Volkswagen Diesel Old Wives' Tale 6: Diesel Is Dirty." You-
Tube. June 25. https://www.youtube.com/watch?v=RMFaBXiBaZA.

Walters, Glenn D., and P. Colin Bolger. 2019. "Procedural Justice Perceptions,
Legitimacy Beliefs, and Compliance with the Law: A Meta-Analysis." *Journal
of Experimental Criminology* 15 (3): 341–72.

Wang, Amy B., and Kristine Philips. 2018. "'Just Shoot Me,' an Armed Man Told
a Cop. The Officer Didn't—and Was Fired, His Lawsuit Claimed." *Washington
Post*, December 8. https://www.washingtonpost.com/news/post-nation/wp
/2018/02/12/an-officer-who-was-fired-after-refusing-to-shoot-an-armed
-man-just-won-175000-in-a-settlement.

Warren, Danielle E., Joseph P. Gaspar, and William S. Laufer. 2014. "Is Formal
Ethics Training Merely Cosmetic? A Study of Ethics Training and Ethical
Organizational Culture." *Business Ethics Quarterly* 24 (1): 85–117.

Warren, Elizabeth. 2016a. "Enough Is Enough." Facebook. https://www.facebook
.com/senatorelizabethwarren/posts/556583621170802.

———. 2016b. "Letter to the Department of Justice Inspector General." https://
www.warren.senate.gov/files/documents/2016-9-15_Referral_DOJ_IG
_letter.pdf.

———. 2016c. "One Way to Rebuild Our Institutions." *New York Times*, January
29. https://www.nytimes.com/2016/01/29/opinion/elizabeth-warren-one
-way-to-rebuild-our-institutions.html.

Waschbusch, Daniel A., et al. 2019. "Effects of Behavioral Treatment Modified to
Fit Children with Conduct Problems and Callous-Unemotional (CU) Traits."
*Journal of Clinical Child and Adolescent Psychology* 49 (5): 1–12.

Waxman, Olivia B. 2019. "Before the Trump Impeachment Inquiry, These Were
American History's Most Famous Whistle-Blowers." *Time*, September 26.
https://time.com/5684536/whistleblower-history.

Weaver, Gary R. 2014. "Encouraging Ethics in Organizations: A Review of Some
Key Research Findings." *American Criminal Law Review* 51: 293–316.

Weaver, Gary R., and Linda Klebe Treviño. 1999. "Compliance and Values
Oriented Ethics Programs: Influences on Employees' Attitudes and Behavior."
*Business Ethics Quarterly* 9 (2): 315–35.

Weaver, Gary R., Linda Klebe Treviño, and Philip L. Cochran. 1999. "Corporate Ethics Practices in the Mid-1990's: An Empirical Study of the Fortune 1000." *Journal of Business Ethics* 18 (3): 283–94.

Webley, Paul, et al. 1991. *Tax Evasion: An Experimental Approach*. New York: Cambridge University Press.

Weekes, John R., et al. 2013. "What Works in Reducing Substance-Related Offending." In *What Works in Offender Rehabilitation: An Evidence-Based Approach to Assessment and Treatment*. Edited by Leam Craig, Louise Dixon, and Theresa Gannon, 237–54. Hoboken, NJ: Wiley.

Weisburd, David, and Lorraine Green. 1995. "Policing Drug Hot Spots: The Jersey City Drug Market Analysis Experiment." *Justice Quarterly* 12 (4): 711–35.

Weisburd, David, and Lorraine Green Mazerolle. 2000. "Crime and Disorder in Drug Hot Spots: Implications for Theory and Practice in Policing." *Police Quarterly* 3 (3): 331–49.

Weisburd, David, et al. 2004. "Trajectories of Crime at Places: A Longitudinal Study of Street Segments in the City of Seattle." *Criminology* 42 (2): 283–322.

Weiser, Kathy. 2019. "The Curse of the Petrified Forest." Legends of America. http://www.legendsofamerica.com/az-petrifiedcurse.html.

Welch, Chris. 2019. "Spotify Launches a Simplified Car View for Controlling Your Music While Driving." *Verge*, January 16. https://www.theverge.com /2019/1/16/18185644/spotify-car-view-now-testing-android-simple-controls.

Wenzel, Michael. 2005. "Misperceptions of Social Norms About Tax Compliance: From Theory to Intervention." *Journal of Economic Psychology* 26 (6): 862–83.

White, Ben, et al. 2012. "What Do Emergency Physicians Think of Law?" *Emergency Medicine Australasia* 24 (4): 355–56.

———. 2014. "Doctors' Knowledge of the Law on Withholding and Withdrawing Life-Sustaining Medical Treatment." *Medical Journal of Australia* 201 (4): 229–32.

Whitebread, Charles H. 2000. "Freeing Ourselves from the Prohibition Idea in the Twenty-First Century." *Suffolk University Law Review* 33: 235–58.

Williams, Allan F., and JoAnn K. Wells. 2004. "The Role of Enforcement Programs in Increasing Seat Belt Use." *Journal of Safety Research* 35 (2): 175–80.

Williams, Kevin M., et al. 2009. "Inferring Sexually Deviant Behavior from Corresponding Fantasies: The Role of Personality and Pornography Consumption." *Criminal Justice and Behavior* 36 (2): 198–222.

Wilson, Richard A. 2001. *The Politics of Truth and Reconciliation in South Africa: Legitimizing the Post-Apartheid State*. Cambridge, UK: Cambridge University Press.

Winter, S., and P. J. May. 2001. "Motivation for Compliance with Environmental Regulations." *Journal of Policy Analysis and Management* 20 (4): 675–98.

Woo, Ayoung, and Kenneth Joh. 2015. "Beyond Anecdotal Evidence: Do Subsidized Housing Developments Increase Neighborhood Crime?" *Applied Geography* 64: 87–96.

Wood, George, Tom R. Tyler, and Andrew V. Papachristos. 2020. "Procedural Justice Training Reduces Police Use of Force and Complaints Against Officers." *Proceedings of the National Academy of Sciences* 117 (18): 9815–21.

Woodward, Aylin. 2019. "It's Been Nearly 30 Years Since the Exxon Valdez Oil Spill. But That Crisis Pales in Comparison to These Recent Ocean Disasters." *Business Insider*, March 21. https://www.businessinsider.nl/exxon-valdez-spill -other-disasters-contaminated-ocean-2019-3?international=true&r=US.

Woodyatt, Amy. 2019. "'World First' Cell Phone Detection Cameras Rolled Out in Australia." CNN News, December 2. https://edition.cnn.com/2019/12/01 /australia/cell-phone-detection-camera-australia-intl-scli/index.html.

Worrall, John L. 2004. "The Effect of Three-Strikes Legislation on Serious Crime in California." *Journal of Criminal Justice* 32 (4): 283–96.

Worsham, Ronald G., Jr. 1996. "The Effect of Tax Authority Behavior on Tax-payer Compliance: A Procedural Justice Approach." *Journal of the American Taxation Association* 18 (2): 19–39.

Wright, John Paul, et al. 2017. "Malevolent Forces: Self-Control, the Dark Triad, and Crime." *Youth Violence and Juvenile Justice* 15 (2): 191–215.

Xunzi. 2003. *Xunzi: Basic Writings*. Translated by Burton Watson. New York: Columbia University Press.

Yates, Sally Q. 2015. "Memorandum on Individual Accountability for Corporate Wrongdoing." US Department of Justice, Office of the Deputy Attorney General. September 9. https://www.justice.gov/archives/dag/file/769036/download.

Yu, Rongqin, John R. Geddes, and Seena Fazel. 2012. "Personality Disorders, Violence, and Antisocial Behavior: A Systematic Review and Meta-Regression Analysis." *Journal of Personality Disorders* 26 (5): 775–92.

Zador, Paul, and Adrian Lund. 1986. "Re-Analyses of the Effects of No-Fault Auto Insurance on Fatal Crashes." *Journal of Risk and Insurance* 53 (2): 226–41.

Zimring, Franklin E., Gordon Hawkins, and Sam Kamin. 2001. *Punishment and Democracy: Three Strikes and You're Out in California*. New York: Oxford University Press.

Zimring, Franklin E., and Sam Kamin. 2001. "Facts, Fallacies, and California's Three Strikes." *Duquesne Law Review* 40: 605–14.

# Index